Reflecting Transformation in Post-socialist Rural Areas

Reflecting Transformation in Post-socialist Rural Areas

Edited by

Maarit Heinonen, Jouko Nikula, Inna Kopoteva, Leo Granberg

CAMBRIDGE SCHOLARS PUBLISHING

Reflecting Transformation in Post-socialist Rural Areas, edited by Maarit Heinonen, Jouko Nikula, Inna Kopoteva, Leo Granberg

This book first published 2007 by

Cambridge Scholars Publishing

15 Angerton Gardens, Newcastle, NE5 2JA, UK

British Library Cataloguing in Publication Data
A catalogue record for this book is available from the British Library

ISBN 1-84718-128-7; ISBN 13: 9781847181282

TABLE OF CONTENTS

LIST OF FIGURES

LIST OF TABLES

PREFACE

The idea of a family farm has played an essential role in the economic and social development of the Nordic countries. The family farm was not only an enterprise; it was also a basis for a particular rural way of life. At the social structure level, family farmers acted as a stabilising force between the opposing classes of the industrial society. During the past decades, we have been witnessing a process in which the family farms have been gradually declining almost everywhere.

In the post-socialist transition period, the idea of a family farm was used again as a key political concept for deconstructing collective forms of agricultural production. Family farms were to be created as a basis for an enterprising middle class. This more general idea of a sacred middle class was culturally constructed in moral terms, which should remind us of the rhetoric concerning the previous *avant-garde* of the proletariat. The independent farmers were supposed to be law-abiding guardians of democracy and the common good.

This book is more or less a story of this most recent – and rather unfortunate – agricultural reform.

In many ways we can see in this book how the idea of the family farm did not work out in the post-communist transition period. We learn that the paths of the reform have been different but the basic lesson is clear. Much poverty and disorganisation has been caused in this process. At the end of the day, not many family farms exist and many of the key features of the previous times seem to prevail. This is especially the case in Russia, which is still dominated by large-scale farms and where the household plots are still very significant.

At this stage, the basic wounds of the radical decollectivisation are gradually healing. We do not want to propose any general key to agricultural problems in transition societies. However, we want to challenge the straightforward reasoning of the previous Western advisers from the World Bank and the IMF, who were so actively proposing the idea of a family farm. In this book's articles many of the unintended effects of this programme are thoroughly analysed.

Within the Aleksanteri Institute, studies on agriculture in transition have been one of the research focuses for many years. This book is one step in the ongoing research process by several leading Finnish scholars in the field. It is based on the fifth Aleksanteri Conference in November 2005 attended by some of the most prominent specialists from the international research community.

We have previously dealt with issues of democratic transition and Western aid to Eastern Europe.

This book brings an essential viewpoint of our common intellectual effort when we want to face the most significant social processes in contemporary Europe.

Markku Kivinen
Director of the Aleksanteri Instute

INTRODUCTION

JOUKO NIKULA

The world's inherent complexity is a common cause of unintended consequences in social and economic action. This has been a classical theme in social sciences since the Scottish Enlightenment. Unintended consequences are more the rule than the exception in policy making. However, it is extremely difficult to take them into consideration in a real policy making process. Some years ago Markku Kivinen returned to this topic in his book *Sociology and Russia.* He analysed how the basic guiding principles and distinctions of the Bolsheviks, based on the spirit of the Enlightenment, resulted in a number of unintended consequences; certain issues became taboos, everybody knew about them, but nobody was aloud to talk about them. For example, instead of science prevailing over religion, reality was demonised when developments did not proceed in the way the Bolsheviks thought they should. Instead of a strong and powerful working class, the nomenklatura appeared, and instead of urbanization, the rural way of life continued.

In a similar manner, rural reforms in many post-soviet countries produced a number of unintended consequences. These reforms were guided by the ideal of a romanticized society of family farmers, living and working on their well-kept farms and enjoying a decent standard of living in rural communities. These farmers were to be the basis of a new rural middle class and – together with the owners of non-agricultural small and medium sized enterprises (SME's) – the guardians of patriotism, democracy and the common good. Guidelines were set down by advisers from the World Bank and the International Monetary Fund (IMF), who preferred family farms or individual farms to collective enterprises (Lerman et al., 2001, Chapter 2, 1). To their way of thinking, all corporate forms of agriculture were inherently disadvantaged economically and socially, and just a transitory stage on the way to efficient family farming. There were certain differences in the adoption and realization of rural reform amongst post-socialist countries: in some countries reformers adhered firmly to the rules and recommendations set down by their advisors, while in other countries more independent decisions were in evidence.

In most countries the results were nothing like those envisaged by reformers. The "creative destruction" of the rural sector was evident in the struggle that agricultural companies had just in order to survive and indeed many of them went bankrupt. Instead of efficient and productive family farms, the result was the almost complete de-capitalization of agriculture and a collapse of production. For example, the level of production in the late 1990s in Latvia was less than one third of its pre-reform level. At the same time in Russia, production had "only" halved, but the result would probably have been worse, if the direction of reform had not been revised, after the initial stage, away from complete decollectivisation towards the reconstruction of the collective sector. Most of the rural population relied on household plots for their survival. Reform was destructive not only as far as production was concerned, but more importantly, for rural communities. Social ties, which had been based on the collective farm as the main economic and social resource for the local community, were eroded, unemployment and general uncertainty sowed anomie, which in turn resulted in increasing social problems, alcoholism, and criminality.

Given the absence of economic resources in most villages, all sorts of organizations and cultural activities either disappeared completely or were much reduced. No modern public sphere or civil society emerged to fill this void, or replace the collectivity once provided by the *collective farm*. Local communities were characterized by the disintegration of social relations outside the family network. Considerable difficulties were met in creating local party organizations, interest organizations, and the third sector in general. Organized civic activity was effectively confined to study circles, the distribution of humanitarian aid and leisure activities.

Only since 2000 have the early signs of some developments in economic and social life in post-socialist rural areas become evident. In many of the Central European and Baltic countries this has been the result of joining the European Union, the accession funds and support programmes that membership has brought and revised agricultural and rural policies in these countries. In Russia, a slow recovery began shortly after the rouble crisis in 1998, which greatly improved the competitiveness of agricultural producers and the food industry in Russia. Another, even more important factor for development has been the arrival of external investors, who have seized the chance to invest in agriculture and created the necessary conditions for a general increase of agricultural production. The result is that now, more than fifteen years after the beginning of these agricultural reforms, the key agricultural producers in Russia, the Baltic countries, and elsewhere are very large capitalist farms or large agricultural holding companies.

This anthology is based on presentations given at the Aleksanteri Institute's the fifth Aleksanteri Conference on 10 – 11 November 2005, in Helsinki, Finland, and it is devoted to the analysis of some of the above mentioned issues.

The volume is divided into two parts. In the first part, the focus is on the patterns and problems of transformation in post-socialist agriculture and agricultural policies, while the second part is focused mainly on efforts to revitalize rural communities and issues of local development.

The first two articles discuss developments in and the distinctive features of Russian agriculture from the early 1990s until now. Eugenia Serova analyses these issues from the perspective of the agrarian economy and agricultural policy, while Alexander Bedny's study is based on the institutional approach of economic sociology, where *institutions,* understood as formal and informal constraints, play a central role.

Both authors point to failures in Russia's agricultural reforms as the main cause for the current state of Russian agriculture, along with, until quite recently, inconsistent and faulty agricultural policies. These failures have contributed to the perennial problem of loss-making agricultural enterprises, which only manage to exist with the help of artificial respiration in the form of soft-loans and debt restructuring by regional authorities. The shoots of a successful transformation of the Russian agricultural sector have gradually withered away due to an insufficient and misplaced agricultural policy and the lack of necessary institutions of finance, training, regulation and interest representation.

Leo Granberg analyses the reasons for the survival of some of the key features of Russian agriculture, namely, the dominance of large-scale farms, the durability of household plots and the marginal role of family farms. According to Granberg, popular explanations – resistance, rational calculation or deficient skills – provide only a partial and, therefore, unsatisfactory answer. Instead, he focuses attention on other factors such as paternalistic management and the symbiotic relationship between large-scale farms and household plots, which preserve existing structures, even though they are disadvantageous for the company farm. Together with a deficient institutional environment, these factors prevent new paths of development from evolving in Russian agriculture.

In his article Ivaylo Vassilev takes a critical stance towards both the simplified liberal understanding of rural transformation and towards the simplified interpretation of path-dependency theory. According to Vassilev, an "emphasis on path-dependency suggests that *nothing can change* because past trajectories re-assert themselves, and a one-sided emphasis on path-shaping leads easily into a voluntaristic position that radical *change is always possible*." For him, there are no identifiable paths in post-socialist Bulgaria, but the notion of legacy is more satisfactory for capturing the complex interrelationship of continuity and discontinuity in political, economic and legal processes. Legacies are "influences from the past that are only actualised by their coupling with certain presents, yet with largely unpredictable, and therefore, often unintended and contradictory outcomes." From this starting point, Vassilev analyses the difficulties structures and practices from the socialist past face in adapting in the current stage of transition and how these difficulties are influenced by present policies and practices, such as mechanisms for land restitution, lost markets and reduced subsidies.

Katalin Kovács reports on land use and ownership structures in three Central European countries, Hungary, Slovakia and the Czech Republic. After introducing the patterns of late socialist ownership and land-use systems and the scale and nature of the duality of large-scale and small-scale farming in these countries, she makes a short comparative analysis of privatization approaches to landed and non-landed assets and present land-use patterns. The second part of the paper focuses on the role of small-scale farming in the livelihoods of families living in rural areas and considers the impact of the dramatic fall in agricultural employment and the break up of formerly operating integration channels for dwarf-farm products.

Irina Râmniceanu and Robert Ackrill analyse the European model of agriculture and rural development policy choices in the new member states. They identify the policy choices made by the eight Central and Eastern European New Member States by classifying measures as either primarily competitiveness-oriented measures or primarily multifunctionality-oriented measures. The balance of these measures is then analysed in terms of the public funds attached, allowing a judgement to be made about the extent to which the New Member States are promoting multifunctionality and the European Model of Agriculture. Economic and policy factors that might explain the policy choices made are examined, and conclusions are drawn as to what policy-makers can do if they wish to promote rural multifunctionality in the area.

Maarit Heinonen in her article evaluates the role of multifunctionality in post-socialist agriculture. According to her, multifunctional agriculture is a new concept in the new EU Member States of Central and Eastern Europe (CEE). However, even now very little is known about the role of different farm strategies in multifunctionality, their relevance, the degree to which multifunctional activities are taken up by farm households and used in rural policies, and their contribution to economically, ecologically and socially sustainable rural development. There is a need to challenge current analytical frameworks on multifunctional agriculture and rural areas, which are based mainly on the farm structures and other characteristics of Western agriculture.

The second part of the anthology begins with two articles on the village movement in Lithuania. After a short overview of developments in Lithuania over the last ten years, Arunas Poviliunas analyses the main features of the Lithuanian village movement. The dynamics that have geared the growth of the movement include rural policies adopted by the government which emphasize only the development of agriculture, not rural areas as such. This political exclusion of rural communities is reflected in the growth of social transfers, poverty and in the lack of the necessary investment. On the other hand the dominant view in social policy is one where poor people are seen as an underclass rather than active members of the local community. Poviliunas argues that an effective rural inclusion policy must be based on an interactive interpretation of social exclusion. Empowerment and destigmatization are also necessary preconditions for effective strategies of social inclusion.

Aine Macken Walsh in her paper analyses the factors that make a village movement a success. She compares two rural villages and identifies historical and current social, economic, cultural and traditional factors. According to her, success is based on positive previous experiences with collective farms. These experiences include a trusted leader and good leadership which promoted the welfare of the village. This has helped preserve the feeling of community. The continued presence of local professionals – especially female – who had played a prominent role in social activities before was also crucial for a successful movement.

In her article Ingrid Oswald analyses rural life through the concept of an industrialized village. According to her, the concept contrasts with the "old European village of family farms" concept, and her analysis starts with the basic elements of the socialist and post-socialist rural way of life and then proceeds to compare them in Bulgaria, Russia, Estonia and the former GDR. Oswald argues that the peasant village no longer exists and that it will not be revived. Instead, new rural ways of life are emerging which are different from those in the West and those found in the pre-Soviet period.

Karina Lukin presents a study about the changing attitudes of the Nenets-people to nature and the village, beginning with Soviet efforts to settle nomads and create a new way of life for them. According to Lukin, rapid and often violent reforms from the 1930s through to the 1970s left little room for the Nenets to adapt to their new circumstances. However, they did adapt and shape the life in the village. Over the years, the village became part of the Nenets structure of places, and therefore the abolishment of the *kolkhozes*[1] has been an attack against these "imagined communities" that have become very real.

Nathalie Ortar analyses the social differentiation of Russia's rural community through an analysis of *dachniki*[2] and their social relations. Some *dachniki* have stable roots in rural communities but there is also a large number of "newcomers", urban workers with different habits. These newcomers maintain social networks with other *dachniki* and other villagers on the basis of

[1] Collectively owned, large agricultural enterprise.
[2] Summer cottage owners.

an active family network and reciprocal exchanges of services amongst the *dachniki* themselves and between the *dachniki* and other villagers.

Maria Djakonova's article concentrates on the problems of youth employment in Russian Karelia. In contemporary Russia, the rural youth is particularly exposed to the pressure of social and economic problems. The article highlights the main factors which influence changes in the labour market and describes the youth's position on the rural Karelian labour market. She also identifies features of youth employment and unemployment and makes some recommendations how to mitigate social exclusion on the rural labour market and suggests some ways of solving youth employment problems.

All in all, the common tone of the articles in this book is a questioning of the merits of ultraliberal reforms in the countryside. In most post-socialist countries, the reconstruction of a new peasantry from former members of collective farms was a delusion. This delusion had very severe and unintended outcomes socially, economically and ethically. The articles also show that conclusions about a deepening destitution and anomy in post-socialist rural areas are premature. Indeed, rural people are innovative, adaptive and even entrepreneurial. A necessary precondition for success in the transition of rural areas in post-socialist countries is the adaptation of a consistent policy of rural development in its widest sense. In addition to developing agriculture, alternative forms of employment have to be created, such as tourism or small-scale non-agricultural entrepreneurship. It is especially important to support local communities in promoting development from below.

Current global tendencies suggest an increasing degree of concentration and vertical integration in agricultural production, both in Europe and in Russia. However, recent experiences have proved that it is not possible to "fabricate" a future based on western models, nor are future developmental patterns predestined by history. This means that the rural transition, transformation and restructuring of rural production, social and community structures, and cultural and normative patterns, is still very much an uncompleted process. Therefore the *Agrarfrage* will be with us for many years to come.

PART I

INSTITUTIONS AND TRANSFORMATION OF AGRICULTURE

CHAPTER ONE

RESULTS OF TRANSFORMATION OF RUSSIAN AGRI-FOOD SECTOR

EUGENIA SEROVA

Introduction

In order to assess the progress of agrarian reform in post-communist Russia one should consider not only the final point that has been reached but also the distance covered in the course of its implementation. Unlike in Central and Eastern European (CEE) countries, in Russia agriculture had experienced severe problems for long periods. Nevertheless, it had been the granary of Europe before 1917; 50% of the value of all Russian exports was in grain. In addition to this historical backwardness, seventy-four years of communism had left a deep imprint on the perceptions of the population, on the spatial and sectoral structure of production and on the rural infrastructure. Inevitably, Russia's reforms took much longer than, for instance, the reforms in Hungary or Slovenia, and even in these countries not all the problems associated with the reforms have been overcome.

Russia's reforms faced a communist legacy which not only considered the private ownership of land a crime but even outlawed the possession of a private tractor. The state was in charge of agriculture and fixed the parameters of the agricultural sector, and entrepreneurial activity was invariably prosecuted as a crime. Only if one considers this legacy, can one fully understand the new agricultural structure and system of land tenure that has emerged in Russia over the past 15 years and realize the achievements and limitations of Russia's attempt to introduce a market-oriented agricultural system.

The most complicated task was simply to change the state's agrarian policy from one based on a central plan to one based on the market. This change was strongly affected by the federal structure of the state and the degree of independence given to regional administrations in implementing agrarian policy. Another problem was the inexperience of policy makers and the agricultural establishment in regulating an agri-food sector in a market environment. In CEE countries, this lack of experience was partially overcome by accepting an EU rules and regulations as a precondition for their accession as new member states. In Russia, a new political concept emerged only after a series of continuous contradictions and failures.

The evolution of Russia's new farm structure

The evolution of a new farm structure in Russia was the product of several social and economic developments over the last decade. In fact, it also bore the impact of Russia's history as a whole, but in this particular paper, I shall not examine, to any great extent, the historical background. In this section, I shall only consider the most important developments which affected the new farm structure.

As is generally known, Russia's land reform and the restructuring of farms were based on a procedure called land sharing. The workers of the *kolkhoz*es[3] and *sovkhoz*es[4] as well as pensioners and employees in social service sector (teachers, doctors, etc.) received equal conditional[5] shares of the landed property of their particular parent farm. These conditional shares were not marked out on the ground. Rather, they can be considered as a kind of option: the shares gave the holder the right to withdraw from his/her parent farm with a physical plot of land at any time without the permission of the other shareholders. Only the location of the plot had to be agreed with them. These land shares were legally transferable. In the reform of 1992-1994, around 12 million such shares were allotted to rural residents.

About 300,000 households used their right to withdraw from the parent farm enterprises and set up their own family farms. The remaining rural residents preferred to retain their original status as members of the collective farm. In the majority of cases they leased their land shares back to the farm enterprises. There was also the option of contributing their land shares to the equity of the parent farms, in which case the shareholder lost his/her right to claim a plot and instead became a shareholder in either a joint stock company or a co-operative. In practice, this option was rarely used.

Due to Russia's poor legal culture, weak law enforcement, and the federal structure of the State[6], the land share arrangements were not registered properly: shareholders were unaware of the benefits and responsibilities involved in

---

[3] Collectively owned large agricultural enterprise.

[4] State owned large agricultural enterprise.

[5] Each member of collective farm received a certificate of ownership of parcel of land, which they could transfer for establishing their own farm or lease back to the large-scale farm. The shares were not converted into physically demarcated plots of land.

[6] Land tenure issues are a subject of both federal and regional legislation, and a number of regions did not offer land sharing arrangements.

possessing shares. The agricultural enterprises which used the land did not actually pay for doing so. Besides, land which was leased in the form of shares was not identified on the map.

The situation changed somewhat after a presidential decree in 1996, which obliged all land users to enter into legal contracts with the owners of land shares. Since then, the average size of individual farms has grown due to the leasing of land shares. There is no official data, but only anecdotal evidence on the land share transactions that were made between farm enterprises. Obliged to enter into formal lease contracts, land shareholders were encouraged to choose more preferential lease terms. In this way a kind of market in land shares sprang up.

There was a further development concerning land shares after the crisis of 1998. The rouble's devaluation led to a noticeable increase in import substitution, and to a significant growth in agriculture over the following three years (see below). Due to this growth, there was a sudden demand for land and its value increased. In these circumstances, the conditional character of land shares played a positive role in the development of the land market. Attracted by a high net return in agriculture and enforced for a vertical integration due to high transaction costs in food chain, external investors began to acquire farmland for their own farming operations. On the other hand, land shareholders had become aware of the rising value of their land and were not eager to sell their shares. Therefore, the leasing of land shares had become a major way to acquire land in this period.

If farmland as a result of land reform were divided into physical plots, the big companies, which now lease up to 300,000 hectares each in several regions, would have been obligated to invest in land consolidation and divert financial resources from their productive investments for this consolidation. Now they could accumulate a big number of the leased shares and only afterwards claim the lands in the corresponding farm enterprises for allocation in the physical terms and allow them to get these lands in big fragments.

On the other hand, the shareholders, who remained the owners of these shares, can claim a plot of land on the edge of the land used by the tenant after the expiry of the lease. In the case of physical land shares, this might result in a situation where someone's plot was in the middle of a crop rotation of a tenant. Such a situation could release the land shareholder from the terms of the lease.

Thus, after 1998 the market in land shares developed very rapidly. In accordance with our estimate, 5-6% of the land shares changed hands annually. This large market required a sound legal basis, and for this reason a new Land Code and a Law on Farmland transactions was passed easily in the Duma in late 2001 and the spring of 2002, after several years of heated but unsuccessful public debate.

The evolution of farmland tenure

In the former USSR, all the land belonged to the state and was allocated to the *kolkhoz*es and *sovkhoz*es for use free of charge and without any time-limit. The *kolkhoz*es and state institutes (such as factories, research institutions) also used to allot small plots of land to individual households for domestic subsistence production. There were several attempts to reform land tenure in the Soviet period but a radical reform of land tenure in Russian agriculture only started with the break-up of the USSR at the end of 1991.

In accordance with the Russian Constitution (1993), land regulation is simultaneously within the competence of both federal and regional authorities. The relevant part of the Constitution is not very precise and clear and has, therefore, created a certain contradiction in land legislation. In general, this provision concerning the various authorities' competence in this matter is taken to mean that the federal power has the right to impose the *principles* of land legislation, while regional (level of the subjects of the Federation) administrations are authorized to issue *detailed land laws*. This legal ambiguity led to a situation where several regions used to have laws which contradicted federal legislation, and furthermore, the federal authorities have no real power to prevent regions adopting such laws.

All the land in Russia is divided into several categories such as farmland, municipal land, industrial land, land used for transport and other non-farming purposes, land for nature conservation, forest lands, land under water, and other land. Each of these land categories has its own legal regime. The most profound land reforms were carried out in relation to farmland, while other categories of land remained mostly in state ownership.

For the first time since 1917, private ownership of land was introduced by the Constitution of the Russian Federation in 1990. This property right was limited by a moratorium on the sale of land for ten years after the acquisition of land plots by individual citizens[7]. Only the state was allowed to sell land freely. In the autumn of 1990, two laws were adopted which detailed the private ownership of farmland: the Law on Peasant Farms and the Law on Land Reform. These laws allowed citizens to have in private ownership a plot of land for household production, for gardening, for house construction, and for some other purposes. These two laws also envisaged land sharing by *kolkhoz*es and *sovkhoz*es, which meant that *kolkhoz* and *sovkhoz* workers could get a plot of land as their private property for individual farming. However, these laws did not make such arrangements obligatory. The terms of these laws were further

---

[7] Free right to sell was restricted by the right of first refusal provided to other employees of the enterprise and the restriction to sell only for agricultural use (see Wegren 2005, 67).

consolidated in the Land Code of the Russian Federation, adopted in the spring of 1991. This Code was limited by the Constitution and did not allow free land transfers between enterprises or between individual land owners.

Farmland reform in Russia was accelerated by the break-up of the USSR in late 1991. A Presidential decree and Government decision in December 1991 started the process of farm restructuring and land privatization. In accordance with these two pieces of legislation, the employees of *kolkhoz*es and *sovkhoz*es received land and assets in collective ownership. They were stipulated to share received lands into the conditional shares of workers and pensioners (lands were allotted also for social workers in the villages). The shareholders had a right to transfer these shares to their personal use for setting up individual farms. The shareholders could sell and rent their shares to the members of the same collective, pass them to their heirs, or realize them in the form of landed property when withdrawing from the collective farm.

A new Russian Constitution, adopted by referendum in late 1993, provided for the complete and unfettered right to own private property. So, the previous moratorium on the sale of land was lifted. In accordance with the new Constitution and endowed with a temporary extraordinary power to issue decrees equal in force to laws, the President issued a decree which abolished most of the articles of the acting Land Code of the Russian Federation. The remaining ruins of this Code became the most liberal land legislation in Russia in so far as it does not prohibit almost any type of land transaction. Only two restrictions remained in this piece of legislation: (1) the purpose for which the land is to be used cannot be changed voluntarily, and (2) regional authorities could impose upper size limits for individual land ownership.

At the same time, the incomplete nature of Russian federal land legislation coupled with the weakness of the federal powers and political uncertainty prevented the proper implementation of this land legislation. In addition, incomplete and inaccurate information created in the public's mind the impression that legal prohibitions on private land ownership in Russia still existed and caused endless discussions as to whether it should or should not be introduced.

On the other hand, a plunge in agricultural production that lasted several years led to a lack of demand for farmland in the majority of Russia's regions with inevitable repercussions for the land market. Consequently, obtaining a mortgage to buy land became rather problematic.

Fig. 1-1 Farmland ownership structure in Russia, 01/01/04

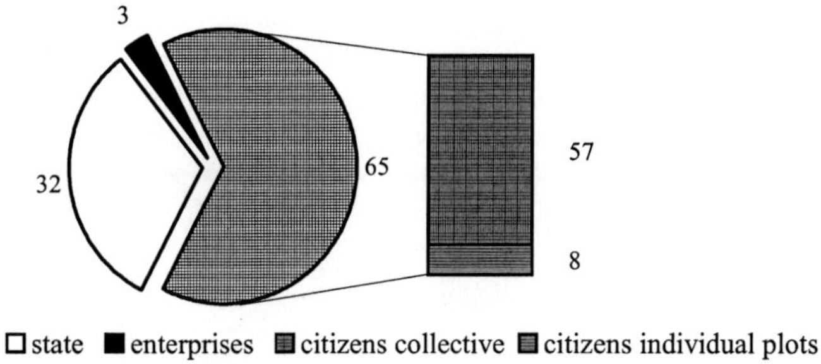

Source: Shagaida 2005.

The structure of farmland ownership has not been monitored properly so here we can only present estimates. As can be seen from Fig. 1-1, 65% of farmland in Russia today is in private ownership (if land shares are considered as private ownership) with 32% of farmland owned by the state and municipalities.

Land transactions were very rare before the crisis of 1998. So, in accordance with federal legislation, almost all types of transactions (excluding mortgages since 1998) were permitted after 1998. Moreover, since the rouble's devaluation and the start of a recovery of the agri-food sector, demand for farmland rose and a rather energetic agricultural land market emerged. However, the economic agents (farms, refining industries and trade) were in a constant state of uncertainty regarding the stability of the current land tenure system, due to the perpetual public debate on whether the sale and purchase of land was legal. This uncertainty has become a substantial impediment for the development of the agri-food sector[8].

This was the state of farmland tenure in Russia on the eve of new land legislation in late 2001 when a new Russian Land Code was adopted. However, the issues concerning farmland turnover were excluded from this code in order to make its passing through the legislature easier. In the spring of 2002, a special Law on Farmland Turnover was adopted.

Bearing in mind the system of land tenure in Russia before 2002, one should admit that the new land law does not herald a revolutionary change either in Russia's agriculture or agrarian structure. The new law, coupled with the earlier adopted Land Code, codifies, normalizes, and completes Russia's land legislation. This is the first significant aspect of this new land legislation. The

[8] A totality which consists of agricultural enterprises, food-processing and production input (fertilisers, machines, etc) industries and trade.

second significant aspect is that it sends a clear message to the economic agents that the current land tenure system is here to stay.

The new law on the farmland turnover has imposed a ban on the non-residential ownership of farmland. Foreign persons, legal entities with more than 50% foreign participation in equity can only rent farmlands on long-term (up to 49 years) leases. In this way, the new law sends a message to the substantial number of Russian citizens who were concerned about the acquisition by foreigners of Russian land. It also means that non-residents can only own urban and industrial lands.

It is worth noting that in almost every East European post-socialist country (excluding Latvia and Estonia) the ownership of farmland by non-residents is restricted. In this respect the new Russian law is no exception to mainstream developments in other transitional countries. On the other hand, under current Russian economic and legal situation this restriction will have circumstance no serious effects on the *status quo*. First of all, the ownership of farmland by legal entities is permitted in Russia, and it is almost impossible to trace the real ownership relations of affiliated holdings. Therefore, through several affiliates, foreigners can control the final entities which own farmland. Also the ban on ownership by foreigners provides a reason for foreigners to enter into formal marriages with Russians to get access to farmland in Russia.

The law on farmland turnover envisages a right for subjects of the Federation to put an upper limit on the amount of land in the ownership of one owner. However, this limit cannot be less than 10% of the total amount of farmland of rayon (the smallest administrative unit in Russia). This norm has an anti-trust nature: it prevents the monopolization of access to land for agricultural production.

The new law announces land shares[9] a right in a common property. It means *de facto* the prohibition of land shares renting; now only collective renting is possible. The sale of a share involves such a sophisticated procedure that it becomes impossible for rural people. Therefore, under the new legal conditions land share holders will tend to contribute there shares into equities of their parent agricultural enterprises and lose their property rights to the land. It is a result, which reformers of agriculture tried to avoid throughout the years of the reforms, because it deprives people of their right to own land.

Both the collective rent and the rent from agricultural enterprises will increase the price of land for outsider investors. This in turn will result in a reduction of productive investments, which agriculture is in so much need of nowadays.

[9] See footnote 3.

Other consequences of this norm are linked with the social support of rural people. The land shares were rather often given for rent with a life-long support: elderly rural residents usually passed their shares on to new owners, who in return undertook some life-long services and payments to these people. This was a significant social guarantee for the elderly rural residents, who have much less social security services than urban residents. With the new law this mechanism was also abolished.

It can be concluded that the new law (1) gave society a clear message about the long-term development strategy of private land ownership in agriculture; and (2) provided a legal ground for farmland turnover. It did not cause any revolutionary change either in agricultural production or agrarian structure. At the same time, the law may lead to a certain reduction of investment flowing into the primary sector and reduce the level of social protection of the rural elderly.

The structure of agricultural production

The current structure of agricultural production in Russia has an ambivalent nature. Farm enterprises worked an overwhelming majority of Russia's farmland and accounted for 86%, whilst private farmers accounted for 8 % and households for 6 % in 2000 (Calculated from the Russian Cadastre Service's data). This despite the fact that since 1991 the total area used for farming fell by 7.5% while the area worked by farm enterprises fell by almost 20%. However, less than half (40% in 2003) of gross agricultural output (GAO) originated from farm enterprises while the households' share was 55% (Calculated from the Russian Statistic Service's data). The deepest point of recession in Russian agriculture was in 1998 when the whole sector produced only 56% of the GAO of 1991, and the GAO of farm enterprises represented just 35% of the pre-reform level.

At first glance, it seems that farm enterprises held onto most of the land, while actual production was concentrated in individual farms. However, the data on household production (Fig. 1-2) shows that this sector has not significantly increased its output; potatoes, vegetables and fruit constitute a certain exception. In the pre-reform period, household plots mainly produced for self-consumption, and official data confirms that only 13% of their total output went for sale (Serova 1999, 7). Therefore, the noticeable fall in the contribution of farm enterprises to GAO simply reflects the equally noticeable fall in food consumption in the Russian Federation since the beginning of the reforms. Demand for agri-food products contracted due to a drop in the purchasing power of the population; the output of commercial (market oriented) farm enterprises fell to the same extent, whilst households kept on producing for their own subsistence at the same level as before the reforms or perhaps with an even stronger orientation towards producing food for their domestic needs. The contribution of individual farms to GAO increased.

Fig. 1-2 Production of selected products by households in Russia, in mln tons

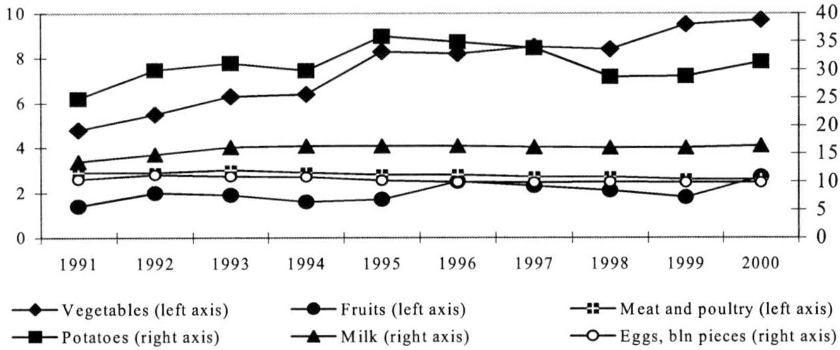

Source: Calculated from Goskomstat data.

The second reason for the remarkable growth in the share of households in GAO is linked to changes in relative agricultural prices: crop prices rose much more slowly than prices for livestock product. Households are more involved in livestock husbandry and the cultivation of high value products like fruit and vegetables, while farm enterprises specialize in cereal crops, oilseeds, and fodder crops. Thus, given these price ratio changes, the share of households in GAO has grown.[10]

The growth in agriculture which has occurred since 1998 resulted in an increase of the contribution of farm enterprises to GAO. This means that this type of farm unit was the first to react to changes in the market. Individual farms also reacted to the market positively and their share in GAO has also increased since 1998.

This period of growth in agriculture caused acceleration in farm differentiation in Russia. On the one hand, a certain number of farms fully utilized the window of opportunity opened by the rouble's devaluation in 1998. Their revenues increased, they managed to pay back debts, they re-invested profits, and they attracted external capital. On the other hand, a certain number of farm enterprises and some of the area used in the past for agriculture were marginalized in terms of production and profitability. Some farms continued to

[10] The shares of various types of farms in the GAO are computed in current prices.

record losses over a period of several years, other farms accumulated hopeless debts, assets were depreciated, and land abandoned.

On the role of the most prosperous farms, one can observe not only a trend towards concentration, but also a trend towards new ownership structures. These farms are very different from collective enterprises (co-operatives) and are usually organized as a joint-stock company. Although production co-operatives are still the predominant form of farm enterprise (around 46% of total farm enterprises), the best farms are usually either a joint stock company or have a very strong manager who runs the farm almost as if he was the owner. A lot of farms (especially in the most profitable sectors) are bought by outsiders, such as mineral oil companies (Gazprom) or financial companies.

Farm enterprises have experienced not only a process of differentiation, but also increasing specialization. Fig. 1-3 depicts the products which farm enterprises currently produce. One can see that farm enterprises have specialized in extensive crops: cereal and oil crops, and sugar beet. The first two types of crops are exported and are the cash crops with the highest profitability level. Farm enterprises produce hardly any potatoes or other vegetables, honey or wool. As for basic livestock products, they produce less than half of total production. However, the line on Fig. 1-3 indicates the loss in the share of production of selected products by enterprises since 1991 in percent age points.

The most significant losses in production share for farm enterprises were in milk, meat, vegetable and wool production. This was a natural result of the irrational agricultural policy of the Soviet period. There were plenty of huge and highly specialized greenhouses, milk and fodder farms (mostly *sovkhoz*es around big cities). They were operated on the basis of cheap energy, subsidized grain feed and negligible transport costs. Naturally, price liberalization made these farms heavily insolvent. During the reform these farms were subsidized (subsidies for heating green houses, subsidies for grain feed for huge feed lots), but in vain. On the other side, the consumption of meat and dairy products was adversely affected by the much reduced purchasing power of the population. Therefore, the biggest greenhouses and feedlots, faced with a rapid rise in costs and reduced demand, went bankrupt. At the same time, households maintained and even increased their level of production.

Fig. 1-3 Share of farm enterprises in the output of selected agricultural products in Russia, 1991 and 2000, in percent

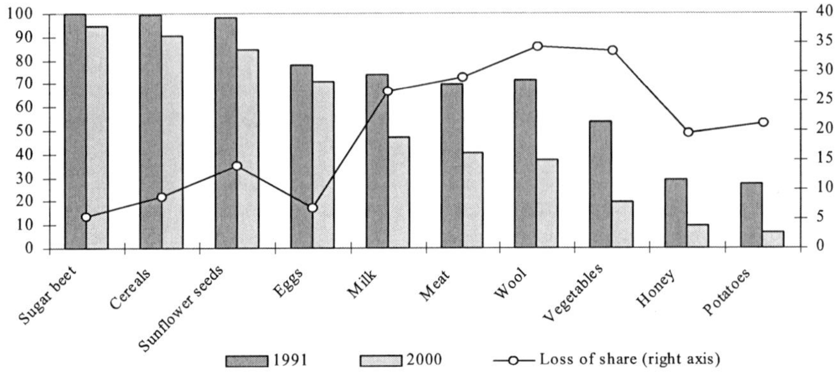

Source: Calculated from Goskomstat data.

However, after the rouble's devaluation demand for livestock products from the domestic producers was gradually regained, which made feedlots profitable again. They became attractive for external investors and are now booming. The contribution of households in GAO exceeded 50% whereas earlier, since 1998, its share had been falling. As noticed earlier (see Fig. 1-2) the production of selected products in subsistence farms remained quite steady during the period of the reforms and has not very significantly grown since the Soviet period.

In the middle of the 1990s, various studies of Russian agriculture began to register the emergence of a new organizational form in farming which was quite different from the main type of agricultural production unit in all the other post-Soviet economies (E.g. Rylko 2005, Serova & Khramova 2002, Uzun 2001, Koester 2003). This process has become especially evident since the crisis of 1998 when growth in the agri-food sector began to recover. There is no commonly accepted name for this type of farm in the literature: Rylko calls them "New Agricultural Operators" (NAO), Serova and Khramova "vertically integrated companies", and in Russian official practice the term "agroholdings" is used. Whatever the name it unites a number of quite different kinds of agricultural companies, established in different ways and motivated by different incentives. Moreover, sometimes the structure of these forms differs dramatically. They are not necessarily organized as holding companies and not every firm is vertically integrated into a supply chain. In this respect the term "new operators" reflects the essence of the phenomenon in the most adequate way – something new in a seemingly traditional, large scale form.

These firms are the big – much bigger than the traditional Soviet farm enterprises and their current heirs – farm operations, established with capital arrived outside the primary sector. Sometimes, this external capital comes from the downstream sector, for instance, when a processor invests in raw material (such as meat, milk, flour) supplying farms, and sometimes it comes from the upstream sector when a supplier (machine dealer, seed producer, etc.) tends to control a buyer of inputs, i.e. the farms. In many cases, capital originates from outside the agri-food sector entirely – mainly from the most profitable sectors of the Russian economy such as energy, finance and metallurgy. In some cases, several farm enterprises are held by one holding company, but there might just be one huge farm enterprise. Sometimes these companies are organized under the control, and with the participation, of the regional and/or local administration, although in the majority of cases they are purely the result of private initiative. The management structure also differs considerably from company to company. Land tenure can also be arranged in different ways: huge areas may be owned by the company, but usually these companies rent land.

What distinguishes these new operators from traditional farm enterprises is not only, or even predominantly, the scale of their operation but the remarkable flow of investment they bring to the primary sector, new types of management, new technologies, the commercial orientation of the business and their aggressive market behaviour.

There is still no clear understanding or even definition of this new phenomenon in Russian agriculture, but it has grown rapidly in the last decade and now plays a significant role in the agri-food sector. It is a quite opposite direction to the one Russia's agricultural development was supposed to take after the collapse of the Soviet system: the former collective and state farms are not being split into individual farms but are being united into even bigger agricultural companies. We do not pretend to develop a comprehensive theory for the emergence of these new operators in this paper, but we will discuss the preconditions for their emergence, their motivation and scope and the possible consequences of their operations.

Agri-food policy

Despite the protectionist rhetoric of Russia's agricultural establishment, Russian agri-food policy is rather liberal. The level of support of the agri-food sector, according to the conventional measure, that is, the Producer Support Estimate (PSE), is one of the lowest in the world and on the decline: in 2002 in Russia it was 9%; in the USA, 21%; in Australia, 4%; in Switzerland, 73%; and in the EU-15, 35% (OECD and Centre AFE Data).

After the sharp decline in support in 1991-1992 with the start of the reforms, the PSE grew steadily until 1997. However, this growth was to a large extent explained by an appreciation of the national currency. After the crisis of 1998, the PSE remained very low, making Russia a member of the group of low-support countries such as New Zealand, Australia, Kazakhstan, and Ukraine; and Estonia in pre-accession period to the EU.

Budget transfers to agriculture are also declining (Fig. 1-4).

Fig. 1-4 Budget transfers to agriculture in Russia, million RUR*

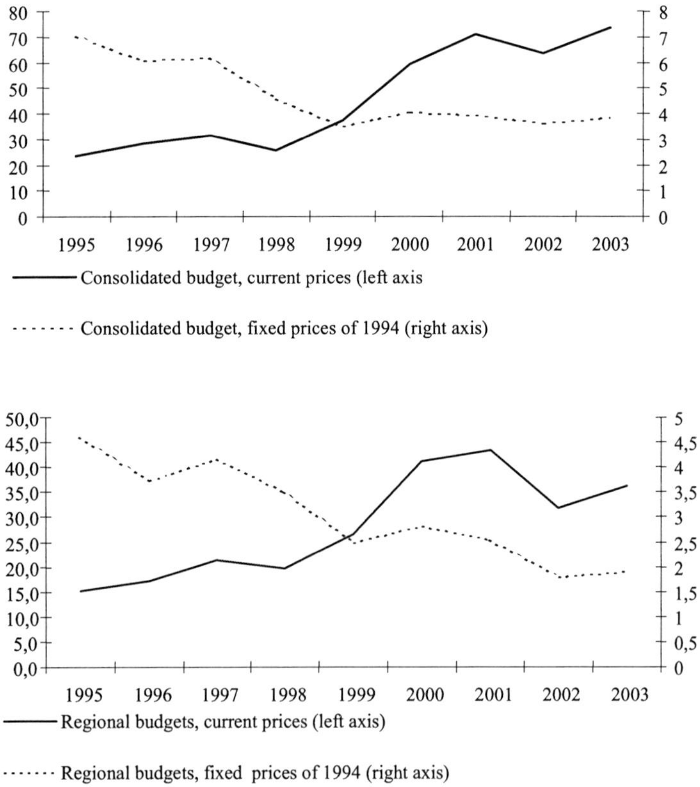

* currently US$~28,5 RUR.

Source: Centre AFE.

Their share in GDP and in gross agricultural product has steadily declined as well. The consolidated budget involves transfers from three budget levels: federal, regional and local. Therefore, Fig. 1-4 depicts the dynamic of both federal and regional budgets. Later we shall discuss the distribution of budget support between these three budget levels. This is particularly important for Russia as a federal state with such different natural conditions for farming across the regions.

The trade regime in the agri-food sector in Russia is also one the most liberal in the world if judged by added value equivalent (AVE) import tariffs. Russia not only has one of the lowest mean import AVE tariffs in the world but also has very low tariff caps. A cap of 50% is imposed on cocoa, but for all the other agri-food commodities there is a cap of 25%. However, one should be aware that apart from ad valorem import duties, Russia has since 2002 imposed import volume quotas for poultry and TRQs[11] for beef and pork. In 2004, a variable import duty for sugar (bound to New York commodity board prices) was adopted. In addition to simple import duties, combined duties are broadly applied, and Russia actively uses phytosanitarian (sanitary regulations of all agricultural products) measures for domestic market protection. Therefore, the efficient level of protection is notably higher than mean import tariff. Hence, taking into consideration the fact that other countries use the same import tools in their trade policy, one can conclude that Russia allows greater access to her domestic agri-food markets than her main trade partners allow to their agri-food markets.

The structure of budget agricultural transfers can be assessed in three main ways: (1) by budgets level; (2) by measures of green and amber boxes[12]; and (3) by particular measures of support. Each method has its own particular set of problems.

Russia is a federation of 86 constituent subjects; each region has its own budget, and the rules of governing the drawing up of these budgets are subject to federal tax and budget codes. Currently less than 10 regions offset their budgets with a surplus. All the rest have budget deficits and receive budget transfers from the federal budget in order to implement their budget obligations. It is evident that regions with budget surplus have more potential for supporting agriculture than other regions. Russian legislation sets no limits on the kind of support measures that the regions may use; regions can use all sorts of measures. As a rule, regional administrations copy federal programmes of support with minor changes and/or simply co-finance federal programmes on their territory. However, there are a few exceptions to this rule. A problem arises the moment a region starts to intervene in regional markets with price

[11] TRQs – tariff rate quotas, one of several import regulation measures.
[12] See WTO Uruguay round Agricultural Agreement.

support measures which are normally coupled with inter-regional trade limitation measures. Apart from these tools of direct support for their producers, the regions conduct real trade wars. Thus, Tartarstan is enjoying high budget revenues from oil prices and applies substantial subsidies for each unit of fresh milk sold. As a result, the small neighbouring Republic of Chuvashia, with a similar agricultural sector, similar organizational and historical backgrounds, and similar technical and production potentials for its dairy sector, has to slaughter its cattle, which is uncompetitive compared with Tartarstan's production on the regional market, because it is deprived of oil budget revenues. In other federations such as the USA and Germany, the federal proportion in total budget transfers to agriculture is 90%. In 1998, in Russia this was just 20%. For a time, the growth of the federal contribution was considered a positive trend by policy makers. (Fig. 1-5) However, in 2004 a piece of legislation was adopted which shifted all agricultural subsidies to the regional budget level.

Fig. 1-5 Structure of budget transfers to agriculture in Russia according to budgetary level, in percent

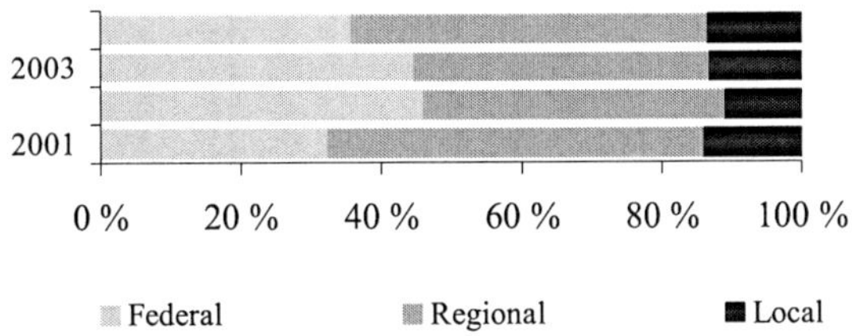

Source: Centre AFE.

Besides interregional trade wars and the disintegration of national agricultural markets, this shift of agricultural subsidies to the regional budget level leads to a non-optimal use of national resources: Russia's "rich regions" are predominantly located in the north of the country, which is the least suitable area for agriculture. Agricultural production is mostly to be found in regions with budget deficits. This is a particular element of inefficiency of agricultural policy in Russia, which differs from most other transitional economies.

The share of green box measures in total budget transfers to agriculture in Russia is slowly growing (Fig. 1-6), though it still lags behind many other countries: in Russia the share was 0.25; in USA 0.62; in Australia 0.23; and in Switzerland, 0.83 (Centre AFE data). At the same time, one should note that it is precisely green box measures that are intended to facilitate the development of market institutes and infrastructure, which are mostly lacking in a transitional economy, and which we needed for the efficient growth of the economy, including the agri-food economy.

Fig. 1-6 Structure of budget transfers to agriculture in Russia by green and amber box measures, in percent

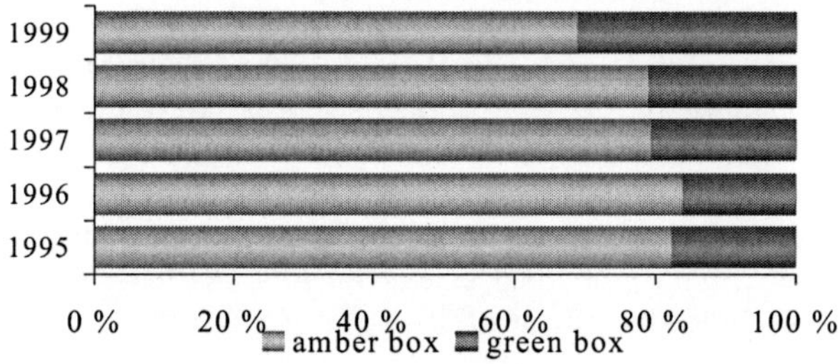

Source: Centre AFE.

At the federal level, input subsidies dominate the structure of budget transfers to agriculture (Fig. 1-7) From the very beginning of the reforms, the government subsidized the cost to producers of acquiring mineral fertilizers, seeds, pedigree animals, planting sticks for vineries and orchards, and in some years, for mixed fodder. In 1994, a state programme of machinery and cattle leasing was introduced. From the first year of transition, various schemes of preferential farm credit were also implemented.

Fig. 1-7 Share of input subsidies in the total value of federal agricultural subsidies in Russia, in percent*

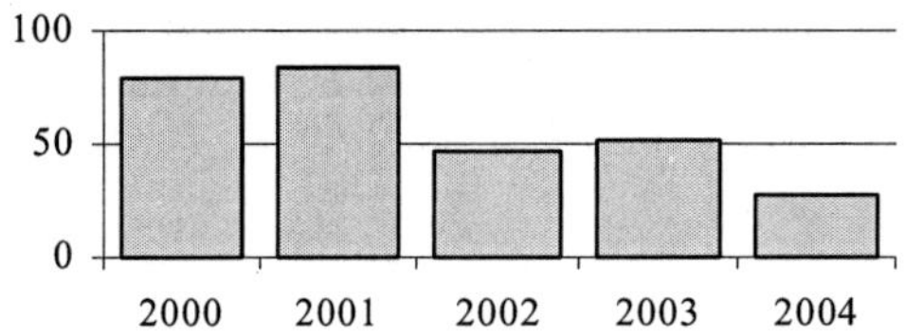

* 2004- provisional
Source: Centre AFE: Farm differentiation and farm efficiency

Fig. 1-7 depicts the decline in the share of these subsidies in the total value of subsidies to agriculture. This reduction is explained by that fact that some budget expenses were given to the equity of the state enterprises (a state agricultural bank and a state leasing company) for implementing these programmes. These sums are not explicitly reflected in the budget outlays for agricultural subsidies.

Farm structure and farm efficiency

Russian agriculture continues to be rather inefficient. In the first half of the 1990s, the average profitability of the agricultural sector as a whole was permanently negative, and although after 1998 this indicator was positive, it still remained very low. Up to 50% of farms, even after 1998, were recording losses, which testifies to the deep crisis in farm performance. There are many studies (e.g. Uzun 2001) which deal with individual causes for this inefficiency and loss-making. Authors have studied the effects of the lack of capital, the terms of trade for agriculture, management issues and labour quality. However, it is clear that in spite of the importance of all these reasons they can not explain the loss-making of up to half of Russia's farms.

Notwithstanding the background of chronic inefficiency for the sector as a whole, one can divide Russia's agricultural producers into two groups. The first group consists of relatively profitable and modernized producers, who are attractive to outside investors, and the other group consists of marginal, chronic loss-making producers. The first group produces the dominant share of gross agricultural product and is expanding its landuse and assets. The second group is steadily loosing its share in production, in terms of acreage, level of technology and productivity. This differentiation of Russia's farms has already been discussed in the literature (see e.g. Epstein & Schultze 2005; Uzun & Gataulina 2005).

In other words, the inefficiency of the entire agricultural sector is the product of this second – marginal – group. It is this group of producers that is recording losses and contributing to a reduction of the entire sector's profitability. It is reasonable to ask why these producers still exist in the national economy and have not gone out of business. To what extent their survival is the result of the soft budgetary constraints that the agri-food policy has provided? This part of the paper proposes to answer this question.

It is reasonable to assume that the level of a farm's viability is random variable with a normal distribution of frequency. A significant deviation from normal distribution may be the result of two kinds of external impact: first, it may be the result of a transitional process when producers adjust at different speeds having experienced some kind of a shock; second, it may be the result of some long-lasting political influence.

Fig. 1-8 Theoretical frequency distribution of producers by viability with, and without, external impact[13]

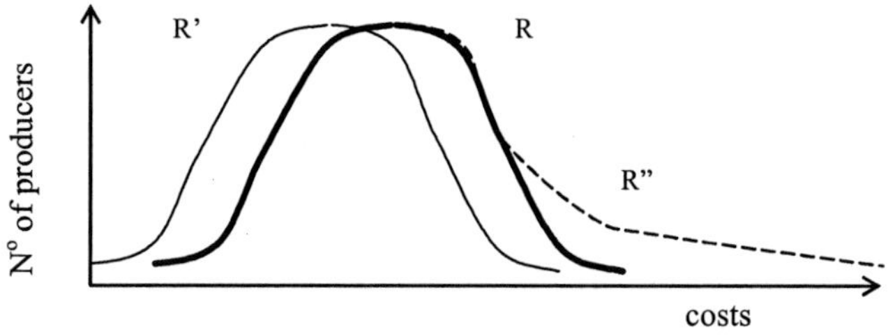

A shock associated with an economy's transformation or some specific government policy, for instance, targeted support for inefficient farms, results in an increase in the number of farms with a viability level below the sample mean (curve R" in the figure). In practice, this means that regardless of the relatively high number of producers with a high level of performance, the number of badly performing producers is too high and this reduces the average viability of the sector.

For the purpose of our study, we will use production costs as a measure of farm viability. It can be assumed that within one region there is a unified market for a product at a particular price. Therefore, the cost of production can be considered as a proxy for profitability and viability. In order to demonstrate the significance of the "right tail"[14] problem for Russia, let us consider the difference between the frequency distribution of Russian and American farms by cost of production in, for instance, the grain sector. At the same time, one should note that the grain sector is supported by the state, and some deviation from the normal curve can occur there as well. However, in spite of this, US farms are distributed by grain production costs much closer to the normal curve than farms in Russia.

Fig. 1-9 depicts the distribution of grain producers in Rostov oblast' region, which is one of the major grain producing areas in Russia, and of American wheat producing farms by the production costs of corresponding commodities. The horizontal axis indicates percentage of farms in their total number whilst the vertical axes indicate actual production costs. The figure shows that it is

[13] In Fig. 1-8 the bold line depicts a theoretical normal frequency distribution of farms' viability (curve R). As a result of the positive impact of a sound governmental policy which aims to increase producers' viability, this curve can move to the left (curve R'), which in turn means that all producers are more viable.

[14] The share of less viable and cost-effective farms of all farms.

more likely that production costs will be higher for Rostov producers than for American producers. Actually it means that the frequency distribution of production costs for Rostov has a longer right tail than the same distribution for American producers.

Fig. 1-9 Distribution of US wheat farms (1998) and Rostov's grain farms by production costs (2000)*

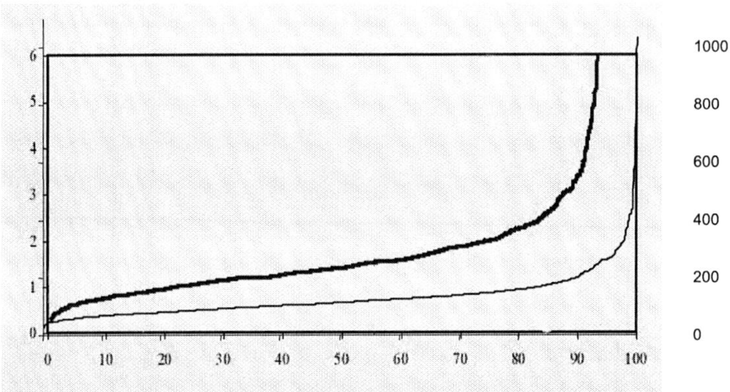

* Rostov – thin curve; USA – bold curve; right axes – RUR/100 kg; left axes US$/bushel

Sources: USA: http://www.ers.usda.gov/publications/sb974-5/sb974-5.pdf; Rostov area: Russian Statistic Agency.

To a certain extent this difference can be explained by the transition in Russian agriculture from a centrally planned economy to a market one: it is possible that in this transition not all the producers succeeded in adjusting – modernizing their production and reducing their production costs. However, almost 15 years of reform is too long a period for such an adjustment. Therefore, it is possible to hypothesize that the difference in production costs between US and Russian farmers is the result of Russia's policy of explicitly or implicitly supporting loss-making farms, by setting them soft budgetary constraints, thus, allowing them to operate despite these high costs and to avoid bankruptcy.

Why don't production factors move from the "tail farms" towards the model farms? One of the main reasons for the current situation is the state's support of non-viable large farms. This support is not implemented through direct budget transfers, but largely through various state programmes for the financial restructuring of non-viable farming enterprises.

It is precisely this policy which results in the existence of weighty right tails in the frequency distribution curves for the viability of farms, and which, at the same time, reduces the average profitability indicators for Russia's agriculture as a whole. Moreover, the disappearance of these loss-making farms will open up the market for more productive farms, which will be able to expand their output, and thus increase their productivity even more.

The right-tail effect is not only the result of measures designed to allow loss-making farms avoid bankruptcy. This effect can also be attributed to a market failure of the major production factors. Land, financial and labour markets in agriculture are all very unsatisfactory. Access to farmland is associated with tremendous transaction costs, which create a considerable barrier to outside investors; land transactions between one producer and another, are conducted more like administrative arrangements than commercial deals. The distribution of financial recourses is not fully ruled by market forces either, since price and non-price rationing in credit access is widespread.

An agricultural labour market hardly exists. On the one hand, there is a lack of alternative jobs in rural areas and an excessively large amount of labour in agriculture, thus reducing labour productivity in the sector. On the other hand, there is a severe shortage of social and technical infrastructure in rural areas and they lag behind urban infrastructure. Low wages, the enormous size of Russia and the underdevelopment of communications all serve to isolate rural areas from the national labour market. The rural economy suffers from an excess of unskilled labour and a severe shortage of skilled labour and managers.

One other problem related to the imperfect factor markets is the inadequate reaction of the government to the lack of market institutes (financial, trade, advisory, etc) and infrastructure. In particular, this trend is evident in purchased inputs.

Conclusion

Since the beginning of the reforms in 1992, enormous structural changes have been made in Russian agriculture. The initial expectations that individual farming would serve as an engine for growing efficiency throughout the agricultural sector were not realized. Nowadays, agricultural units are severely polarized with very efficient producers at one end of the spectrum and extremely marginal producers at the other. At both ends, there are corporate and individual producers. Current federal and especially regional policies still support loss-making farms, mainly large-size enterprises, in the hope of maintaining household incomes in rural areas. As a result of these policies Russia's agri-food sector as a whole suffers from low efficiency and competitiveness. The only way out of this situation is a sound rural development policy which will create new sources of income in rural areas.

References

Agricultural Policies in Transition Economies (2002) OECD, Paris.

Epstein, D. & E. Schultze (2005) *Two picks of farms distribution by their size.* Paper presented on the Moscow session of the XI Congress of EAAE. Unpublished paper.

Koester, U. (2003) *A revival of large farms in Eastern Europe? How important are institutions?* Paper delivered on the 25th Conference of IAAE, Durban, 16-22 August, 2003. http://www.iaae-agecon.org/conf/durban_papers/papers/Koester.pdf

Lerman, Z., C. Csaki & G. Feder. (2004) *Agriculture in Transition.* Lexington Books, Lexington.

Review of Agricultural Policies. Russian Federation (1998) OECD, Paris.

Russian Economy in 2000: Trends and Outlooks (2001). IET, Moscow. http://www.iet.ru/trend/2000/2000en.html

Rylko, D. & R. M. Jolly (2005) Development of Agroholdings in Russian Agriculture. *Comparative Economic Studies* 47(1), 115-26.

Serova, E. (1999) Privatization and Farm Restructuring Impact on Russia's Agriculture, in *Farm Restructuring: Efficiency and Sustainability.* Golitzino-I. Ed. by E.Serova. Proceedings of the international conference. AFE, Moscow, 4-35.

Serova E. & I. Kharamova (2002) *Non-Agricultural Capital in Russia's Agriculture: Vertical Integration or Business Diversification?* Unpublished report.

Serova, E. & I. Khramova (2003) Farms and Factors Markets in Russia's Agriculture, in *Transition, Institutions, and the Rural Sector* ed. by M. Spoor. Lexington Books, Lexington, 61-80.

Serova, E. (2000) Public Opinion Concerning Russia's Agrarian Reform, in *Russian Views of the Transition in the Rural Sector* ed. by A.Northworthy. The World Bank, 67-86.

Serova, E., M. Prokopjev & I. Ivanova (2001) *Prognoz potreblenia osnovnykh prodovolstvennykh tovarov in Russia v srendnesrochnoj perspektive.* [The midterm forecast of consumption of the basic foodstuffs in Russia] www.iet.ru/afe

Shagaida, N. (2005) *Russia's land market functioning in current constrains.* Paper delivered on the Conference Enhancing Competitiveness in Agriculture in Transition Economies, December 1-3, 2005 in Budapest.

—. (2002) The Land Market, in *Factor Markets in Russia's Agri-Food Sector: Framework of Further Analysis* ed. E. Serova. AFE, Moscow, 81-107.

Wegren, S.K. (2005) *The Moral Economy Reconsidered. Russia's Search for Agrarian Capitalism.* Palgrave Macmillan, New York.

Uzun, V. & E. Gataulina (2005) *Adaptation of agricultural producers of Russia to the market.* Paper presented on the Moscow session of the XI Congress of EAAE.Unpublished paper.

Uzun, V.Y. (2002) Organizational Types of the Agricultural Production in Russia, in *Factor Markets in Russia's Agri-Food Sector: Framework of Further Analysis* ed. by E. Serova. AFE, Moscow, 16-44.

CHAPTER TWO

INSTITUTIONAL FACTORS OF RUSSIAN AGRICULTURAL DEVELOPMENT

ALEXANDER BEDNY

Introduction

The socio-economic crisis of the Russian agro-industrial sector has since the beginning of 1990s been accompanied by considerable discussion concerning possible ways and models of further developing agriculture. A plurality of forms of ownership in agricultural production is one of the most important consequences of Russia's agricultural reforms. However, efficient ownership structures in agriculture have yet to receive widespread acceptance. The fact that collective agricultural enterprises survived the lengthy period of transition and still dominate the agricultural scene despite policy-makers' best efforts, testifies to powerful social resistance, which was not catered for in the planning of the agricultural reforms.

Thus, there is a need for an in-depth scientific analysis of the impact of the socio-cultural norms and values of rural communities, of formal and informal constraints, on the optimization of the economic activities of agricultural enterprises. The institutional approach of economic sociology has been particularly useful in this context. *Institutions* as formal and informal constraints in society, which structure political, economic and social interactions, are at the centre of this scientific approach. Any analysis of the efficiency and viability of different organizational forms in Russian agricultural production must emphasize the specificities of the cultural and national traditions of Russia's rural inhabitants, their value preferences and norms, which may be referred to as embedded institutional characteristics of the rural society. This paper is an attempt to analyse the socio-economic problems of Russian agriculture and the prospects for its development from the point of view of the institutional approach of economic sociology.

The empirical evidence for the research consists of the results of a sociological survey conducted among managers of agricultural enterprises; a number of in-depth interviews with experts of in rayon[15] administrations and agricultural enterprises, and with ordinary rural inhabitants; and the materials of working meetings and consultations with leading agricultural specialists from Nizhni Novgorod Region (Russian Federation) in 2003 and 2004. All of the above research was conducted by the University of Nizhni Novgorod within the framework of two international projects. One of these projects[16] was targeted at the development of new institutional relations in the agricultural sector of Nizhni Novgorod region by training managers of agricultural enterprises and other relevant officials in the most advanced European organizational and managerial practices in agriculture, in the protection of farmers' common interests and in the sustainable development of rural areas. At the same time as the project was being implemented, a survey of the heads of 317 agricultural enterprises in Nizhni Novgorod region (which is just under half the total number of enterprises registered in the region) was conducted The survey was aimed at finding the search of effective strategies for the development of agricultural enterprises, and drawing a sociological "profile" of what makes an efficient agricultural manager. In addition, in September 2004, within the framework of another international project[17], we conducted thirty-five in-depth interviews with representatives of different social groups of the rural population of Nizhni Novgorod region

An institutional analysis of socio-economic relations in agriculture

Institutional theory emerged as a reaction to orthodox economic doctrines at the turn of the nineteenth and twentieth century. Institutionalists do not accept the basic principles of classical economics, such as the existence of an isolated, independent and rational "Homo Economicus", who has certain preferences and is exclusively driven by utility maximization motivation. They also believe that there is a problem in obtaining and using the information that is required for taking rational decisions.

The ideas of F. List, K. Marx, M. Weber, E. Durkheim, T. Parsons, J. Schumpeter, T. Veblen and J. Commons played a crucial role in the formation

[15] Rayon is the main unit of administrative and territorial division of Russian rural areas.
[16] The European Commission Tempus project "The Democratic Mechanism of Agricultural Development" (IB_JEP-21100-2000).
[17] The international research project called "Specialisation and Diversification of Enterprising during Transition – a Comparative Study of Development in the Estonian and Russian Countryside (LOCAL PATHS)" funded by the Academy of Finland.

of modern institutionalism. The emergence of the New Institutionalism in the second half of the twentieth century was made possible thanks to the contributions of R. Coase, D. North and O. Williamson. The institutional approach in modern economic sociology has been significantly affected by the contributions of American scholars (V. Nee, R. Swedberg, and P. DiMaggio). The work of V. Radaev, S. Kirdina and others are dedicated to the development of the institutional approach in Russian economic sociology.

The concept of an institution in socio-economic studies

In our research, we use the definition of an institution developed within the framework of the institutional approach of economic sociology. The institution in this approach is defined as a system of interrelated informal and formal constituents – customs, shared beliefs, conventions, norms and rules – governing social relationships within which actors pursue and fix the limits of legitimate interests (Nee 2003, 23). The formal components of institutions are comprised of a set of political (legislative, legal) rules, economic rules and contracts. At the same time, the informal components of institutions are comprised of cultural traditions, norms and social values.

Private property is a key institution in transforming Russian agriculture. It governs agrarian actors' socio-economic relations in relation to producing income and the turnover of the agricultural means of production. The formal constituents of this institution include, for example, the legislation which regulates land ownership relations, and the statutes of agricultural enterprises which structure their internal property relations. On the other hand, the informal components of the institution of private property in agriculture include the attitudes of agrarian actors towards private ownership of agricultural lands, and informal agreements, concluded by the heads of enterprises, which regulate the use of the land plots when no efficient land legislation is available.

Discovering the social mechanisms which determine the relationship between formal and informal components of institutions is one of the major methodological tasks of modern economic sociology. The informal components of the institutional environment deserve special attention when analysing the effectiveness of various forms of agricultural production. We have to study carefully the attitudes of agrarian actors in order to reveal the sustainable and self-replicating types of motivation, the standards of behaviour and the norms of interrelations between social agents which actually form the social reality (Efendiev & Bolotina 2003, 99). Decision makers often ignore these factors, although they form the most complicated area of economic transformation. This area cannot be changed by a governmental decision, a new law, or by structural reconstructions.

The informal constituents of institutions are much harder to change rather than the formal rules. In contrast to the formal constituents, the mechanism of monitoring informal ones is "embedded" in the system of social relations and enforcement is done informally; it is actually a side-effect of social interactions.

The inert nature of institutional change is called path-dependency. We speak about this phenomenon when yesterday's institutional framework remains effective but limits people's choices today and in the future (North 1990, 93). A dangerous for transforming societies phenomenon is conditioned by the inert nature of institutions the phenomenon is called "an institutional trap". It assumes the form of inefficient, though sustainable, institutions (Polterovitch 1999, 3).

The so-called "symbiotic relations" between agricultural enterprises and the private plots of rural residents is a good example of the institutional trap phenomenon. Such stable relations may be characterised as a complicated socio-economic form of living together on the part of employees, their family members and the enterprises which employ them (Nikulin 2002, 44). The enterprise is interested in exploiting as cheap and obedient a labour force as possible. At the same time, the employees aim at securing access to the resources of the enterprise, in order to use them for the needs of their private plots. A sort of semi-regulated trade-off between the interests of the enterprise, and the interests of the enterprise's employees is formed on that basis.

Transaction costs and ownership structure as factors of efficiency of an agricultural enterprise

Transaction costs are those caused by conducting negotiations and the protection and enforcement of transactions within a market economy. In other words, these are the costs connected with the exchange of information and the protection of contractual rights (Oleynik 2000, 133). Transaction costs may represent a significant obstacle to the implementation of various economic opportunities.

The absence of informational transparency in Russian agricultural markets hampers the reaching of agreements between potential contractual partners. Inefficient institutions increase transaction costs and adversely affect the division of labour in the agricultural economy.

The competitive advantages of various forms of organisation of agricultural production are, to a significant extent, determined by the characteristics of the institutional framework. Whereas private family farming is common and relatively efficient in countries with established market economies, the institutional environment of Russian agriculture provides more favourable conditions for large-scale enterprises than for private farmers.

The opportunistic behaviour of agrarian stakeholders, which implies persuading of individual interest through malfeasance (Williamson 1983, 362), is one of the major sources of transaction costs in this sector of the economy. Information asymmetry forms the basis of opportunistic behaviour. In its turn, opportunistic behaviour leads to transaction costs in the form of acquiring protection against that kind of behaviour. Institutions, in the form of sustainable rules of behaviour, are tools for resisting opportunistic behaviour.

Ownership structure is an important issue in the institutional analysis of agrarian relations in countries in transition. In accordance with the institutional approach, the system of ownership relations is a socially approved mechanism which regulates the extraction of economic goods' utility based on the system of powers (Nesterenko 2002, 337).

The existence of any particular form of ownership is determined by a society's ability to establish and protect the institutions of that particular form of ownership. The ownership structures that survive are those with the lowest transaction costs in a particular society with a particular institutional framework.

The results of fifteen years of agricultural reform in Russia show that collective forms of ownership in agriculture are sustainable and secure. This sustainability is not supported by the high level of economic efficiency of collective enterprises. Most of them are unprofitable. Moreover, analysis shows that collective enterprises[18] are not widespread in the world, and that they are characterised by instability, weak labour motivation, and low competitiveness on the market (Uzun 2003, 15). In spite of this, most of Russian agricultural enterprises retain a collective form of ownership.

It is evident that practically all Russia's rural residents are disappointed by the results of the agrarian reform and are protesting against the current socio-economic situation in the agricultural sector. In spite of this, the workers seem to want to stay with the "*kolkhozes*" (Efendiev & Bolotina 2002, 115). Thus, the institutional framework directly affects the organizational forms of Russia's agricultural enterprises.

[18] We use the term "collective enterprise" for agricultural enterprises (which are legally registered, for example, agricultural cooperatives, joint stock companies or limited liability societies), the property of which is almost evenly distributed among current and former employees (shareholders), and where a collectivist organizational culture is re-produced.

Trust and social capital as components of the institutional environment

The world's agricultural experience shows that producers are not able to effectively stand up for their interests when they are not united in some form. In isolation, they face such well-known problems as overproduction, low incomes due to price instability, exposure to foreign competitors and a lack of investment. The commercial and political organization of farmers illustrates the potential for self-organisation in agriculture, which is an inevitable component of agricultural development.

Sociology postulates that a social system cannot effectively exist if fundamental conditions of collective co-existence are not observed, if vices such as lies and theft are socially justified and if mechanisms of social control are absent. Norms and values contribute to the development of social partnerships and cooperation and thus build up the social capital of society (Fukuyama 2002, 24). Social capital allows individuals to combine resources to protect their rights and interests, and to organize joint action in order to solve common problems.

Trust is the basic ingredient of the concept of social capital. It is one of the factors in the institutional framework, a link between expectations and reality. Trust makes it possible to pursue given aims rationally and to plan economic activity. Any transaction requires the parties concerned to trust each other, to believe their partners' promises and statements.

The high level of agricultural self-organisation in Denmark, Sweden, Austria and other Western European countries illustrates the role of social capital in the success of this sector's development (Bedny et al. 2002, 23). The relatively high level of trust and the common interests of agrarian actors form the basis for this successful development. The sustainable development of rural areas in the modern global economy is only possible with an intensive development of horizontal and vertical partnerships in society.

Social capital played a crucial role in the success story of the Danish agricultural cooperative movement. Undoubtedly, the level of impersonal trust in rural society is crucial in creating social capital and for the development of self-organisation in agriculture. Along with this, the joint economic interest of farmers was a necessary precondition for the success of the Danish cooperative movement. Social capital may be considered as an important factor when analysing economic growth or assessing the efficiency of economic decisions.

An overview of the socio-economic development of Russian agriculture

The agrarian reforms which started in 1990 were targeted at transforming the Russian agricultural sector into a market based economy. The tasks included the privatization of land and the property of agricultural enterprises; the structural reorganization of *kolkhozes* and *sovkhozes*; creating favourable conditions for the development of independent private farming; raising the efficiency of the food industry; and reducing the burden of State agricultural subsidies.

Deep economic crisis of the majority of agricultural enterprises along with rural poverty are the characteristics of Russian agriculture after the fifteen years of its reformations. The agricultural managers interviewed for our survey on average assessed the condition of their enterprises as poor. The average monthly wage of employees was less than 62% of the cost of living in 2002 (Fig. 2-1). The heads of the enterprises thought that the most painful problems in rural areas were poverty (76% of the respondents), hard drinking (47%) and the shortage of labour (33%)[19].

The socio-economic crisis has led to an erosion of employees' values. Instead of creating an "owner's" psychology, market reforms have actually contributed to increasing the level of estrangement between employees and the results of their work. Stealing, drinking at work and the spreading of illegal practices among the peasants are the typical examples of the destruction of labour motivation in agriculture. The main cause of stealing was accompanied by its social justification (legitimatization). There was a common perception that people were forced to steal in order to survive (Efendiev & Bolotina 2002, 98).

These practices are especially intensive at weak enterprises. On the other hand, the positive development of a rise in labour discipline may be observed at stronger enterprises. The formation of a plurality of types of ownership systems in agriculture is the main structural result of the reforms. The Russian agricultural economy includes the following basic forms of agricultural production units: large-scale agricultural enterprises, family farms, and individual household plots. The main contributors to the gross agricultural product are the large agricultural enterprises and private plots. One may note that the latter are generally highly inefficient in economic terms due to the dominant role played by manual labour and the small size of the plots. They primarily have a social security role for rural and to a lesser extent urban residents. The contribution of private farmers to the gross agricultural product of the country remains at a symbolic level.

---

[19] In addition, bad living conditions were mentioned by 26% of the respondents, and unemployment by 13%.

Fig. 2-1 Average monthly wage in agriculture in Russia in RUR, by the results of the year 2002 (currently US$~28.5 RUR)

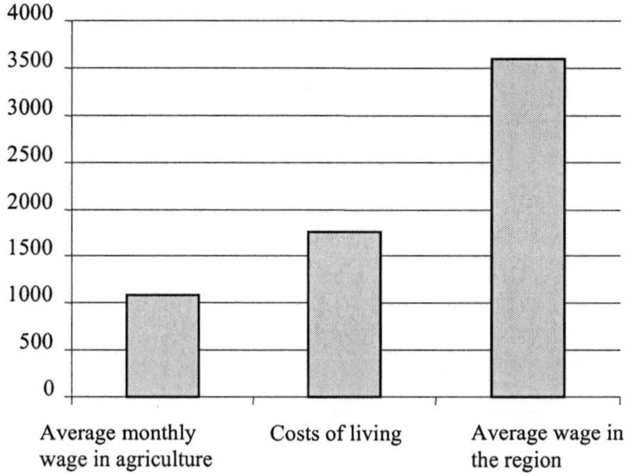

After fifteen years of agricultural reform, it is still too early to speak about the completion of the structural transformation of this sector of the economy. Basically, the reorganisation of *kolkhozes* and *sovkhozes* has not led to the appearance of an efficient owner in the Russian countryside. Inefficient legislation adopted together with the complex system of social relations within agricultural enterprises has constrained such an appearance. As a result, the collective type of enterprise still dominates Russian agriculture, and the number of employees who decided to leave the old collective farms with their conditional shares (see Serova 2007) to start private farming turned out to be very small. According to specialists from the rayon administrations of Nizhni Novgorod, there are few if any farmers operating in their raions. Thus, it is obvious that private farming has not become the basis for the development of a rural middle class in Russia. In the following section, we will concentrate on examining the strategies of middle- and large-scale agricultural enterprises.

Sociological portrait of a head of an agricultural enterprise

The personality of a head of an agricultural enterprise requires special attention in analysing agrarian socio-economic relations and the prospects for rural development in Russia. This actor is actually a "moving force", defining the general direction of the enterprise and his area's development. A *kolkhoz* chairman (who is now a director of a joint stock company or a chairman of an agricultural cooperative) is a key figure in the Russian countryside.

A sociological portrait of a head of an agricultural enterprise has been built on the basis of our survey's results: He (it usually is a man) is 40-50 years old, was born in a rural area, has a higher education and has been working as head of an enterprise on average for five years (Table 2-1).

Table 2-1 A portrait of a manager

Age	**%**
30 and less	2
31 – 40	21
41 – 50	53
51 – 60	20
Education	**%**
Secondary	4
Secondary professional	23
Higher	73
Length of occupation of current position	**%**
less than 1	9
1-2,5	25
3-5,5	20
6-9	18
10-19	20
20 and more	8

Informal constraints, which include norms, socio-cultural attitudes and the patterns of social actors form the informal component of the institutional environment, and thus affect the economic behaviour of agrarian actors. As part of our research we tried to reveal the socio-cultural attitudes of the managers of agricultural enterprises in order to discover their opinions and views on the problems facing their enterprises in terms of development and management and their perceptions of the current situation within the Russian agro-food industry. The liberalization of agricultural markets has been at the centre of controversy for a long time. This question assumes particular significance in light of Russia's future membership of the WTO. The heads of agricultural enterprises who were interviewed expressed well-defined opinions on Russian membership: 91% believe that agricultural imports would ruin Russian agricultural producers. Almost none of them believed that imports would have a positive impact on domestic production, as it would make the market more competitive.

These managers were convinced that Russian agricultural products would be unable to compete with Western products because of the incomparably higher level of State support given to European and American farmers.

The question about the role of State regulation in agriculture also elicited an almost unanimous response: 87% believed that active intervention was necessary. The managers made the following comments on this question. They believed that the State must

support domestic agricultural producers;
lower taxes and energy prices;
increase the wages of people in the countryside;
and set prices for agricultural products according to their costs.

Basically, the respondents' attitudes may be characterized as traditionalist. Most of them perceived the State's functions in an old Soviet manner. At the same time, most of the respondents were convinced that it is better to have a guaranteed albeit modest income; that there should be no income stratification in society; and that the State should be responsible for citizens' guaranteed life maintenance. On the other hand, twenty percent of the agro-managers exhibited more liberal views; they can be characterized as the more entrepreneurial managers.

Obstacles to Russian agricultural development and ways of overcoming them

The respondents' opinions about the obstacles facing Russian agricultural development mirror the complexity of the problem. Almost all of them (96%) mentioned the so-called imbalance between the prices paid for agricultural products and those for material and technical inputs.

The problem of the imbalance between the prices of agricultural products and the prices for the energy and other resources or inputs consumed in the production process is one faced by most agricultural producers in the world. The traditional and most effective way of resisting the monopoly of the processing industry among Western farmers has been to establish a processing capability within agricultural enterprises. According to the results of our survey, only 23% of these agricultural enterprises had their own processing capability and even less (20%) their own retailing outlets.

European and American farmers stand up for their economic interests in the market by establishing agricultural cooperatives, thus "enlarging" their production potential. An agricultural cooperative is a commercial structure owned by farmers. It guarantees its members that their products will be sold, it creates a joint ownership of the processing enterprise, provides profits and access to professional services. The individual farmers preserve their economic independence, but gain all the advantages of a large-scale enterprise.

The situation is totally different in modern Russian agriculture. Despite facing severe problems, agricultural producers remain fragmented and isolated and are, as a result, economically and politically weak. The inability of agricultural stakeholders to stand up for their collective interests is one of the most serious obstacles for agricultural development in Russia, according to the respondents' opinions (this was mentioned by 40% of them). At the same time, only 11% of them were members of agricultural unions (cooperatives, associations), and 92% of the respondents believed it was necessary to develop such organizations.

Table 2-2 Managers' opinions on

Obstacles for Russian agricultural development	**%**
Price imbalances	96
No clear "rules of the game"	70
Insufficient subsidies	69
Inability of agro-stakeholders to stand up for their interests	40
The existence of processing units at the enterprise	**%**
Yes	23
No	77
The existence of a retail outlet	**%**
Yes	20
No	80
Agricultural self-organisation	**%**
Members of agricultural unions (associations)	11
Believe it is necessary to create such organisations	92

It is characteristic that the respondents believed that insufficient State support was one reason for the lack of independent voluntary organisations in agriculture (which, by definition, are supposed to ensure a balance between the State and civil society). Among the other most important reasons, the absence of strong leaders (52%) and the lack of traditions of self-organisation (34%) were the most notable.

We assume that the reasons for the lack of professional organisations in Russia are of an institutional nature. The lack of trust between agricultural stakeholders is seen as the result of a misperception about the functions of independent organisations and civil institutions on the part of key agricultural actors.

Nevertheless, the unfavourable environment does not necessarily mean that institutional changes are impossible. We believe that a very important role in this process will be played by the implementation of various national and international training programmes aimed at acquainting agro-managers with the most modern techniques and forms of agricultural organization and with the potential of commercial and political associations of agricultural stakeholders (Bedny et al. 2005, 77).

Fig. 2-2 Level of trust

1: One should be very careful dealing with people
2: Uncertain (or neutral) view
3: Most people are trustworthy

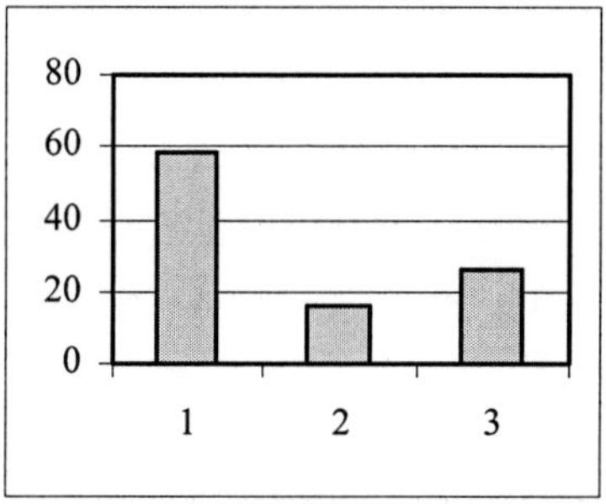

The lack of success of government policy and the absence of clear rules of the game in agriculture are perceived as the biggest problems for Russian agriculture by 70% percent of the respondents. Specifically, land ownership and the issue of agricultural assets are still the most painful problems for the agricultural sector in Russia. The uncertainty surrounding ownership rights is still a big problem for those involved in agriculture, despite new land legislation. This legislation has not had sufficient time to yield effective results. A senior agronomist from a large agricultural enterprise describes the current state of affairs: "We have been trying to exchange land plots with the neighbouring *kolkhoz* for 12 years... We are actually using the land, but it is impossible to legalise this." Such problems significantly increase the risks of investments, raise transaction costs and limit interaction between agrarian actors. This results in the establishment of informal practical arrangements between agrarian actors.

We shall now attempt to analyse the effect of ownership structure on the economic performance of agricultural enterprises. The empirical evidence shows that most of the enterprises are still characterized by an even property distribution. At the same time, symbolic wages are insufficient to provide even a basic standard of living for the employees of agro-enterprises.

Individual private plots serve as an extra source of income for virtually all rural residents. The main factor which determines the success of individual plots is the support provided by the agricultural enterprises, where the household plots' owners are working, or used to work before. Forage, fertilizers and use of machinery granted by the agricultural enterprises makes an individual plot a sustainable tool in the hands of rural residents. This is a characteristic feature of the so-called economic symbiosis between large-scale enterprises and the personal plots of their employees. Almost every interviewed manager (97%) confessed that his or her enterprise supports its employees' personal plots at its expense.

We show that current property relations do not encourage agrarian actors to increase the long term efficiency of their enterprises. On the contrary, the current situation forces them to rent-seek at the expense of the enterprise. This raises the production and transaction costs of enterprises and results in stealing and poor decision-making. A loss-making enterprise is unable to provide its employees and shareholders with a satisfactory income, which forces them to steal. This is the way an institutional trap is formed.

We conclude by examining the alternatives for agricultural self-development within the current institutional environment. One scenario is that the rent-seeking behaviour of the employees results in the exhaustion of an enterprise's resources, which inevitably leads to the enterprise going bankrupt. The serious social and economic effects of this scenario are especially painful: villages and rural areas fall into decay as a result of the collapse of the agro-enterprise. A more optimistic scenario involves a change of ownership, which could force the new heads of such enterprises to stop rent-seeking and start conducting an economically efficient policy.

Such a change in ownership at the current stage of socio-economic reform may involve concentrating ownership in the hands of the managers of agricultural enterprises either by these managers redeeming the property shares of the bulk of small shareholders or by including the enterprise in an agri-food holding company. In both cases, the change in ownership leads to the appearance of a new owner in control of the enterprise. An owner, having invested his own resources in the enterprise, is interested in receiving the maximum profit from his investments and in raising the value of the business. Vertically-integrated agro-food corporations are often successful, though isolated, examples of the change in property relations in the agricultural sector. However, the separation of ownership from management causes a number of serious problems. The incompatibility of managerial practices at the higher levels of such a vertical structure with institutionalised practices of agricultural management at the enterprise level, and contradictions between the long-term interests of the owner and the short-term interests of the manager may be listed among them.

Fig. 2-3 Ways out of the institutional trap

Ways out of the institutional trap:
1. Resources are exhausted – bankruptcy of the agricultural enterprise
2. Change in ownership relations at agro-enterprises

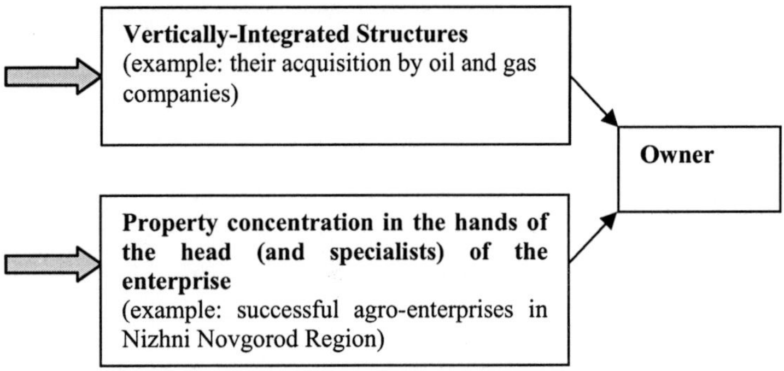

We have also conducted a comparative analysis of the economic performance (profitability, average monthly wage of employees, production volumes per employee etc.) of the enterprises whose heads believe that collective property is the best solution for Russian agriculture, and those whose heads believe that the major property share should be concentrated in the hands of the managers.

The results of the analysis show that enterprises in the second group are doing much better than those in the first group in all of the mentioned respects. Moreover, the heads of the most successful enterprises, that is, those in group 3, aspire to share ownership with their enterprise's leading specialists. Over the period of our research, we have managed to study the practical experience of the heads of the most successful agricultural enterprises in the Nizhni Novgorod region, all of whom have chosen to concentrate ownership to some degree (groups 2 and 3 in the Table 2-3). We can give the following interpretation of the results received: the *heads of relatively strong enterprises have more market-oriented attitudes and are more interested in the concentration of ownership.*

Table 2-3 Relationship between an enterprise's performance and the attitudes of its manager

Managers who prefer (groups of enterprises):	**The indices of performance averaged[20] by the group of enterprises**				
	Turnover in the last reporting year, in RUR	**Commodity output per employee in 2002, in RUR**	**Profitability in the last reporting year, %**	**Average monthly wage of regular employees in 2002,in RUR**	**Share of wages paid in kind, %**
(1) collective distribution of property	3,000,000	36,041	0	994	15
(2) to be the owners of the enterprise	6,650,000	50,000	1,5	1,220	10
(3) to share the ownership rights with the leading specialists of the enterprise	7,194,500	55,000	5	1,250	10

Obstacles of a financial, social and legal nature remain insuperable for many of the heads of agro-enterprises in their attempt to concentrate ownership. To overcome these obstacles, the concept of equality and the current perception of social justice that prevails in Russian rural communities nowadays will have to be replaced. Providing agro-managers with information about sources of credit and legal schemes for concentrating ownership of their enterprises plays a crucial role in overcoming the mentioned obstacles. The experience of managers who have already become the major owners of their enterprises in demonstrating the advantages of these new property structures constitute the most effective arguments for convincing other agro-managers. This was clearly revealed during our seminars with agricultural officials and the heads of agro-enterprises in the different districts of Nizhni Novgorod region. In our opinion, wider discussion of such issues could switch the search for agricultural

[20] The median mean is used (that is, the point at which the data is divided into two equal parts in respect of the particular criterion). We consider this indicator to be more reliable than a simple average, because the latter is too dependent on isolated "pips".

improvement away from traditional responses such as drawing up new budget subsidies to wards more promising alternatives such as efficient management and the development of a conceptually new layer of landowners – rural entrepreneurs.

Conclusion

The uncovering and analysis of institutional factors, which affect the socio-economic development of agriculture, is an essential issue in modern economic sociology. The consequences of the agrarian transformation currently taking place in Russia are evident in the poor economic condition of most agricultural enterprises and in the socio-economic crisis that has affected most rural areas in the country. The formation of a plurality of ownership forms in the agricultural sector is the main structural result of the agricultural reforms. Nevertheless, there is still no general development of private farming in the agricultural sector. Most of the middle- and large-scale enterprises have retained collective forms of ownership. This has meant that the former (collective) schemes of corporate relations between employees and management have been preserved.

The institutional approach of economic sociology is especially important when attempting to understand and explain the significant divergence between the actual results of the reforms and their initial intentions. The fundamental concepts of the institutional approach include institutions, transaction costs, opportunistic behaviour, property rights, trust and social capital.

The heads of agricultural enterprises are among the most authoritative and influential agrarian actors; their values and attitudes play a substantial role in forming the informal components of the agrarian institutional framework. Most heads of agricultural enterprises are 40-50 year-old men, and native rural residents. The majority of them follow traditional ways of economic behaviour: they prefer a guaranteed albeit modest income rather than a high income with no special guarantees; they believe that there should be no stratification in society; and they think that the State should be responsible for guaranteeing a basic standard of living for its citizens. At the same time, the community of agricultural managers is not totally homogeneous. Our research has discovered that about one fifth of the agrarian establishment is more liberal and entrepreneurial in its attitudes and beliefs. These managers support the liberalisation of land; they are ready to take risks to obtain higher incomes; and they believe that social stratification is inevitable and that the individual is personally responsible for his/her own welfare.

The following obstacles were considered the most significant by the agro-managers interviewed: the imbalance between the prices of agricultural products and those of material and technical inputs; unsuccessful government policy; the absence of clear "rules of the game" in agrarian relations; insufficient subsidies; and the inability of agricultural producers to stand up for their collective interests. It has been shown that these obstacles are of an institutional nature.

The formal components of the agrarian institutional environment in Russia are the result of a lack of clearly defined rules and either inefficient mechanisms or mechanisms that don't work for their enforcement. First of all, it is characteristic for the property market. Due to this fact, the practical actions of agricultural actors in the sphere of land relations are either frozen, or become "grey" in accordance with settled informal arrangements (e.g., interpersonal relations). It results in high transaction costs for agricultural producers, which puts an extra burden on them.

One of the major causes of the price imbalance is the low level of independent organisational activity of Russia's agricultural producers. This is conditioned by the low level of trust in society and by managers misinterpreting the role of independent voluntary organisation. Traditional attitudes make the heads of enterprises believe that the State is fully responsible for the fragmented and isolated position of agricultural managers. The main way to resolve this problem is to increase the level of managers' awareness of the institutional mechanisms of agricultural development.

The ownership structure also affects the course of development of an agricultural enterprise. Most of the enterprises covered by the survey have retained a collective type of ownership, where the shares are equally distributed among both current and former employees. This implies that the "old" (kolkhoz type) model of management has been preserved together with the old mechanisms of interaction between management and workers. This leads to a situation where many different agents have access to the resources of the enterprise. Each of these agents is encouraged to put the minimum into the enterprise whilst seeking to extract as much as possible. Symbiotic relations are being established between agricultural enterprises and their employees' private plots.

The even distribution of property in no way counteracts the socio-economic inequality that exists in rural areas, but in fact promotes it through rent-seeking. Opportunistic behaviour and rent-seeking both lead to the exhaustion of the resources of the enterprise and to low productivity and profitability. The institutional trap is being formed.

The rent-seeking behaviour of employees may come to an end with the complete exhaustion of the enterprise's resources, which inevitably leads to the bankruptcy of the enterprise. A more optimistic scenario is based on changing the ownership structure of enterprises, which would force the management to stop rent-seeking and adopt economically effective ways of management. Such a change would lead to the appearance of an owner who has invested his funds in the enterprise, and who would, therefore, be interested in maximising profits and business value. There are several ways of introducing more efficient ownership practices in agricultural production. One of them has become quite popular in Russia nowadays – it is the creation of vertically-integrated agro-holdings. Another way is connected with the concentration of an enterprise's property in the hands of its management through the redemption of property shares from a majority of its shareholders.

It is impossible to destroy the vicious circle of inefficiency of agricultural producers with paternalist State policies. On the contrary, such measures promote the conservation and replication of inefficient institutions. The State should not subsidise "losers", but should support "winners" by providing them with a legal framework to encourage and protect them, and by creating an efficient institutional environment favourable for the development of agricultural entrepreneurship.

References

Bedny, A., E. Balabanova & A. Groudzinski (2005) Ownership Concentration in Agriculture as Pathway for Efficient Enterprise Development. *Sociologicheskie Issledovaniya* (4), 69-78.

Bedny, A., E. Balabanova & Y. Rozova (2002) *Commercial Organizations and Systems of Protection of Collective Interests of Farmers in Developed Countries*. Nikolaev, N.Novgorod.

Fukuyama, F. (2002) Social Capital and Development: The Coming Agenda. *SAIS Review* XXII (1), 23-37.

Efendiev, A. & I. Bolotina (2002) Modern Russian Countryside: At the Break of Ages and Reforms. *The Experience of institutional Analysis in Mir Rossyi* XI (4), 83–125.

Nee, V. (2003) The New Institutionalism in Economics and Sociology. *CSES Working Paper Series,* Paper No. 4, Cornell University.

Nesterenko, A. (2002) *Economics and Institutional Theory*. Editorial URSS, Moscow.

Nikulin, A. (2002) Kuban' kolkhoz – to a holding or a hacienda? *Sociologicheskie Issledovaniya* (1), 44.

North, D. (1990) *Institutions, Institutional Change and Economic Performance.* Cambridge University Press, Cambridge.

Oleynik, A. (2000) *Institutional Economics*. Infra-M, Moscow.

Polterovitch, V. (1999) Institutional Traps and Economic Reforms. *Economics and Math Methods* 35 (2), 3-27.

Serova. E. (2007) Results of Transformation of Russian Agri-food Sector. In *Reflecting Transformation in Post-socialist Rural Areas*, ed. by M. Heinonen et al., Cambridge Scholars Publishing, Newcastle, 8-29.
Uzun, V. (2002) Organisational Forms in Agricultural Production in Russia, in *The proceedings of the scientific conference in Golitsino* 6-7 July 2001, Moscow.
Williamson, O. (1983) Organizational Form, Residual Claimants, and Corporate Control. *Journal of Law and Economics* XXXVI (2), 351-66.

CHAPTER THREE

RURAL PATHS IN RUSSIA

LEO GRANBERG

Introduction[21]

Five years ago, our research team began a tour of Russian Karelia in order to study the post-socialist countryside. In the Priazha district[22], we interviewed dozens of people, many of whom worked in various positions in a former *sovkhoz* that had been converted into a limited liability company or who worked for the local government or private enterprises. Because it was May, their porches were filled with sprouting potatoes and their window sills were groaning with tomato plants. Every one of the people we interviewed, except

---

[21] This article is part of the research project funded by the Academy of Finland in 2004-06 called "Specialisation and Diversification of Enterprising during Transition". Special thanks go to all those who took part in the fieldwork and helped us gather the material.

The earlier versions of the text has been published in Finnish in "Maaseudun uusi aika" in 2006, 14 (29); and in Swedish in "Nordisk Østforum" in 2006, 3.

[22] This refers to our first field study in May 2002, which took place in the Priazha district about 50 kilometres west of Petrozavodsk. We made two further visits in spring 2003 and 2004 and extended our interviews to villages in the Olonets district on Lake Ladoga. Each trip consisted of a busy week of thematic interviews with people selected from opposite positions in local government, enterprises and agriculture. In 2004 and 2005, we applied the same method as we gathered material from around Nizhny Novgorod; for two weeks in 2005, some of the team also conducted field interviews in the arctic countryside of the Republic of Sakha (Yakutia), and for one week in Yakutsk, the Republic's capital. There was also comparison material gathered from Estonia. The composition of the team working in the field varied. In Karelia, the participants were Ilkka Alanen (University of Jyväskylä), Leo Granberg, Inna Kopoteva and Jouko Nikula (University of Helsinki) and Svetlana Pasti (University of Tampere). The team for field research in Siberia also included Ulla Partanen and Katriina Soini (Agrifood Research Finland, Jokioinen), and Anu Osva. Russian researchers Alexander Bedny and Eugenia Balabanova (University of Nizhny Novgorod) were in charge of gathering material from the Nizhny Novgorod district, while the material from Estonia was gathered by Helvi Põder, Anna Põder and Kristel Maidre (Estonian Agricultural University).

those who were very ill or were chronic alcoholics, told us that they kept a small plot where they grew potatoes for the winter and raised hens, goats and cows, although usually no more than one cow at a time since there was no market for milk.

Russia is a huge country, and Karelia is one of her distant border regions, with forestry playing a significant role in the region's economy. Nizhny Novgorod, too, is located in the northern part of Russia. As in Karelia, the main type of agricultural production there is dairy farming, while agriculture in the southern parts of Russia relies heavily on the various forms of grain cultivation. Despite huge differences in natural conditions, various field studies show that certain essential features remain surprisingly similar in different parts of the Russian countryside (e.g. Amelina 2000; Pallot & Nefedova 2003; O'Brien et al. 2004; Visser 2005, Patsiorkovsky et al. 2005;).

In their study on cucumber and cabbage farmers around Moscow, Judith Pallot and Tatyana Nefedova (2003, 354-7) noticed that the farmers showed little interest in expanding their production. The population of villages on the Oka River specialises in cultivating radishes and cucumbers. Each household cultivates an area of 25-30 *sotok* (2,500-3,000 m^2). There are no glasshouses, no paid labour is used, and cucumbers are sold to intermediates who visit the villages daily during the harvesting season, a consequence of rising transport costs and domination of Moscow markets by "the black people" (*chernye*). Nearby households specialize in the production of cabbage, which is processed in the households into the Russian version of sauerkraut (*kvashanaya kapusta*), and stored in large wooden barrels for transport to Moscow (ibid. 356). After decollectivisation, cabbage farmers were entitled to take possession of the lands of the local *sovkhoz*. However, they were not interested in acquiring more land, and most of them gave it up; ten years later, only half a dozen small private farms of 8-12 hectares were still in existence. An exception was the former manager of the *sovkhoz*, who set up a successful 160-hectare private farm, employing 24 people.

Cucumber cultivation in the region pre-dates the collapse of the USSR. Cucumbers and tomatoes were the business of state farms, where they were grown in giant glasshouses. Gradually, however, production shifted from the socialised to the "private" sector. The tradition of cabbage cultivation is even longer, dating from before the 1917 revolution. It has been very profitable in recent years, which is why the villagers' houses are in better condition than in most other parts of the Russian countryside. In other words, people would rather spend the income they get from cabbage or cucumber production to improve their housing than to establish family farms, which would require more modern production methods and the acquisition of new land. They would rather stick to conventional activity than opt for change that would include both a risk of failure and a hope for financial success.

The rapid change in certain things in Russia is linked with the stability and constancy of others. This article will tackle the issue by recalling first the main stages of the agricultural reform in Russia. This is followed by an introduction to the theory of path dependence and an outline of certain features of the constancy of Russian institutions, and, finally, a discussion on the path of rural Russia.

The three stages of the Russian agricultural reform

In the Soviet times, collective farms – either state farms (*sovkhoz*es) or cooperatives (*kolkhoz*es) – controlled rural Russia in a number of ways. They were large enterprises that extended their operations to several villages and were in charge of other rural industries as well, except forestry. Practically everybody worked for them, but people also cultivated their own little plots. In addition to a field and a vegetable garden, there would be shelters for a small number of livestock. There were also *dacha*s[23] belonging to city dwellers, or groups of summer cottages rather like garden allotments, which provided an important supply of food for people living in cities. After the agricultural reform, the *dacha*s assumed even greater importance.

After the collapse of socialism, there was a rush of Western experts and consultants into Eastern Europe and Russia, many of whom recommended that the state should quickly drop its support for agriculture, an idea embraced by the leaders of the new Russian government. With regard to the structural change in agriculture, many aimed at transferring agricultural production into the hands of *fermery*[24], or family farms. This change would have been identical to the process seen in Western and Central Europe during the first half of the 20th century and the trend of land reforms in a number of developing countries. In Eastern Europe, however, the actual goal was not achieved, least of all in Russia.

The rural transition started in Russia in 1990, when agrarian reform replaced state land ownership with private ownership, which also was written into the Constitution in 1993. In the same year the establishment of family farms (*fermery*) was also allowed and it received strong economic support in the beginning. It was stated, however, that there would be a transition period of ten years for a free land market. A free market did not become reality until the

---

[23] See Ortar (2007) for analysis of *dacha*s and *dachniki* in Russia today.

[24] The Russian word *fermer* (pl. *fermery*) is borrowed from the English language (farmer) and is used here as a synonym for a family farm.

enactment of special legislation on the purchase and sale of farmland, which came into effect in January 2003. However, farmland leases had been on the increase since the 1990s (Wegren 1998, 159; Nikula et al. 2005, 28-29; Serova 2007).

The reform can be divided into three distinct stages: the era of privatisation under Yeltsin (1990-94), the subsequent period of reorganisation (1995-98) and the current state agricultural policy (from 1999 on) activated under Putin.

Stephen W. Wegren considers the reform launched at the beginning of Yeltsin's term of office mostly as a strategy of minimal state intervention and at the same time aiming to destroy Communist-era institutions, behaviour, and attitudes (Wegren 2005, 40). The objective was rural change, motivating rural actors to adapt and adjust their behaviour. However, this led to a rapid fall in production to half of what it used to be – in many industries even less. At first, the government supported the establishment of family farms, which began to start up in promising numbers. At the end of Yeltsin's era, however, government subsidies for *fermery* were abolished. After that, most of these farms existed on paper only, as only a few of them were able to establish production on a permanent basis. At this stage, employees of agricultural enterprises became shareholders. They were able to decide on the form of ownership of the enterprise – at least in principle – and also had an opportunity to resign from the enterprise. Most chose to stay on the large farms and lease or transfer their own lands to the enterprise.

The reorganisation from the mid-1990s to 1998 covered large farms, the wholesale trade, and the food industry. Soviet farms had to be reorganised, but the road taken by the Russian government was different from what Western experts had recommended. While the World Bank experts believed that the importance of large farms was only temporary, Russian leaders were planning a permanent role for these.

After 1999, in Putin's era, the state launched a new agricultural policy, aiming to develop market relations and stabilise food production. The policy includes debt arrangements for large farms, protection of domestic production, creation of a credit system for agriculture, and improvements in farming machinery. The most recent efforts have focused on strengthening food supply chains, modernising mass production in agriculture and improving rural living conditions. Critics say that Putin's agricultural policy is still overly reliant on maintaining the existing structure and applying protectionist means instead of providing real opportunities for the development of a competitive agricultural sector (Serova et al. 2004; Serova 2007).

The structure of Russian agriculture

At the initial stage of the reform, mass production began to lose ground and private farmers launched their own production. The main responsibility for food supply in Russia, however, was borne by households, as it had been in the socialist era. As the new large enterprises were starting to face problems, households had an even greater responsibility for the production of food, especially potatoes, vegetables, meat and milk. Mass production dropped to half of what it used to be and remained at that level as things stabilised in the late 1990s. Most employees were sacked. In the current decade, the proportion of households of all agricultural production has slowly begun to decline as the standard of living rises and private farmers expand to grain, sugar beet and sunflower cultivation and, to some extent, to other industries as well.

Table 3-1 Structure of agricultural output by categories of producers in Russia, 1992-2004, in percent

	1992	1995	2000	2004
Large enterprises	67.1	50.2	43.4	43.1
Private farmers	1.1	1.9	3.0	5.9
Households	31.8	47.9	53.6	51.0
Total	100	100	100	100

Source: Rossiia v tsifrakh, 2004 and 2005; Ref. Patsiorkovsky et al. 2005.

Between 1992 and 2004, the number of officially registered private farms (*fermery* and private large-scale farms) grew from 49,000 to 264,000. Nevertheless, they still account for only a small proportion of the total agricultural output (6% in 2004). During our tour of southern Karelia a few years ago, we only found two *fermery* in business: one of them was a milk producer who had moved to the Priazha district from southern Russia, the other was a highly educated seed potato farmer in the Olonets district. Despite the fact that both were very successful in their business, others had not followed their example in either district.

As we can see, rural vitality still depends primarily on the workability of large farms, reorganized forms of former collective farms. These may be successful, struggling or in liquidation. In terms of production structure, management style and operating culture, the large farms we examined were much like the *sovkhoz*es of old times. Their employees still frequently call them *sovkhoz*es even if they have been turned into limited liability companies years ago.

At the macro level, international trends are ruled by globalisation, privatisation and the triumph of the market economy. The entire Russian economy is going through an upheaval, and yet large farms try to remain as they are, households in Russian Karelia keep to their little plots of land, and small-scale production of cucumber and cabbage continues without any inclination for expansion into new markets. Why?

Explanations of changes in post-socialist Russia have been based on transition theories (such as the general modernisation theory), which stress the attractive power of the future. The huge differences between Russia and other post-socialist countries imply that the end result of change in a political system cannot be considered as a given. The direction of a change should therefore be explained on the basis of the effect of the present and the past rather than the end result (Nikula 2004). This approach will turn our attention to institutions. According to Douglas North, the institutional framework of the past limits current possibilities for institutional change (North 1990, ref. Kaneva 1999). This idea provides the foundation for applying the theory of path dependence to the research in post-socialism. What is it about?

Path dependence and radical innovation

According to the idea of path dependence, "initial moves in one direction elicit further moves in that same direction; in other words there are self-reinforcing mechanisms or positive feedbacks" (Kay 2003, 406). The direction of moves in society is controlled by institutions, which can also resist any change in the course of such moves. The nature and tasks of institutions can be viewed very differently in different traditions in theory (Scott 2001). Institutions are based on shared concepts which are fairly established and which control people's behaviour in one way or another. Such control can be based on externally confirmed rules or internalised rules and customs.

The above is illustrated by the strengthening role of peasant farms in many northern European countries at the turn of the 20th century. As the market for butter increased with urban growth in Europe in the late 19th century, more and more farmers switched to dairy farming. The growing number of farmers learnt new production methods from each other and established common institutions: they created safety networks of cooperatives, dairies, savings associations, extension organisations for small farmers, political parties and Farmers' Unions. Also, the birth of political democracy gave farmers political clout in countries, which relied heavily on agriculture. Peasant farms, and later family farms, became central institutions in agriculture and rural life for more than half a century. This self-reinforcing path continued until the changes caused by the European Union (Granberg & Peltonen 2001, 290-302). But what is the path for rural Russia like?

Explanations for the permanence of structures in rural Russia have been sought from resistance and rational decision-making. Some have suggested that the transition to a genuine market economy has been prevented by the resistance of the management and workers of agricultural enterprises (Barnes 1998). Others believe that workers on collective farms have a realistic, rational view of the risks and opportunities as they choose not to become *fermery*. The system of family farms certainly often lacks all the main ingredients for success: machinery, subsidies, loans, advice centres and marketing channels (Wegren 2004, 560-61). It has also been suggested that rural people might not have sufficient skills for farming since most of them did not actually work the land during the socialist era but carried out various administrative duties or highly specialised tasks at *sovkhoz*es (Oswald 2007).

The first of these explanations is not supported by evidence from recent Russian history. Despite some local resistance, the changes in Russia have actually been incredibly peaceful. The second theory is partly accurate: it is only rational and sensible for private plot holders to be cautious about giving up their long-standing benefits. The third theory certainly holds true for many workers on collective farms: most of them have indeed become estranged from traditional agriculture. Yet many of them are directly engaged in agriculture and dairy farming, with enough potential for setting up farms of their own. This applies to households described above, for instance, which produce food for the Moscow market and even know how to market their goods in Russia. None of the three theories is therefore fully accurate: it is impossible to understand the rural situation without considering the socio-economic structure of agriculture and the cultural and psychological factors keeping it together.

We shall now focus on three features with a profound impact on Russian agriculture: the paternalistic management culture, the symbiotic relationship between large- and small-scale production, and the role of central government. All these are affected by an institutional deficit in rural Russia.

A paternalistic management culture

The socialist tradition runs deep on farms through the paternalistic relationships between managers and employees. The background for these relationships can be traced to the Russian patrimonialism, which, according to Max Weber, had been medieval Russia's alternative to feudalism since Peter the Great (Weber 1978, 1065). Typically, the Russian style of management is based on the strong authority of the superiors, direct personal relations, and the manager's obligation also to look after the workers and their families.[25]

An important element maintaining the tradition of paternalistic management is the institution of collective farm managers. Alexander Bedny has drawn a typical portrait of a manager from the managers of collective farms in the Nizhni Novgorod district (Bedny 2006). A manager is usually a 40- to 50-year-old man born in the country whose education is relatively high and who has an average of five years of experience in managing an enterprise. He has a conservative attitude towards economic change, for instance, he believes that the agricultural import kills a Russian agro-producer (91%), he believes that an active state intervention is necessary (87%) and feels there is lack of impersonal trust between the agricultural stakeholders, nor is he a member of agrarian unions (89%), even if he finds it necessary to develop such organisations (92%).

Sometimes these managers break away from failing collective farms and set up their own, more successful private farms, which is also what the manager of a *sovkhoz* in the Moscow cabbage production region did. However, there are also many who struggle to save their enterprises. Some remain in their jobs after changes in the ownership or even after the business has gone bankrupt. Good managers are also respected by their workers. The interviews we carried out on both sides of the Fenno-Russian border illustrate the difference between the two countries: when asked about the main strengths of the local countryside, Finnish farmers frequently mentioned natural resources and scenic beauty, while a typical answer of farm workers in Russian Karelia was "a good manager".

A symbiotic relationship

The manager-worker relationship extends to a wide range of things, including production arrangements. Ilkka Alanen, who has studied Russia's legacy in the Baltic countries, stresses that large farms and private plot holders have never been mutual opposites, quite the contrary: the prosperity of *sovkhoz*es was largely dependent on private plots even in the Soviet era, as these were a significant supplement to production and compensated for workers' low

[25] Paternalism is undoubtedly deeply rooted in the mental structures. This explains the difference between the developments in Estonia and Russia, for instance. Despite the introduction of the Soviet system of *sovkhoz*es and *kolkhoz*es to regions taken over after the Second World War, the system worked differently in Russia and the Baltic region. Two former Estonian managers of collective farms told us in an interview in 2006 that the difference was that a manager in Estonia would obtain his position through his competence at work, while what mattered in Russia were personal relations rather than achievements. This would also make the manager's authority over the workers more unquestioned, providing a foundation for paternalism.

wages. Private plot holders could use the resources of the collective farm – animals, fertilisers, machinery and marketing channels – for their own benefit. In agriculture, this connection was evident in the division of labour between the collective farm and the plots of its workers and in certain practical arrangements. These can be considered to have formed a symbiotic relationship, which has protected small farms from the full rigours of the market (Alanen 1998, 145; Pallot et al. 2003, 361). A collective farm would provide a lot of help for private plot holders, who fulfilled their own obligations to the collective farm.

As collective farms were turned from *sovkhoz*es into limited liability companies, many of the old practices were discontinued or were no longer free of charge. The change has been more rapid and more complete in Estonia than in Russia. According to our field study, Russian collective farms continue to provide help for the workers and shareholders. A dairy farm manager told us in 2003 that he tried to keep the farm in business and the work collective together by offering ploughing and transport services, firewood, fertilisers and a variety of other fringe benefits to the workers to compensate for their low wages. The company would help the local population with housing construction and sold its products to the workers at a discount. In the manager's view, all this was natural and even vital: "If we do not support our people, nobody else will do it either. We live as one big family."

Although this support and aid provided to the workers and local inhabitants were an economic burden for the company, the idea of cost-cutting was pure folly for the manager:

> […]Well, you understand it all as urban citizens. It is your urban opinion. The thing is that our wages are very small and people could not live without help. If we give a driver 50 litres of petrol for work, he will take 5 to 10 litres for his own needs. It is the truth. He will sell it to survive. (Nikula et al. 2005, 43)

The symbiotic relationship between collective farms and households gave the workers the right to use, borrow and even steal the property of the collective farm (see Alanen 1998, 145). It was the mainstay of collectivism, mutual trust and management's obligations to the workers on the collective farm. For a worker in an agricultural enterprise, giving up his share of the company and setting up a private farm would mean severing this relationship. It is therefore quite understandable that most of the workers at these companies have been unwilling to take up private farming. Maintaining a symbiotic relationship has strengthened the path dependence, ensuring that the combination of mass production and private plots remains a fundamental element of the structure of agriculture. The change in the legal ownership of Russian farms (from collective farms to limited liability companies) did not bring a structural change in the form of the disintegration of collective farms and an emergence of a system of family farms, which would have been what the West had expected to happen. This path dependence was based on decisions that private plot holders working on collective farms had been forced to make on the basis of rational calculation and a fear of cultural change.

In terms of rational thinking, these decisions are related to a fear of losing the protection and support provided for private plots by the collective farm. The risks involved are also connected with the lack of organisations in rural Russia that would help small producers. A more irrational fear affecting the decisions is the fear of cultural change. Detachment from a symbiotic relationship means leaving an institutional arrangement that has served several generations. The first family farms were in fact established by urban people – most of who have since then had to give up production. The farmer from southern Russia mentioned earlier was an exception: although he had no previous ties with the local culture, he had sufficient skills and starting capital that he had acquired elsewhere. Family farms and farming enterprises with paid labour have also been established by those with enough strategic and practical knowledge of farming and markets. These people used to work as experts or managers in agricultural enterprises in the socialist era. Most workers have remained as paid employees on the farms or, after retirement, continued to cultivate their own plots together with their families.

Central government and rural areas

The Russian government is used to a top-down development of the country, an approach which remains very much the same for the current government as well. The continuity of the structure of power is part of the path dependence.

For generations, food production in Russia has relied on mass production, and investments in it continue even today in southern Russia and around Moscow and St. Petersburg, for instance. Some of these investments are made by private capital investors, particularly energy companies. The state has now become an important player as well: it was recently decided that milk production around St. Petersburg was to be raised to a new level through a 94-million-euro funding programme. This funding will not be aimed at creating family farms or institutions that would help family farms; according to a spokesman of the St. Petersburg regional government, it will only focus on farms with 500 to 3,000 cows (MT 2006)[26].

[26] For problems connected with this trend, see Tekoniemi 2003, 7; Visser 2004, 181; Ioffe 2005, 189-190; Serova 2007.

This is not a one-way road, however. New enterprises and industries are gaining a foothold in rural areas. There is also an ongoing process of creating a system of democratic decision-making in Russia. The reform of local government launched at the beginning of 2006 will reduce the distance between central government and citizens, and the agricultural reform programme will entail modernisation projects. However, it is still too early to tell how successful these reforms will be.

An institutional deficit

Rural Russia still suffers from an institutional deficit – in other words, a lack of organisations that have long had an established role in Western Europe and could help small enterprises and farms solve their problems. Unlike Finland a hundred years ago, Russia in the early 1990s did not produce organisations or national systems of providing funding, advice or marketing channels for small family farms or private entrepreneurs. Entrepreneurs were on their own, local government in villages disintegrated, and farmers failed to organise. The deficit was made even more severe by the fact that non-governmental organisations were far too underdeveloped to be able to address the needs of farmers, entrepreneurs, consumers or rural families in matters related to economy, leisure, social assistance or new types of cooperatives.

The path of rural Russia

The development of rural Russia seems to focus on mass production and to cover the range from agriculture to food processing and food supply chains reaching shops. There is no rush of *fermery* in sight yet, although studies carried out in some regions (e.g. Patsiorkovsky et al. 2005) show that *fermery* have strengthened their economic return in both agriculture and business. Our field studies show that private plot holders are in no great hurry to change their modus operandi and become *fermery*. They will, however, engage in more non-agricultural activities, either as registered companies or in the grey economy.

The path dependence theory seeks to help economists to understand the dynamics of change and history scholars to explain the nature of historical evolution. It seems to provide appropriate tools for understanding the differences and special features in the development of Eastern Europe and Russia.

Studying the path dependence in transition conditions is an application of the general path dependence thinking. It can be seen as a heuristic framework combining sub-theories which can, in this particular case, be operationalised into empirically testable hypotheses on formal and informal institutions and factors affecting them. The development of Russian agriculture is affected by paternalism, symbiotic relationships and the power relations between state and citizen. These factors cannot be excluded from explanations of the operation of formal institutions or Russia's particularity compared with a number of other eastern European countries.

An essential lesson learnt from the path dependence theory is the importance of taking time into account in social research. While social research is often static and covers only a short span even when the subject is social change, the path dependence theory provides an opportunity to examine long-term change processes. Beating a new path in the context of social and political development requires difficult, long-term institutional changes (See North 1997, 17; Dahrendorf 1990). As we know, any changes on traditional farms are usually made when new generations take over. Whatever the political system, the land itself has the inherent feature of curbing radical changes. Russia's transition from socialism to market economy and from central planning to pluralism will involve not only structural changes but also changes in values and mentality, which may not take effect for several generations but are nevertheless possible.

The road to family farms in Russia was taken right at the beginning of the transition even when no road signs had yet been erected. It has remained a muddy, narrow, winding path, overgrown with thickets, because there are still not enough institutions or non-governmental organisations to help keep the road clear. It seems that people will remain private plot holders even if more land were available for them. Unemployed rural families will primarily seek income from their own plots and the grey economy. At the same time, however, local circumstances are beginning to change as new enterprises, for instance, are gradually being established in the countryside as well.

We have good reason to expect that the next generation of cucumber and cabbage farmers in the Moscow region will consider modernisation of their production methods. It is also quite certain that the values adopted by the new Russian generation will be rather different from those held by socialist-era generations.

Reforms of basic institutional elements will provide new openings for development in Russia that will be created locally rather than controlled centrally in a top-down approach. The 2006 reform of local government provides good opportunities for this. Local organisations are being founded here and there that show a new kind of trust between the rural players. Institutional changes, however, are measured in generations, not years. With twenty years now gone from the start of the perestroika, we can gradually see signs of change. Nevertheless, fundamental changes in the system will not be seen for at least another generation.

References

Alanen, I. (1998) Baltic Agriculture after the Decollectivisation, in *Actors on the Changing European Countryside*, ed. by L. Granberg & I. Kovách. Institute for Political Science of the Hungarian Academy of Sciences, Budapest, 144-67.

Amelina, M. (2000) Why Russian Peasants Remain in Collective Farms: A Household Perspective on Agricultural Restructuring. *Post-Soviet Geography and Economics* 41 (7), 483-511.

Barnes, A. (1998) What's the difference? Industrial privatization and agricultural land reform in Russia. *Europe-Asia Studies* 50 (July), 843-54.

Bedny, A. (2007) Institutional Factors of Russian Agricultural Development, in *Reflecting Transformation in Post-socialist Rural Areas*, ed. by M. Heinonen et al. Cambridge Scholars Publishing, Newcastle, 30-48.

Dahrendorf, R. (1990) Reflection on the Revolution in Europe. NY:Times Books, New York.

Kaneva, K. (1999) Organisational Restructuring of Bulgarian Agriculture. Partial Project 3c in 3rd KATO Workshop, Prague.

Kay, A. (2003) Path Dependency and the CAP. *Journal of European Public Policy* 10(3), 405-20.

MT (2006) Maaseudun Tulevaisuus [The Future of Countryside], 19.4.2006, Maataloustuottajain keskusliitto, Helsinki.

Nikula, J. (2004) Path-dependency Theory and Post-socialist Transition, in *Plussat ja miinukset* [Plusses and Minuses], ed. by R. Blom & J. Nikula. Lumikki-kustannus, Tampere, 57-64.

Nikula, J., I. Kopoteva, L. Granberg & I. Alanen (2005) Traditional in Modern – Local Economy and Community in Priazha, in *Social Structure, Public Space and Civil Society in Karelia*, ed. by H. Melin. Kikimora Publications B 34. Saarijärvi, 25-59.

North, D. (1990) *Institutions, Institutional Change and Economic Performance.* Cambridge University Press. Cambridge.

—. (1997) The Contribution of the New Institutional Economics to an Understanding of the Transition Problem. *WIDER Annual Lectures* 1, UNU/Wider, Helsinki.

O'Brien, D. J., S.K. Wegren & V.V. Patsiorkovski, (2004) Contemporary Rural Responses to Reform from Above. *The Russian Review* 63 (April), 256-76.

Ostrom, E. (1999) Institutional Rational Choice: an Assessment of the Institutional Analysis and Development Framework, in *Theories of the Policy Process*, ed. by P. Sabatier. Westview Press, Boulder (CO), 35-72.

Oswald, I. (2007) "Industrialized villages" in Post-socialist Countries – Steps Towards an Integrative Research Concept, in *Reflecting Transformation in*

Post-socialist Rural Areas, ed. by M. Heinonen et al. Cambridge Scholars Publishing, Newcastle, 215-35.

Ortar, N. (2007) Villagers and *Dachniki* in Post-soviet Russia: A Complex Relation, in *Reflecting Transformation in Post-socialist Rural Areas*, ed. by M. Heinonen et al. Cambridge Scholars Publishing, Newcastle, 257-68.

Pallot, J. & T. Nefedova (2003) Trajectories in People's Farming in Moscow Oblast during the Post-socialist Transformation. *Journal of Rural Studies* 19, 345-62.

Patsiorkovsky, V.V., D.J. O'Brien & V.V. Patsiorkovskaya (2005) Agrarian Reform and Multi-Functional Rural Areas in Russia. Paper Presented in 21st Conference of the European Society for Rural Sociology, 23-27 August, Keszthely.

Scott, R. W. (2001) *Institutions and Organizations*. Sage, Thousand Oaks.

Serova, E., N.Karlova, T.Tikhonova, I.Khramova & I.Shik (2004) *Prospects of Reforming of an Agrarian Policy of Russia.* Society and Economics. Russian Academy of Sciences, Institute for International Economic and Political Studies. Moscow.

Serova, E. (2007) The Results of Russian Agri-Food Sector Transformation, in *Reflecting Transformation in Post-socialist Rural Areas*, ed. by M. Heinonen et al. Cambridge Scholars Publishing, Newcastle,8-29.

Tekoniemi, Merja (2003) Venäjän maatalous 2000-luvulla. [Russian Agriculture after 2000] *BOFIT online* 9/2003. Helsinki.

Weber, M. (1978) *Economy and Society*. (Ed. by G. Roth & C. Wittich.) University of California Press. Berkeley.

Wegren, S. K. (1998) Agriculture and the State in Soviet and Post-Soviet Russia, University of Pittsburgh Press. Pittsburgh (PA).

—. (2000) State Withdrawal and the Impact of Marketization on Rural Russia. *Policy Studies Journal* 28(1), 46-63.

—. (2004) Rural Adaptation in Russia: Who Responds and How Do We Measure It? *Journal of Agricultural Change* 4 (4), 553-78.

—. (2005) *The Moral Economy Reconsidered.* Palmgrave Macmillan.

Visser, O. (2004) Coping with Crisis in the Post-communist countryside, in *New Countryside. Culture, Local Governance and Sustainability in Rural Development*, ed. by I. Sihc-Mihanovic & M. Máteffy. Sapient-Hungarian University of Transylvania, Miercurea-Ciuc, 177-210.

CHAPTER FOUR

LEGACIES AND PATH-DEPENDENCE: CONTINUITIES AND DISCONTINUITIES IN THE ORGANISATION OF BULGARIAN AGRICULTURE

IVAYLO VASSILEV

Introduction

"Reform" in post-socialist Bulgaria has been associated with the large-scale privatisation of state property, the liberalisation of trade regimes, and the withdrawal of the state from the market. In agriculture these measures involved land restitution and the privatisation of co-operative property, as well as the withdrawal of state subsidies and the liberalisation of the market for agricultural goods. Most of these reforms were inspired by the desire for a swift and radical break with the past, which, although initially painful, was expected to lead quickly to the building of new efficient and well-tested institutions. These hopes rested on the belief that a totally new beginning was possible, where the old would be erased, and the resulting void would be quickly filled with well-tested, functioning institutions from Western Europe. A new history could be written on a clean slate (*tabula rasa*).

Compared to some other Eastern European countries, the reforms were introduced in Bulgaria rather more slowly, but, as in other cases, their implementation coincided with a staggering decline in production levels[27] and living standards[28]. While the decline affected the economy as a whole, it was especially marked in agriculture and its impact most severe in rural

[27] For example, the yield (tonnes per hectare) of wheat was 4.8 in 1989, 4.6 in 1990, 3.7 in 1991, and 3.1 in 1992, with other crops following similar patterns. With the exception of the low wheat yield in 1985, the levels in the mid and late 1990s were similar to levels at the beginning of the 1970s. The production of meat dropped from 820,000 tn in 1989 to 612,000 tn in 1992. (See Cochrane, Schmitz & Bojnec 1994; Davidova & Batchvarova 1995)

[28] Bulgarian GDP fell by 28% between 1989 and 1993 (Davidova & Batchvarova 1995).

communities[29]. In many respects, Bulgaria's post-1989 experiences can be described as reliving history in reverse (Fitoussi 1997). One of the explanations of this decline was that agricultural production in socialist Bulgaria was not sustainable and was, therefore, even before 1989, heading towards an unavoidable collapse. Alternative approaches suggest that the decline was mainly the result of post-1989 policies, which were blamed for annihilating the very grounds (existing institutional arrangements) on which successful reform depended. In this sense, reform could only be gradual and evolutionary (Campbell & Pedersen 1996).

Some authors have suggested using the notions of "path-dependence" and "path-shaping" (Stark 1992; Bruszt 1992; Hausner, Jessop & Nielsen 1994; Offe 1996; Chavance & Magnin 1997) as a way of capturing the importance of history for ongoing changes. However, if overemphasised, this may lead to simplistic and deterministic claims[30]. Thus, while the danger of ignoring the past and local specificity was evident in the failures of the excessively voluntaristic 'shock therapy' policies, an overemphasis on the past, and the significance of some pasts over others, is likely to lead to determinist assumptions, the neglect of major external factors and the possibilities of change and learning. More specifically, emphasising the past as an explanation of the present makes underdevelopment to appear historically and culturally pre-given and inescapable (Trigilia 2001).

I will suggest that, while very useful, the notion of path-dependence seems to exaggerate continuities. If what constitutes a path is the coupling of institutions, the organisation of material reality, practices and habits, then I would argue there are no identifiable paths in post-socialist Bulgaria. The post-socialist context is one of disruption and disorder, of a large-scale de-coupling between regulating institutions, organisational patterns, habits, and natural

---

[29] For example, in 1995, 10-30% of arable land was not cultivated, and between 1989 and 1994 there was a 50% decline in the number of livestock. Between 1989 and 1992 the production of agricultural machinery declined by 59%, while the use of agricultural machinery decreased by 5-10%. Between 1989 and 1993 fertiliser production fell by more than 50% and plant protection chemicals production fell by 56%, while the use of fertilisers and chemicals in agriculture fell by 67% and 86% respectively until 1992. In addition, internal levels of consumption also fell by approximately 15-20%.

[30] For example, differences in the economic and political development of various East European countries after 1989 have been ascribed to their national history (whether a certain country had ever been able to build a nation-state) (Brubaker 1996), their experience with the institutions of private property, and the initial conditions and market relations they faced (e.g. Barlett & Hoggett 1996), the presence of a pre-1989 history of democratic opposition (Higley, Pakulski & Wesolowski 1998), ethnic diversity and nationalism (Jeffries 1993; Bryant 1994), and culture (Sztompka 1995; Miller 1998). In some cases, lock-in effects are assumed to persist for centuries (Huntington 1997).

processes as they existed in the past. Simultaneously, there are also processes in which institutions and practices are re-coupled into new forms, while assuming different functions for individuals, organizations and social systems, and reconstituting forms of conflict and possible solutions. This makes all theoretical pre-conceptions of the relationship between institutional forms and their functions suspect, and makes cross-country comparisons extremely difficult.

While the notion of path-dependence may still prove useful for future analyses of post-socialism, at this stage a weaker notion, such as *legacy,* will be more appropriate for capturing the complex interrelation between past and present in Bulgaria. Here, legacies are understood as influences from the past that are only actualised by their coupling with certain presents, albeit with largely unpredictable and, therefore, often unintended and contradictory outcomes. More specifically, I suggest the following distinction between *legacy* and *path-dependence.* Legacy stands for the independent influence that a single object of analysis (e.g. institution, material structure, habit) might exercise in historical development, while path-dependence stands for a constellation of interdependent influences that tend to establish a definite trajectory that is hard to change. Even where a number of legacies combine to constitute a path this does not mean that this path somehow overrides their individual effects or undermines their openness to being re-functionalised in different contexts or re-deployed for new purposes. A genuine path would involve the establishment of an internal relationship between different legacies so that the path involves more than the mechanical sum of its various elements. This would certainly make it harder to shift.

My priority will be to begin describing the complexity of post-socialist reforms in Bulgaria and to trace some of the continuities and discontinuities in the agricultural sector, whilst focusing mainly on the grain chain. I will argue, in more general terms, that socialist co-operatives, close rural-urban family links, the complicated provision of local welfare, and the large processing and storage units that were developed before 1989, are all significant factors in understanding the difficulties involved with land restitution and with efficient production. However, I will also show how these pasts only became significant within the policies and practices of the more recent changes and specifically with the neo-liberal reform after 1989. Past and present, as well as beliefs and expectations for the future continuously co-evolve, and, therefore, while the present cannot be read through the past, the past is nonetheless essential in understanding the present.

Bulgarian agriculture before 1989

The organisation of production and the centralised state

To begin with, land distribution, land fragmentation, consolidation and efficiency, and, more generally, the large-scale restructuring of agricultural production, are by no means new issues to Bulgaria. The distribution of land has been prominent in all major stages of development and has always been linked not only to broad agendas of modernisation and state building but also to a more narrowly defined political and ideological rationale. The problem of land distribution can be traced back at least to the time of Bulgarian independence from Ottoman rule in the late nineteenth century, as successive governments have sought legitimacy through addressing the land question. This was only one among many factors that marked the specifically Bulgarian route to nationhood. A predominantly rural population and the low level of industrialisation of the country required a gradual process of centralisation. The centralisation of power in the nation-state required popular support, which was gained through giving lots of power to local councils and through an equal distribution of land (the main economic resource at the time).

Thus, immediately after achieving independence, the first Bulgarian government began redistributing the large land holdings that had belonged to members and ex-members of the Ottoman military, administrative and economic elite, who resettled in other areas within the Ottoman Empire[31]. This led to a very high degree of land fragmentation, with a large number, some 1.8 million, of very small family farms. With the division of land among heirs this process of fragmentation was intensified and in 1934 the average size was 0.4 ha. The large majority of these farms were inefficient, with high labour inputs and with production mainly for subsistence. Although there were some attempts to create agricultural co-operatives before World War II, they were largely unsuccessful (for example, in 1944, there were only 15 co-operatives cultivating about 17,000 ha of land) (Davidova & Buckwell 1994), and it was small-scale agricultural production that remained predominant (Meurs, Kouzhouharova & Stoyanova 1999).

In the post-World War II period, land questions re-emerged as politically significant (control over a strategic resource) and ideologically symbolic. Immediately after the war, large land holdings were nationalised and then

[31] After the establishment of a Bulgarian state there was a wave of emigration of Muslims. During the Russo–Turkish war approximately one million Muslims emigrated. Between 1878 and 1883, 250,000 more emigrated for the Ottoman Empire. These were mostly people from the Muslim intelligentsia. Those who remained were the poor and uneducated (Simsir 1988, 18).

distributed among landless peasants. As with previous land reforms, this policy was an efficient tool for consolidating political control. However, for economic and ideological reasons, this was reversed at the beginning of the 1950s. This was also the first time since the re-establishment of an independent Bulgarian state in the nineteenth century that central government directly faced local opposition to its policies. Collectivisation and the creation of co-operatives were resisted by middle landowners but also proved unpopular among small owners. Collectivisation was completed by 1958 when approximately 3,290 co-operative farms covered 90% of the agricultural land (Davidova & Batchvarova 1995), but it was achieved through a mixture of regulatory pressures and intimidation from local communist party activists. Thus, the evolution of the co-operatives followed a pattern of intensified centralisation from the 1950s up until the 1970s, which was followed by a degree of de-centralisation in the 1980s.

The generally high level of centralised decision-making and land consolidation affected the overall shape of the agricultural production cycle. Thus, grain, for example, which occupies over half of all agricultural land, was distributed around the country through large local and regional storage facilities; it was subsequently processed in a small number of large flour and fodder-mills located in the majority of big cities throughout the country. Flour-mills supplied the large bread and bakery plants, which were similarly built on a territorial principle, so that every town and city had its own bread and bakery plant (Slavejkov & Zlatunova 1999). Thus, grain was moving within large production units, both administratively and physically, which were designed to produce economies of scale and reduce the overlapping of functions.

Informal links and the complex functions of the co-operatives

Agricultural production in Bulgaria has never been"truly" or"only" centralised. Indeed, the Bulgarian model combined neo-Stalinist large-scale socialist farms on the one hand and the encouragement of household production after the 1970s, similar to the Hungarian model, on the other (Swain 2001). More generally, agricultural production has always been the subject of negotiation between the central authorities on the one side and the localities on the other, with their different economic rationality and established practices. The rigid and centralised organisation of the party-state was complemented by complex networks of interdependence that ran from the very bottom to the very top of the social hierarchy, but also connected different areas, industries, and occupations. This was complicated by the introduction of personal plots and the complex relations between rural and urban areas. Co-operatives and Agro-industrial complexes were focal points of these relations.

Co-operatives, like other production units, were allowed to keep large social development funds and had a relatively free hand in designing their own social policies. Being the main, and often the only, economic unit in their localities, co-operatives came to play a very special role in that they were both employers and welfare providers for a majority of the population in rural areas. The power of the co-operatives was extended further by the process of de-centralisation in the 1980s and especially the introduction in 1982 of the *accord* system, which allowed co-operatives to subcontract some of their work to groups of workers or individuals. The *accord* system complemented the already existing *lichno polzvane*, or plots for personal use, where individuals and families were given small pieces of land on which they could grow agricultural products for their own consumption, and reinforced the close link between the co-operatives and other forms of production (Meurs & Djankov 1998, Creed 1998). The significance of the plots for personal use and production under the accord system was particularly high in animal rearing, so that at the end of the 1970s the accord system accounted for about 30% of the pork and 50% of the poultry produced, while household plots accounted for about 60% of family income in the 1980s (Swain 2001).

Co-operatives and 'non-co-operative' production

Co-operatives were central for all forms of non-co-operative production in rural areas through the provision of machines, inputs, and markets, and by building and maintaining local infrastructure (Penov 2002). Bulgarian peasants consider some form of small-scale private production very much a characteristic of rural life and an inseparable ingredient of rural identity[32]. However, the importance of such activities for the residents of rural areas goes far beyond identity and used to play a complex economic function as well.

The plots for personal use and *accord* production certainly played an important part in increasing family budgets. Neither the benefits derived from, nor the work invested in, this form of production were restricted to the rural household, rather they were extended to members of the wider family who in many cases lived in urban areas. Thus, family members living in the cities would regularly travel to the villages and assist with production. In return they would share, in one form or another, the produce and/or the cash received from selling it.

Many of these activities involved high inputs of manual labour and a large domestic economy (e.g. the production of jars and alcohol) (Kornai 1997), and

[32] In addition to the complex forms of local interdependence, strong local identities were reinforced by the strict restrictions on resettlement that existed before 1989. For a discussion on agriculture and identity under socialism see, for example, Creed (1995).

therefore would appear to be quite inefficient. But these arrangements were by no means caused by a lack of alternatives in securing subsistence or by the lack of a sufficiently developed infrastructure offering more efficient alternatives. Production on personal plots and under the *accord* system, like the jar economy (where each family was producing their own canned food to be used during the winter months, rather than buying them on the market), was not simply a way of surviving, but would be better described as entrepreneurship under the conditions of a socialist regime that, at least formally, was trying to prevent the emergence of inequalities. For example, such activities increased the availability of disposable cash and, thus, access to, what was defined by the government as, luxury goods. But, privately produced agricultural goods also increased the bargaining power of producers within the 'economy of favours' and thus their access to scarce goods.

The interdependence between co-operatives and the locality was extensive. Despite attempts by the central government before 1989 to diversify the rural economy by opening local branches of city-based enterprises, agriculture remained the predominant economic sector in rural areas. Closely linked to this failure to diversify was a process whereby co-operatives gradually became more efficient and were transformed into sources of funding for municipalities, local infrastructure, and their own expansion into other activities (Swain 1997).

Private production mostly supplemented whatever was available from the co-operative farm and also provided access to resources otherwise unavailable. However, in most cases the people who were privately contracted by co-operatives were the same people who were working in the co-operatives, but who had no incentive to make this effort as co-operative employees. This also reduced the time spent working for the co-operative and increased the time spent in private production (Creed 1998).

Nevertheless, local residents were very important as employees of the co-operative because of their expertise and because alternatives were not easily available. Agriculture has always experienced labour shortages, which, before 1989, were met by the seasonal state mobilisation of the urban population. However, it was the residents of rural localities who were the most reliable, available throughout the whole year, for labour force. Local residents were also highly skilled and could be utilised for pretty much every type of agricultural work on the co-operative farms.

While such arrangements were significantly influenced by the ideology and legal-institutional framework of the central government, it is worthwhile emphasising the essential role of various key factors in making such arrangements possible. These include the availability of large amounts of common land, which could be used by the rural population; the close family links connecting rural and urban areas (a legacy from rapid urbanisation after

World War II); the acceptance of high levels of self-(and family)-exploitation; and the close co-operation, and co-evolution of the relationship, between agricultural co-operatives and local residents. All of these affected the post-1989 agricultural reform and I will refer back to them later.

Thus, co-operatives, as the focal point of agricultural production, came to serve a broader function in the locality by providing different forms of welfare and services to the local community. Similar to enterprises in other economic sectors, they acquired a wide variety of assets broadly related to the welfare of their employees and local residents. In many cases, however, these assets were built with the voluntary (or obligatory, unpaid) labour of local residents, which adds further to the complex interrelations found in rural localities, and later influenced the privatisation of co-operative property and land restitution.

To summarise, after World War II agricultural production in Bulgaria was collectivised and centrally planned. These processes were associated with the creation of large, regionally-based, production, processing and distribution facilities. However, although economic planning was centralised, it was constantly re-shaped through complex negotiations within a locality. The co-operative, which was a creation of socialist planning, outgrew its narrow economic functions and became a major social institution in organising life in rural areas.

Post-communist (dis)continuities

Socialist cooperatives were "total" institutions (Swain 2001) in the sense that, first, within their localities they were to a large degree responsible for the general well-being of the people living in rural areas, and second, that they were also central players and a crossing point between the production and consumption of agricultural products, linking rural and urban areas through consumption and work that were both formal and informal. Although today they have changed considerably, there seem to be significant continuities as well. Thus, in 2003, agricultural co-operatives still had by far the biggest share of cultivated land (40%), while individual entrepreneurs and trading companies cultivated 16% and 12% respectively (MZGAR 2005a).

The cultivation of personal plots (*lichno polzvane*), which was extremely significant before 1989, has recently been described by the Ministry of Agriculture as an extraordinary phenomenon of the present state of agricultural production. Thus, almost all co-operatives and agricultural entrepreneurs (*arendatori*) are offering personal plots (*lichno polzvane*) on some of their land, so that they account for 3% of all cultivated land (MZGAR 2005b). Furthermore, the large processing factories and storage facilities, albeit under new ownership, have generally remained intact with new facilities being predominantly of small to medium size.

So what has actually changed and are those examples clear cases of continuity from the socialist past? And given the presence of a number of other relationships that have been reproduced after socialism, such as the relative inefficiency of co-operatives and the dependence on large buyers such as trading and processing companies, is it justified to talk about the path-dependence of Bulgarian agriculture?

Ownership and control

The reorganisation of agricultural production, in so far as it involved a change in land ownership and land use, meant a radical break with the existing social structure of rural localities as it had developed under socialism. Significantly, land was returned to its owners in its real [physical] boundaries and not as single consolidated unit that equals their share of co-operative holdings (Begg & Meurs 1998), which led to a highly fragmented pattern of land ownership and created a multiplicity of very small landowners[33], the majority of whom did not live in the areas where their land was situated.[34] It was mostly those who were land-less before collectivisation that worked in the co-operatives during socialism, many of them were close or at retirement age[35] (see Swain 1997), and a large number belonged to the Turkish minority, who, in turn, are the main voters of the predominantly Turkish Movement for Rights and Freedoms (MRF).

The question of land restitution raised the much broader question about the grounds on which legitimate claims could be made (and, as it turned out, former

[33] The process of de-centralisation that took place in the 1980s created some problems with boundaries and responsibilities even before the beginning of the reform after 1989. The re-organisation of co-operative units left some unresolved questions about assets between old and new units, which were further complicated by the emergence of small-scale private farming. Thus, in addition to the problems of establishing property relations on the basis of pre-nationalisation ownership, there was also the legacy of the 1980s reform, which blurred the boundaries between co-operatives and agricultural-industrial complexes, and between co-operatives and private plots now used for farming. Although establishing and maintaining the ownership rights of private individuals was the most serious problem after 1989, it was further exacerbated by the blurred control over co-operative assets.

[34] There are an estimated 4 million owners, out of a total Bulgarian population of 8 million.

[35] Among those employed in agricultural production only 12.5% are under 35 years old, while more than half of these employed in agriculture are at, or near, retirement age. Only 1/3 of all those employed in agriculture are women (MZGAR 2003).

ownership was only one such possibility), and about the relationship between ownership, management, and use. Claims for access to land and co-operative property were based on ownership, labour contribution,[36] and custom[37] (Verdery 1994, Creed 1998, Cellarius 2000, Kaneff 2000), and were defended on the basis of moral, economic, political and other discursive strategies. Indeed, contrary to the narrow understanding of ownership as a relationship between people and things, the complexity of land restitution demonstrated that property rights are based on relations between people in respect of things (Hann 2000).

The post-1989 land reform and the liquidation of the co-operatives were quite obviously politically charged processes. Rural areas were often seen as the biggest failure of the pre-1989 regime but were also a stronghold of the new Socialist Party (BSP). Therefore there was a significant ideological as well as political incentive for the anti-Communist Union of Democratic Forces (UDF) to dismantle the existing rural structures, which, indeed, became a priority for the UDF.

The opposing political interests in the rural areas of the BSP and the UDF, as well as those of the comparatively small MRF, which was nonetheless strategically important in parliamentary voting, led to frequent shifts in the direction of the agricultural reform. Thus, depending on whether it was the BSP or the UDF that had the upper hand in parliament at any particular moment,

---

[36] For example, local residents would often be given land plots for personal use, and in other cases they would have participated in the building of co-operative, municipal, and state infrastructure, such as buildings and roads, through either voluntary or involuntary, but in any event certainly unpaid labour.

[37] For instance, in some cases private contractors cultivate land that has been used as pastureland in the past, or has not been controlled by the co-operative. Given the tradition and practices in the locality, this land would be regarded as common land. Such claims are difficult to counter by producers for a complex set of reasons. Local people may consider the continuing use of such land as pastureland as not an entirely illegitimate act because of the "history" of this land. Under socialism, state property was often perceived and treated like common land, and access to it would be considered as socially acceptable, or as something "everyone does".

Access here is discussed through a mixed rhetoric referring to a history of use and morality. On the one hand, local residents might argue against what they see as the excessive enrichment of some private contractors whom they see as exploiting local resources. Sometimes arguments about supposed cases of dishonest participation in the privatisation process were also used as justifications. On the other hand, local shepherds were frequent trespassers, their herds often belonging to local families for whom the shepherds were working on contract. In addition, shepherds are usually poorer people and any excessive measure against them would be considered inappropriate. Taking the trespasser to court would be both inappropriate and ineffective, because in most cases he would not have had enough money to pay for the damage, and because it might be considered morally wrong.

there was a shift towards or away from support for cooperatives. Indeed, the changes in the land law and in the law on co-operatives were so frequent[38] that this led to a common complaint from both practitioners and administrators that they were not entirely sure which version of the law applied.

The land reform and the liquidation of the co-operatives were only one aspect of the reform in agriculture. Other aspects of the agricultural reform included price and trade liberalisation, although agricultural prices continued to be controlled, and the break up of state monopolies in the processing, storage and marketing of agricultural goods. Successive governments after 1990 experimented with different forms of price regulation, which included fixed, minimum purchasing and free-floating prices, trying to achieve 'just' levels of profit, which were calculated on the basis of an estimated production cost.

Unlike the land reform, these processes were much slower and only gathered speed in the mid-1990s, especially under the second UDF government. Unlike co-operative property, which mainly involved units that could be sold independently from each other (e.g. machines, cattle, land), this was not the case with flour-mills, as they could only operate as a whole indivisible unit. In 1991, when the restructuring of the state-owned umbrella holding Zarneni Hrani, renamed Zarno Ltd., began, all large flour- and fodder-mills and 5 million tons of storage capacity, out of a total of 7 million tons for the country, belonged to this one state holding[39]. Eventually, Zarno Ltd. was transformed into a State Reserve, which kept a large number of these storage facilities and remains a major player on the grain market,[40] while the overall process of privatisation

---

[38] For example, Law for the Ownership and Use of Agricultural Land, March 1991, March 1992, June 1993, September 1994, May 1995, issues 79, 103, 104 in 1996, issues 62, 87, 98, 123, 124 in 1997, issues 36, 59, 88, 133 in 1998, issue 68 in 1999. Law on Co-operatives, 3 August 1991, issues 34, 55 in 1992, issue 63 in 1994, issues 59, 103 in 1996, issue 52 in 1997, issue 52 in 1998, issue 81 in 1999.

[39] In 1991 "Zarneni Hrani" was divided into 74 independent entities. Initially the largest of these, Zarno Ltd., still accounted for 11 milling facilities, that is, 20% of the country's storage facilities and controlled 2.4 million tons of storage capacity, that is, 35% of the country's storage capacity as well as 50% of the grain reserves (Cochrane, Schmitz & Bojnec 1994).

[40] Privatisation and de-monopolisation were accompanied by a process whereby the state withdrew from price control, and the deregulation of trade. The process of price liberalisation began in February 1991 mainly under pressure from international financial institutions (see e.g. Campbell 1993). It was introduced simultaneously within an economy with unreformed monopolies dominating many sectors, and was accompanied by removing many of the existing support programmes.

Agriculture was affected both directly by the withdrawal of state subsidies and the deregulation of prices for agricultural products, and indirectly by the deregulation of input prices. The rise of output prices, which doubled in 1991, could not compensate for

was completed at the end of the 1990s. Despite the change in the form of ownership after privatisation, large flour-mills, due to their size and location (they were evenly distributed through the country), continued to influence the grain chain. Similar to the past when they belonged to a large state monopoly, the large flour-mills kept their monopoly position, although, in this case, as regional monopolies. In addition, in many cases they kept their management teams and their relationships with previous partners.

However, while in the past their monopoly position was due to, and guaranteed by, the state, after privatisation it was due to the market situation, where there was little competition, since building new flour-mills was expensive and risky. Consequently, it was mainly small and medium size flour-mills that tended to appear. It was mainly their large size and even distribution around the country, combined with the high cost of entry and the comparatively high risk of investing in a sector with low profits that transformed privatised state companies into regional monopolies.

Large flour-mills also kept their connections with previous partners, but this was also now based on different principles. For example, as a large consumer of grain a big flour-mill might not be interested in developing close links with many small producers, who are difficult to deal with as they tend not to fulfil their contract obligations. But it might be interested in co-operating with a large grain warehouse, and not necessarily, or only, because of the good connections that the managers may have had in the past, but because this also has a strong economic logic. An indication of their changed position is that while they clearly dominate the markets in the cities, large flour-mills are challenged by small local producers in towns and rural areas.

The privatisation of storage space also created independent traders of grain, who in some cases managed to acquire the entire regional warehouse network of former state companies, thereby becoming dominant factors on the regional level. In other cases, state and co-operative warehouses were acquired by small traders and/or by producers of grain. A large number of warehouses remained in the State Reserve Fund. Exporting, which used to be conducted exclusively through state monopolist companies, was liberalised, while remaining subject to

---

increased input prices, such as pesticides, fertilisers and fuel, which increased between 400% and 800% over the same period. However, although direct intervention was reduced, the state continued to intervene indirectly on the market. As early as July 1991, under pressure from both producers and agricultural organisations, the government reintroduced subsidies. To a large extent this was due to pressure from agricultural producers who could not cope with the pressure from, on the one hand, impoverished consumers asking for low prices and, on the other, the import of cheap and often highly subsidised agricultural goods.

a licensing regime (relaxed more recently). It is now mostly dominated by large multinationals[41].

Other new intermediaries in the grain market, which had no equivalent in the period between World War II and 1989, are the three Commodity Exchanges, located in three major cities, Rousse (North), Plovdiv (South) and Sofia (West), but they still, many years after their establishment, represent an insignificant part of the trade. Even more significantly, these exchanges rely for much of what they trade in, on the goodwill and special support of the state, in that they buy and sell through the State Reserve Fund[42].

The restructuring of markets

Grain markets (in this discussion, wheat only) in Bulgaria can be analysed as territorially-defined local, national and export circuits. Local circuits are dominated by subsistence production. Most of the grain is produced on personal plots (*lichno polzvane*),[43] and on co-operative and private farms (*arendatori*) where it is used as payment in kind for rented land (sometimes in the form of flour). Cash payments are rare at this level and are usually for services provided by local flour-mills. For medium size flour-mills local markets are too small and they need to have contracts with big consumers of flour (in addition to small local bakeries), such as former state or municipal bread factories in the bigger towns. In these commercial relationships, the provision of accurate documentation is a necessary requirement.

The majority of Bulgaria's grain exports is controlled by a few large global players such as Louis Drayfus, Glenkor, and Dominion Grain, which, according to data from the MZGAR, are the biggest exporters (Aleksandrova & Velinova 2002). Among Bulgarian companies, there is only one big exporter, Himimport. It is part of a larger holding group TIM, and together with Papas Olio (Multigroup) and 'Zarneni-Hrani' – Silistra are the other big exporters.

---

[41] For example, until the beginning of August 2002 the largest grain (all types) exporters were Louis Dreifus with 154,000 tons; Zarneni Hrani Silistra, 41,000 tons; Bulagro, 35,000 tons; Papas-olio, 28,000; and Dominion Grain, 20,000 tons (Velinova 2002).

[42] Thus according to the 2001 Agricultural Report of the MZGAR (2001) approximately 80% of the turnover of the SCE is based on the trading of goods from the State Reserve. The figure for PCE and RCE is even higher, 98% and 90%, respectively. The actual turnover of the CEs is also very low, BGN 59 million for all three, of which BGN 38 million was the turnover of SCE.

[43] *Lichno polzvane* can take different forms and can start at earlier or later stages of the crop development and very closely resembles the pre-privatisation relations. The land contracted in this manner varies between 0.1ha to 1 ha and most often involves maize, wheat, sunflower, crops that are important for animal rearing and family subsistence (MZGAR 2005a).

Himimport, Multigroup and 'Zarneni-Hrani'—Silistra, together with the State Reserve Fund also dominate the national market. These companies do not buy grain directly from producers but use specially appointed intermediaries that provide the necessary local knowledge and networks.[44]

Trading is most active during and immediately after the harvest. Transactions take place at the local and regional levels. In the period immediately after the harvest, for approximately two months, in July and August, prices are at their lowest. In this period, the main sellers are the smallest and weakest co-operatives, who sell almost their entire stock because of the pressure to pay back creditors. The bigger co-operatives and the large contractors sell very small quantities. There are two main types of buyers. These are, first, local and regional traders and flour-mills (both small and large) and second, traders commissioned by big exporters and the State Reserve.

Most of the grain is distributed during the initial period after the harvest. The main destinations are export markets, which are most active immediately after the harvest, and various storage facilities. Small co-operatives and small land contractors rarely manage to hold on to their produce until prices rise because they do not have sufficient storage facilities and because they are usually pressed for payment by their creditors, namely, input traders, and firms providing fuel and machines. With the introduction of state-licensed stores even smaller producers can afford to wait for higher prices, which restrict the power that large traders and exporters have over producers.

The existing framework provides an incentive for the development of strong local ties between producers and processors of grain, or alternatively for vertical growth at the local level: from grain production through bakery products and distribution networks. Bigger producers or mill owners are gradually taking over the business of smaller producers or bakers, as they are able to produce much more cheaply through economies of scale and tax evasion. However, this is rarely the case with perennial crops and crops that have a very high labour content. The access to personal plots for subsistence production (as well as the local moral economy) offers rural residents a viable exit option from local labour markets and in this respect also operates as a controlling mechanism over the extent to which wages can be pushed down. The latter further affects the profitability of different crops in terms of their land, labour and technology requirements. The tendency is towards a co-existence of medium and large firms, of a very similar kind (combining some form of vertical growth, backwards or forwards, or both), side by side with very small land contractors,

---

[44]Regional representatives and supply networks of traders, as well as some of the companies mentioned above, are popularly associated with racketeering in the past with and insurance firms.

some of which operate in riskier and niche markets, and a very large number of subsistence farms.

New production relations

Most of the people who live in rural areas are somehow involved in agricultural production, but while most of these are subsistence farmers, the overwhelming majority of agricultural products are produced by co-operatives and the newly emerged individual entrepreneurs (private contractors) who cultivate rented land. According to MZGAR (2002) data, in February 2001 there were 768,800 agricultural production units in Bulgaria and they cultivated 3.44 million ha of land. Ninety-nine percent of these units (763,500) were not legally registered[45] and cultivated, on average, 1.15 ha of land. These were mainly subsistence farmers, who, although participating in the market (mainly for a variety of animal products), were receiving an income that was insufficient for accumulation and expansion.

The remaining 5,300 producers, or 0.7% of all production units, were legally registered agricultural production units, 2,900 of which were co-operatives and 2,400 were individually owned farms or traders. These units accounted for the cultivation of 74% of all land (2.54 million ha). The average size of co-operatives was 600 ha, and that of individual farms (earlier also referred to as "private contractors"), 340 ha. In terms of land used for grain production, these units accounted for, on average, 85% of the land. In the case of wheat, co-operatives cultivated 57% of the land, while individual farmers cultivated 29%.

In many cases private contractors and co-operatives are legally indistinguishable from each other, as private contractors may be registered as co-operatives, or vice versa, for tax purposes, for example. But usually, private contractors are individuals, small partnerships, or families, who cultivate (mostly) rented land, while, co-operatives are unions of landowners, many of whom live locally, pool together their land and manage it collectively. However, co-operatives also rent private and state land. Consequently, state statistics, based on official forms of ownership, are only useful in showing some general patterns of production relations.

The attitude of the local population towards private contractors and co-operatives may vary significantly from one region to another. The factors that affect these relations are often specific to the locality concerned, and include the type of land, the type of ownership structure, and the types of crops and cattle traditionally produced. But the main factor is usually the manner in which the

---

[45] This however does not make such units illegal as they are allowed to register in municipalities as producers.

old co-operatives were liquidated in a particular locality. Nevertheless, a distinction between private contractors and co-operatives is useful in revealing some general patterns. There are two main features that differentiate co-operatives and private producers; their internal structure and the relative weight they give to profit and various responsibilities to the locality.

Co-operatives are governed by a landowner committee, but their day to day activities are managed by executive councils and acting chairmen that are appointed by the landowner committees annually. The freedom that the chairman has in making decisions is heavily restricted by a co-operative's rules and regulations, which makes the co-operative decision-making structure relatively rigid compared to private contractors. The internal structure of the co-operatives restricts their flexibility in terms of the types of exchanges in which they can participate and in terms of the time required to make decisions. Both these factors adversely affect the competitiveness of co-operatives within the very dynamic and complex market situation in Bulgaria.

In addition, co-operatives are obliged to be much more transparent in their relations with their employees and partners. The chairman of one co-operative complained that co-operatives paid all their taxes and the full amount of their employees' national insurance contributions, while private contractors only declared a fraction of their profits and wages, and largely operated in a "gray" economy. Thus, while co-operatives are often considered to be less efficient than private contractors, this is often the case because they tend to pay lower wages but higher taxes, and have less choice in terms of partners and terms of contracts. As a result, they tend to make lower profits because they are much less flexible within the existing conditions.

Private contractors are more profit oriented, while co-operatives perform complex social functions. For example, many co-operatives only employ members of the co-operative (who participate with their land) and try to provide employment for as many people as possible. Professionalism and competence are taken into account but they are not the only, and sometimes not the most important, factors. Family circumstances and broader community concerns such as the availability of opportunities for young people and the depopulation and aging of villages, are also taken into consideration. While, private contractors also take into consideration individual circumstances, they are much more concerned with the competence and performance of the individual worker.

The concern of a co-operative for local welfare and their employee's welfare also affect the kind of crops they cultivate. Because private contractors produce exclusively for the market they tend to produce the most profitable crops. Co-operatives, however, produce partly for the market and partly for the needs of their members, therefore their diversification and growth is affected not only by profit considerations but also by the need to satisfy the (dietary) requirements of their members. For example, although the production of vegetables or bean crops (e.g. lentils) may be unprofitable co-operatives might still grow some of these crops as well.

The structure of production units and the significance of their welfare function are also related to the age structure of rural localities. Thus, a large number of rural residents are at, or close to, retirement age, which naturally makes them less geographically mobile (therefore unlikely to look for job opportunities away from home) and more risk averse compared to generally younger urban residents. Forty percent of all managers of agricultural units are over 65 years old, while only 15% are under 45 years old (MZGAR 2005b), and the tendency is also for private contractors to be younger than the managers and employees of co-operatives.

Co-operatives and local relations

The role of the locality and some of the relationships between the co-operatives and local residents remained important factors in shaping the post-1989 agricultural restructuring. But they now performed different functions. For example, whereas before 1989 small-scale private agriculture supplemented incomes from state-run co-operatives, after 1989 this became the main and often the only source of subsistence for many households. The impoverishment of the co-operatives prevented them from paying wages to their members but they continued to provide services, such as machines; inputs, such as seeds, chemicals and fertilisers; sometimes information, and a market for produce for the private subsistence farming of their members.

It is therefore hardly surprising that private producers usually found it necessary to legitimise their profits with references to their "hard work", and how they had "begun with absolutely nothing", and had "risked all of [their] own personal property, apartments and houses, and the property of [their] relatives". Practically all the land contractors whom I interviewed[46] were very proud to point out that they paid high rents to the landowners and to mention their contribution to the local community. Apart from that, it was very rare for producers to boast about their profits. They talked about their "success" mainly in terms of "making all this out of nothing", "contributing to the local community", "paying high rents", "finding ways of making business possible despite all the difficulties created by a number of circumstances, often related to the state".

---

[46] This is based on three short one-week stays with a grain producer from north-east Bulgaria and thirty semi-structured interviews with different participants along the production chain, over a period of four years.

There are two main points that I want to emphasise here. First, some forms of co-operation that had existed before 1989 were reproduced after the beginning of the agricultural reform, but under new conditions they came to serve different functions.[47] Thus, small-scale private agriculture was transformed from being a source of additional income and a way to access goods in short supply into a major source of subsistence, although its existence continued to depend on some form of co-operation between the major land operator (a co-operative or private contractor) and the small farmer.

Second, while the co-operative form of production continued to exist, 1989 also witnessed the emergence of large-scale private land contractors who differed from the co-operatives in terms of the different relationship that they established between work and ownership: whereas private contractors separate the two, co-operatives maintain a strong link between them. However, the experience of ownership and control, as well as participation in decision-making became possible with the destruction of central planning and is certainly new for post-socialist co-operatives. If the new co-operatives resemble those of the past it is not so much because they have revived socialist co-operatives as they really existed in the past. However, both co-operatives and private contractors have a social agenda and in this sense they resemble the old co-operatives. Nonetheless, the balance between the profits they make and their responsibilities to landowners, employees, and the locality in general, do vary.

The links between rural and urban areas continue to be significant and villages tend to 'swell' in the summer (Kaneff 1998) when residents from the cities are temporarily employed in rural areas or come to help relatives. Thus, in 2003, there were 1,333,000 people involved in agricultural production of which only 3% (43,000) were full-time non-family-related employees. The largest number, 74% of all agricultural workers, were part-time family employees (MZGAR 2005).

Conclusion

The shifts in the direction of agricultural reform were intertwined in a complex web of rhetoric, rationalities, and strategies. These included, for example, a moral rhetoric of repairing the wrong doings of forceful collectivisation, emotive memories of a "prosperous pre-World War II past",

---

[47] At present, agricultural production is dominated by two major types of production unit: restructured co-operatives and private land contractors, and though both may vary in size, they continue to coexist with a large number of small subsistence producers. A typical village will have two or three major agricultural production units, which may be different co-operatives or a mixture of co-operatives and private land contractors.

rhetoric of legality, which demanded the reversing of the illegal socialist collectivisation, and an ideological rhetoric proclaiming the magic powers of private property and private initiative. All these were mixed with a variety of changing political and economic rationalities, as well as individual and institutional strategies.

The post socialist years are associated with a massive decline in productivity, job security and living standards; a slow process of land restitution and the privatisation of state assets; a disrupted and fragmented production cycle; the destruction of existing facilities; and the creation of new monopolies. In this sense, the period after 1989 might be regarded as a process of institutional-functional de-coupling and fragmentation, where old institutions and practices continue to exist yet within a totally different context where their meaning and the functions are entirely different from those acquired during the socialist period. I argue that "the reform" cannot be understood as a straightforward and unidirectional process with clearly defined agents. In fact, "the reform" appears to be a contradictory process in which diverse rationalities (economic, social, cultural and political), carried by fluid, changing and ever reconfiguring, actors, come to compete and negotiate.

In addition to being dynamic (and constantly emerging), these processes are also partly path-dependent, and thus their outcomes cannot be fully understood without reference to some social-organisational patterns of the past. The dialectic of path-dependency and path-shaping is therefore a useful concept to respond to simplistic accounts (developed mainly in economics and political science) of the processes in Eastern Europe, and to caution against policies based on the assumption of a *tabula rasa* or "institutional void" (Stark 1992). However, I also argue against the opposite, and similarly simplistic, use of the notion of path-dependence, in which specific events or processes in the past are treated as determining the present (tracing simple cause-effect links), or alternatively are used to make the very general point that history matters.

Thus, path-dependency is a useful, yet under-theorised (or overly deterministic) concept. Therefore, I have tried to suggest some ways of thinking about path-dependency as referring to a set of potentially significant pasts, which interact, in a contingent way, with other pasts and presents, to produce effects that are not in any way determined beforehand. More specifically, I claim that while centralised socialist planning created certain institutions, production capacities, and habits, which continued to matter after its collapse, they did so in ways that cannot be explained by referring to "the socialist past", as has been suggested by some authors.[48]

---

[48] See, for example, Begg and Meurs (1998) who try to explain present conditions by referring to, for example, the traditional Bulgarian form of (communal) *zadruga* production, that was significant in the late 19th century.

To be even more specific, I do not argue that the "socialist past" has not played an important role in the restructuring of Bulgarian agriculture, for it has. This can be seen, for example, in the development of co-operative farms as major welfare providers in rural localities; in the building of huge grain processing plants on a regional basis; in small scale family farming (*lichno polzvane*); and in the nurturing among the rural population of a culture that accepts the use of state property for private use. Indeed, there is good evidence that can allow us to find close links between the above mentioned processes and relationships and the logic of socialist central planning. However, the existence of such a link does not help us to understand the ways in which these pasts came to be important in the present. Why was it that these pasts became important rather than others? Why in this way and not in another?

For example, while central planning and socialist ideology were important in shaping institutions, which in turn found expression in physical structures and habits, it is not necessarily the case that their dynamics follow one single logic. There was a significant de-coupling of these mechanisms, especially with the collapse of the political system, and with it of the overall ideological framework and central control.

Thus, my suggestion here is that a strong claim on continuity assumes a continuous coupling between different institutions, material structures, practices and habits, as well as the ecological, or broad overarching, dominance of, in this case, a socialist ideology. This is not the case in Bulgaria. The collapse of Eastern European governments led to the fragmentation and de-coupling of institutional arrangements. These "fragments" came to influence the present independently from each other and independently from the ideological and organisational logic that created them in the first place. They were incorporated into new organisational strategies that followed different rationalities, which in turn came to operate under an imposed neo-liberal version of capitalism (uncritically accepted as the only alternative). Therefore, while in this case the past remains important, this context also justifies the use of the weaker notion of legacy.

References

Aleksandrova, G. & S. Velinova (2002) Buntat na Seloto. [The Agricultural Goods Market: The village riot] *Capital* 35 (31 August – 5 September). http://www.capital.bg/weekly/

Begg, R. & M. Meurs (1998) Writing a New Song: Path Dependence and State Policy in Reforming Bulgarian Agriculture, in *Privatisation of Land: Rural Political Economy in Post-Communist Societies*, ed. by I. Szelenyi. Routledge, London, 245-70.

Bishop, S., K. Howe, D. Kopeva & P. Mishev (1994) Land Markets and Tenure, in *Privatisation of Agriculture in New Market Economies: Lessons From Bulgaria*, ed. by A. Schmitz, K. Moulton, A. Buckwell & S. Davidova. Kluwer Academic Publishers, Boston, 77-85.

Buckwell, A. & S. Davidova (1993) Economic Implications of Land Reform in Bulgaria. [Working draft] Wye College, Kent, UK.

Campbell, J. (1993) Institutional Theory and the Influence of Foreign Actors on Reform in Capitalist and Post-Socialist Societies, in *Institutional Frameworks of Market Economies: Scandinavian and Eastern European Perspectives*, ed. by J. Hausner, B. Jessop & K. Nielsen. Ashgate, Avebury, 45-67.

Campbell, J. & O. Pedersen (1996) The Evolutionary Nature of Revolutionary Change in Postcommunist Europe, in *Legacies of Change: Transformations of Postcommunist European Economies*, ed. by J. Campbell & O. Pedersen. Aldine de Gruyter, New York, 207-49.

Cellarius, B. (2000) Will Forest Owners Co-operate? Some Preliminary Observations About Bulgaria's Forest Restitution, *Max Plank Institute for Social Anthropology* Working Paper No. 13. http://www.eth.mpg.de/pubs/wps/pdf/mpi-eth-working-paper-0013.pdf

Chavance, B. & E. Magnin (1997) Emergence of Path-Dependent Mixed Economies in Central Europe, in *Beyond Market and Hierarchy: Interactive Government and Social Complexity*, ed. by A. Amin & J. Hausner. Edward Elgar, Cheltenham, 196-232.

Cirtautas, A. (1995) The Post-Leninist State: A Conceptual and Empirical Examination, *Communist and Post-Communist Studies* 28 (4), 379-92.

Cochrane, N., A. Schmitz & S. Bojnec (1994) Agriculture: Diversification and Productivity, in *Privatisation of Agriculture in New Market Economies: Lessons From Bulgaria*, ed. by A. Schmitz, K. Moulton, A. Buckwell & S. Davidova. Kluwer Academic Publishers, Boston, 23-53.

Creed, G. (1995) The Politics of Agriculture: Identity and Socialist Sentiment in Bulgaria. *Slavic Review*, 54 (4), 843-68.

—. (1998) *Domesticating Revolution: From Socialist Reform to Ambivalent Transition in a Bulgarian Village*. Pennsylvania State University Press, University Park.

Davidova, S. & S. Batchvarova (1995) *Agricultural Situation and Prospects in Central and Eastern European Countries: Bulgaria*. Vol. 1, Working Document, European Commission, Directorate General for Agriculture.

Davidova, S & A. Buckwell, A. (1994) Agriculture Reform, in *Privatisation of Agriculture in New Market Economies: Lessons From Bulgaria*, ed. by A. Schmitz, K. Moulton, A. Buckwell, & S. Davidova. Kluwer Academic Publishers, Boston, 1-22.

Elster, J., C. Offe & U. Preuss, (1998) *Institutional Design in Post-communist Societies: Rebuilding the Ship at Sea*. Cambridge University Press, Cambridge.

Fitoussi, J-P. (1997) Following the Collapse of Communism, Is There Still a Middle Way? in *Political Economy of Modern Capitalism: Mapping Convergence and Diversity*, ed. by C. Crouch & W. Streeck. Sage, London, 148-60.

Hann, C. (2000) The Tragedy of the Privates? Postsocialist Property Relations in Anthropological Perspective, *Max Plank Institute for Social Anthropology* Working Paper No. 2. http://www.eth.mpg.de/pubs/wps/pdf/mpi-eth-working-paper-0002.pdf

Hausner, J., B. Jessop & K. Nielsen (eds.) (1995) *Strategic Choice and Path-Dependency in Post-Socialism: Institutional Dynamics in the Transformation Process*. Edward Elgar, Aldershot.

Huntington, S. (1997) *The Clash of Civilizations and the Remaking of World Order*. Simon & Schuster, New York.

Jeffries, I. (1993) *The Socialist Economies and Transition to the Market: a Guide*. Routledge, London.

Kaneff, D. (2000) Property, Work and Local Identity. *Max Plank Institute for Social Anthropology* Working Paper No. 15. http://www.eth.mpg.de/pubs/wps/pdf/mpi-eth-working-paper-0015.pdf

Kopeva, D., P. Mishev & K. Howe (1994) Land Reform and Liquidation of Collective Farm Assets in Bulgarian Agriculture: Progress and Prospects. *Communist Economies and Economic Transformation* 6 (2), 203-17.

Kornai, J. (1997) *Struggle and Hope. Essays on Stabilisation and Reform in a Post-Socialist Economy*. Edward Elgar, Cheltenham.

Mandel, R. & C. Humphrey (eds.) (2002) *Markets and Moralities: Ethnographies of Postsocialism*. Berg, New York.

Meekhof, R., A. Schmitz & I. Penov (1994) The Grain Sector: Wheat is King, in *Privatisation of Agriculture in New Market Economies: Lessons From*

Bulgaria, ed. by A. Schmitz, K. Moulton, A. Buckwell & S. Davidova. Kluwer Academic Publishers, Boston, 235-62.

Meurs, M & R. Begg (1998) Path Dependence in Bulgarian Agriculture, in *Theorising Transition: The Political Economy of Post-Communist Transformations*, ed. by J. Pickles & A. Smith. Routledge, London, 243-61.

Meurs, M. & S. Djankov (1998) The Alchemy of Reform: Bulgarian Agriculture in the 1980s, in *Privatisation of Land: Rural Political Economy in Post-Communist Societies*, ed. by I. Szelenyi. Routledge, London, 43-62.

Meurs, M., V. Kouzhouharova & R. Stoyanova (1999) Bulgaria: From Cooperative Village to Agro-Industrial Complex, The Rise and Fall of Collective Agriculture, in *Many Shades of Red: State Policy and Collective Agriculture*, ed. by M. Meurs. Rowman & Littlefield Publishers, Lanham, 87-123.

Mitev, P., I. Tomova & L. Konstantinova (2001) The Price of Procrastination? The Social Costs of Delayed Market Transition in Bulgaria, in *Poverty, Ethnicity, and Gender in Eastern Europe During the Market Transition*, ed. by R. Emigh & I. Szelenyi. Praeger Press, Westport, 37-53.

MZGAR (2005a) *Agricultural Report 2004*, Bulgarian Ministry of Agriculture and Forestry.

—. (2005b) Prebrojavane na zemedelskite stopanstva 2003: momentna snimka na balgarskoto zemedelie [Census of the agricultural production units: the current picture of Bulgarian agriculture], Report No 69, June 2005. Publication of the Bulgarian Ministry of Agriculture and Forestry.

—. (2002) Agraren Doklad 2002 [Agricultural Report 2002]. Publication of the Bulgarian Ministry of Agriculture and Forestry.

—. (2001) Agraren Doklad 2001 [Agricultural Report 2001]. Publication of the Bulgarian Ministry of Agriculture and Forestry.

Schmitz, A., K. Moulton, A. Buckwell & S. Davidova (eds.) (1994) *Privatisation of Agriculture in New Market Economies: Lessons From Bulgaria*. Kluwer Academic Publishers, Boston & London.

Stark, D. (1992) From System Identity to Organisational Diversity: Analysing Social Change in Eastern Europe. *Contemporary Sociology* 21 (3, May), 299-304.

Stark, D. (1992) Path-Dependence and Privatization Strategies in East Central Europe. *East European Politics and Societies* 6 (1, Winter), 17-53.

Swain, N. (1997) Agricultural Restructuring and Rural Employment in Bulgaria. *CCEES,* Working Paper 41.
http://www.liv.ac.uk/history/research/cee_pdfs/index.htm

—. (2001) Transitions of Household Farming and Gardening in Central Europe. *CCEES*, Working Paper 51.
http://www.liv.ac.uk/history/research/cee_pdfs/index.htm

Trigilia, C. (2001) Social Capital and Local Development. *European Journal of Social Theory* 4 (4), 427-42.

Verdery, K. (1994) The Elasticity of Land: Problems of Land Restitution in Transylvania. *Slavic Review* 53 (4), 1071-109.

CHAPTER FIVE

STRUCTURES OF AGRICULTURAL LAND USE IN CENTRAL EUROPE

KATALIN KOVÁCS

Introduction[49]

The questions this paper seeks to answer are, what kind of agriculture has emerged in the Czech Republic, Slovakia and Hungary, and, in Hungary's case, how, in different contexts, are these new structures functioning. These three countries were selected because the author was involved in several projects in the mid-1990s that covered these countries.[50] The first part of the paper relies on material from these research projects, recent literature and on an analysis of other available data. Empirical research findings have been processed in the second part of the paper and are restricted to the Hungarian experience.

To start with the broader perspective, it seems safe to say that what has been emerging in the 15 years of the so-called transition of Eastern and Central European agriculture is a production structure fundamentally different from that of the Western model. The strongest pillar of the farm structure here does not consist of family farms as in the old member states of the European Union. On the contrary, *the production system is based one a duality of large-scale corporate, and small-scale, often dwarf, farming*. This is certainly true for the three countries concerned, but also seems to be relevant for most of the countries of Eastern and Central Europe.

---

[49] The author wishes to thank Michal Lostak, Tomas Doucha and Gejza Blaas for the provision of information and writings on farm structures in the Czech and Slovak Republics. She is also grateful to Kata Rácz and Monika Váradi for their willingness to provide the first summary of a joint empirical research on rural restructuring. The broader project has been led by the author and funded by the National R&D Programme (Project No. 5/051/04).

[50] The most important of these projects was the one titled "Intermediate Ownership of Farming Structures" funded by the Research Report Scheme of the Soros Foundation (no 481/1994).

The weak position of family farms in this part of Europe can be seen as a long-lasting legacy of socialism, which, paradoxically, preserved the duality of pre-World War II farm structures consisting of large manorial estates and small peasant farms, again with some differences between the various countries. Before going into details and describing the roots of today's farm structure with all its variations in the three countries selected, let us dwell upon the features that are more or less common to Central and Eastern Europe's agricultural transformation.

Agricultural restructuring in Central and Eastern Europe

The land is a special and very sensitive issue in all these countries. It is defended by cleverly drafted laws aimed at retaining land in the "hands of the nation", despite the fact that market prices already provide a degree of protection. The uniqueness of land derives partly from the fact that it cannot be reproduced, and partly from the values and cultural constructions that have been and still are attached to it. These factors help, perhaps, to explain why a legal entitlement to land was retained in most of these countries throughout the communist period. Two exceptions have to be highlighted: the former Soviet Union, where land was nationalised, and Hungary, where, from 1967 on, through compulsory or pressured sales[51], 55% of the agricultural land (the lands of those who left agriculture) was gradually transformed into the so-called "indivisible" property of co-operatives.

Of course, the retention of legal entitlement was worthless under socialism, since owners were deprived of all ownership rights except for that of inheritance, but it turned out to be useful when socialism collapsed, and the new democracies embarked on restoring land ownership. Even in Hungary this solution was applied to the 35% of agricultural land that had remained in the hands of its original owners. For these owners, the separation of their land from the co-operatives had been made possible by an amendment of the 1967 co-operative law passed by the last socialist government. But for the 65% of the land used by co-operatives, another solution was required. Hence a system of compensation with vouchers and land auctions was invented as a means of – to use Swain's categories (Swain 1994) – *partial* (because in addition to an upper limit, a digression key was applied), *indirect* (because the beneficiaries received financial instruments, not the property they had lost) and *universal* (because all

[51] If a land owner, who had been forced to become co-operative member, died and nobody from among her/his children continued in the co-operative her/his land was "sold" to the co-operative via compulsory sales on a dictated and very low price. When somebody left agriculture for – for example – an industrial job s/he was pressed to sell her/his land as well.

forms of loss were treated similarly) restitution. Everywhere else, where people's entitlement to their lands remained in place, or, as in the Baltic States, where lands were returned, the principles of restitution were *full*, *direct*, and *specific*. Some countries, however, favoured a restitution "within the historic boundaries", or, as in the former Czechoslovakia, permitted the return of an equivalent amount of land. A common consequence, however, was that despite the full restoration of property rights over agricultural land, people did not necessarily have an exclusive right to a clearly identified plot (or, more frequently, plots) of land even after more than a decade had passed since the system had been changed. For technical and financial reasons (parcelling costs money[52]), for many, ownership represented an entitlement to a notional area within a collectively cultivated indivisible field.

Although during the first years of transformation (before the "velvet divorce" in the case of the former Czechoslovakia) the political climate in each post-socialist country was characterized by a marked political hostility towards collective farms and an equally marked desire to move towards family farming, there is no evidence that legislators wanted to destroy collective farms altogether. They could hardly have done so without risking serious food shortages, and it was scarcely realistic given that most agricultural equipment and buildings were suited to large-scale farming. Thus, the idea of de-collectivising what had previously been collectively used assets and carrying on large-scale farming based on shared ownership emerged. Various voucher schemes facilitated the process of de-collectivising the assets and transferring them to those who had a legitimate claim to them. Whatever the specific details, the result everywhere was that the new successor farms had to cope with a large number of "outside owners" who were no longer members of the co-operative and might not even be local residents. In this respect, the legal solutions of the former Czechoslovakia were probably the most biased in favour of outside property holders (See Námerová & Swain 1998), with Hungary's, perhaps, the least, in that they gave more emphasis to labour contribution (i.e. the duration of active years in the co-operative) and salaries. All in all, land restitution and decollectivisation policies resulted in *a fragmented property structure*, which did not coincide totally with land use. Although there has been a clear tendency everywhere for the large-scale sector to shrink (not always in numbers, but in the amount of land controlled) and the small-scale sector to grow, economies of scale have prevailed in the Czech Republic, Slovakia and Hungary, and, to a lesser extent, in Bulgaria, less so in the Baltic states, and have been almost fully abandoned in Romania and Albania.

---

[52] People have to pay for the service.

Central and Eastern European countries have adopted various approaches towards the issue of foreign and corporate ownership of landed property; corporate farms of all sorts have been excluded from the land market for example in Bulgaria, in Estonia and in Hungary, but in the successor states of the former Czechoslovakia they were not.

Another feature which is common to these countries is the wide variety of business forms that have emerged. Agricultural structures that were once dominated by socialism's unique experiment in extending Taylorist organisational principles to agriculture, have been replaced by numerous forms of business entities, which have increasingly abandoned the Taylorist mould both in terms of management structures and the scale of operation: they have fewer managers, fewer employees, and do not attempt to involve themselves in all branches of farming. The earlier the structures were changed and the least Taylorist they had been, the more likely it was that the transformed large-scale farms would survive within the harsh circumstances of a collapsing economy, shrinking state support, weak state control over business deals, and the rise in competition of the 1990s. The origin of these emerging new corporate farms, companies acquiring ever larger landholdings everywhere, goes back to those former collective farms that successfully tailored their organisational and ownership structures to the new era.

Compared to the rich variety of company forms, the case of co-operatives might be expected to be simpler, but this is not the case. For example, a wide variety of organisations can be classified under the umbrella term of a "co-operative": such as production cooperatives, service-providing co-operatives, specialist co-operatives in Hungary (Sárkány & Hann 2003) and Slovak "co-operatives", which, in terms of their ownership and decision taking structures (Námerová & Swain 1998), are more like joint stock companies. Where foreigners and/or unfamiliar company forms are regarded with suspicion because of rumours about unfair business deals, local managers might opt for a company form, while using the term co-operative to make it more acceptable to the locals. Kaneff (1998, 167), in a report on Bulgaria, notes that this is a necessary condition for some companies' operations. As one millionaire manager explained: "People are scared when they hear the word 'firm', so we call it a 'co-operative'".

The pluralism of corporate farming entities, cooperatives and companies alike, which was particularly evident in the 1990s, also reflects the immature and "experimental" character of these organisations, particularly during the early years of change. The weakness of the state and the culturally-constructed nature of ownership as well as the roles and expectations attached to a certain formation locally, be it a co-operative or a company, foreign or domestic, are also visible. The choice of one or another corporate form might also have been influenced by the links and overlaps between the local elite and the group of managers of the transforming organisation as well as by popular opinions, the prevalence of the principle of egalitarianism in the community, and the strength of control constructed by the moral expectations and judgements of ordinary community members over the local elite and the managers amongst them.[53] What distinguishes post-socialist companies from their Western counterparts is, according to Fertő (1999), that property in this region is managed in a way that favours the managers' instead of the owners' interests.

As was already mentioned above, and is worthwhile emphasizing again, *family based commercial enterprise represents an important and desired,* but in most cases *weak and vulnerable element of the system* everywhere. These units are no longer traditional peasant undertakings, because the people operating them are generally not culturally separated from the wider society in the way traditional peasant societies were (they do not belong to a "part society"[54]). They are no longer the "household plots" of the socialist period, because they are larger and run according to the rules of the market economy, and are therefore increasingly major sources of livelihood rather than supplements to a steady socialist sector income. They most closely resemble an enterprise operated by a permanent and seasonal workforce that is not necessarily made up of relatives. Surviving or newly established family plots in most cases produce a supplement to various kinds of social transfers: elderly or disability pensions, unemployment benefits, as well as social assistance jointly provided by central and local governments.

Commenting on the post-socialist picture of hundreds, even thousands, of holders of tiny plots leasing their land to a handful of people per village who are willing to rent land, Alanen (1998) warns that an Eastern European equivalent of English land tenancy might emerge. But, as Swain (1998b) has noted, these rental structures are the opposite of the historical norm: many own, but few rent, which is not only historically unprecedented but economically absurd too, and is, therefore, explained – probably correctly – by many commentators as a transitional phenomenon. He also notes that agricultural developments in Southern Europe suggest that plots smaller than viable small farms but larger than gardens can persist as long as overall economic development is unable to guarantee non-agricultural employment for the bulk of the rural population. The same was found in the context of a Hungarian market town, where all three major types of small-scale farming (subsistence, semi-subsistence and

[53] Relevant reports include those about Estonia by Alanen 1998; Slovakia by Torsello 2003; Bulgaria by Kaneff 1998 and Meurs 2001; Hungary by Kovách 2001, Váradi 1998, Kovács 1998a, 1998b.

[54] "... peasants are parts of larger, complex societies, whilst primitive tribes are not." (Wolf 1973, 322)

commercial) were commonly pursued before and after the change in the system. However, when a Japanese company producing parts for electronic equipment appeared and offered hundreds of jobs mainly to semi-skilled female workers, many people substantially reduced, or even stopped farming their plots happily changing to industrial work (Rácz 2005).

Pre-accession farm structures

The large-scale-farm sector

To start with assessing the importance of agriculture as compared with other branches of the economy in the Czech and Slovak Republics and Hungary, it is quite small in each of them. The average Gross Value Added in 2001-2003 was 456 million Euros in Slovakia; roughly half this sum (961 million Euros) in the Czech Republic, which was approximately half as much as in Hungarian agriculture (2,056 million Euros) To continue with the similarities of the agricultural transformation of the three countries, the privatisation of landed and non-landed property has taken place relatively smoothly in the three countries, although not without conflicts, dramas and clashes between divergent interest groups. Large farm holdings have been retained in each country, although there are differences in scale and form, as well as in the degree of adaptation to market relations.

The most important factor that generates variations among the agricultural production systems in the countries under investigation is the level of market-penetration, in other words, the extent to which farms are profit-oriented due to government policies.

The Czech Republic seems to have been the most consistent in favouring agricultural companies (they use 45% of the agricultural area), particularly after the "Velvet divorce" when free access to the land market was secured for corporate farms and foreigners. Furthermore, no pro-co-operative policies compared to Slovakia existed, and a small but relatively strong individual commercial farm sector has been able to develop on 12% of the utilised agricultural area, whilst capitalist ventures (limited liability companies, joint stock companies, commercial family farms) operate on 57% of the land.

In contrast to the Czech Republic, in Slovakia, transformed production co-operatives still have the strongest hold, due to uninterrupted pro-cooperative policies. As Blaas (2003) remarks:

> Slovak (co-operative) farm managers seem to have been in a better position than in most Central East European countries to apply survival strategies based on payment arrears, soft state budgets and bad debts; they also have enjoyed more effective political representation and support.

Consequently, the small-scale commercial farm sector is least developed in Slovakia: there are as few as some 5,600 commercial family farms, accounting for 4-5% of the agricultural area.

Hungary stands in between the other two countries: the major political parties have still not come to an agreement as far as structural policies are concerned; rightwing "pro-family-farm" governments have been succeeded by left-wing, "pro-cooperative" ones and this has slowed down the country's transformation. On its second return, in 2002, the left-wing government gave up its pro-co-operative stand and shifted to a sector-neutral pro-capitalist enterprise policy, which speeded up the disappearance of successor co-operatives. Due to this shift, co-operatives in Hungary, which used to control 60% of the agricultural area and owned some 55% of it under socialism, are close to the "final stage": the agricultural area used by this kind of entity was as little as 8% in 2002.[55] The inevitable decline out of successor co-operatives in Hungary was accelerated a few years after the heroic completion of their transformation, and it was also documented in some case studies (Váradi 1998; Kovács 1998a & 1998b). Alongside the decline of the co-operative sector in Hungary, agricultural companies (LTDs and JSCs) increased their share of land usage from 26% in 1990 to 37% in 2002, whilst land-usage by individual small-scale farms grew from 14% to 55% during the same period.

Comparative data about the farm sectors of the three countries from 2000 and 2001 (NIAE 2004, 14-15) confirm the picture described above of large-scale farming; co-operatives retained the strongest position in Slovakia, controlling 46% of the agricultural acreage. Slovakia was followed by the Czech Republic, where co-operatives farmed 28% of agricultural land, whilst in Hungary; their share was around 10% in 2000. State farms had already stopped functioning by 2001, except for a single enterprise in Slovakia. However, data on land ownership show that the state's interest in agriculture did not disappear – on the contrary, the state increased its share in ownership everywhere: the proportion of state-owned agricultural land was highest in Slovakia (24%), followed by the Czech Republic (17%) and Hungary (11%). (Table 5-1.) Beyond operational state holdings, the relatively high figures also reflect unsettled restitution claims and/or un-identifiable landed properties. A significant part of the area registered under state funds[56] is not the object of purposeful agricultural production, but rather serves as a kind of land reserve.

---

[55] This share has obviously been shrinking since then. However, a new system of statistics does not allow one to track changes in the position of farms within the category of corporate entities.

[56] Not all of the land registered under state farms was state owned.

Table 5-1 Ownership of agricultural land in the Czech and Slovak Republics and Hungary, in percent

<table>
<tr><th rowspan="2">Land owners</th><th>Czech Republic</th><th>Slovakia</th><th>Hungary</th></tr>
<tr><th>2003</th><th>2000</th><th>2004</th></tr>
<tr><td>Natural persons</td><td>72</td><td>76</td><td>83</td></tr>
<tr><td>Legal persons</td><td>28</td><td>24</td><td>17</td></tr>
<tr><td>of which state</td><td>17</td><td>24</td><td>11</td></tr>
<tr><td>Cooperatives</td><td rowspan="2">10</td><td rowspan="3"></td><td>2</td></tr>
<tr><td>Companies</td><td>3</td></tr>
<tr><td>Others (LGs, civic organisations, churches)</td><td>1</td><td>1</td></tr>
<tr><td>Total</td><td>99</td><td>100</td><td>100</td></tr>
</table>

Sources: Dorgai at al 2004, 34; Doucha at al 2005, 141; Blaas 2003.

The small-scale-farm sector in Central Europe

Table 5-2 illustrates the differences between the small-scale farming sectors in the three countries, which seem to be much deeper than the structural differences in large-scale farming. In Slovakia, both the number of small-scale farms and their share in land use are low (about 155,000 producers on 23% of the agricultural acreage). Roughly 150,000 household plots cover as little as 16% of the agricultural land, whilst 7% is cultivated by agricultural entrepreneurs[57]: and this represents the weak point in the Slovakian production structure. In the Czech Republic, the total share of small-scale farming is not much larger than in Slovakia, namely, 26%. In this respect, the Czech Republic is next to last among the new Member States. However, the proportion of commercial farms is higher, accounting for 12% of rented property (the latter amounts to 90% of all agricultural land – see Doucha et al., 2005). This, as Blaas (1997) has pointed out, is connected to their respective pre-war land ownership structures. Due to an inheritance system that favoured the oldest son in the family, a viable farm size was preserved more successfully in Silesia, Moravia and Bohemia than within the boundaries of "historical Hungary", that is, in those areas that now make up Slovakia. Full restitution of ownership secured a much better start for a would-be farmer in the Czech Republic than for her/his counterpart in Slovakia.

[57] The farm enterprises they manage are not classical family farms; therefore we use the terminology of agricultural entrepreneur (used in the Hungarian statistical system as well.)

Table 5-2 Number of farms and their share in agricultural land-use by legal titles in the Czech and Slovak Republics and Hungary, 2000-2001

Countries	Legal type of farms	Nr of farms	%
Czech Republic	State undertakings	0	0
	Co-operatives	728	28
	Commercial companies	2,055	43
	Individual farms	35,219	26
	Other	168	1
Slovakia	State undertakings	1	0
	Co-operatives	695	46
	Commercial companies	707	29
	Individual farms	5,292	7
	Household plots	n.a.	16
Hungary	State undertakings	0	0
	Co-operatives	1,886	50
	Commercial companies	9,479	
	Individual farms	949,005	49

Source: NIAE 2004, 14-15.

What small-scale production of the successor states of the former Czechoslovakia have in common is that subsistence farming does not seem to function as much as a social buffer here as it does in some other countries, both among new Member States and those yet to "accede". The most radical example of the role of subsistence farming in forming a social buffer is found in Romania, where more than four million small-scale plots account for 80% of the agricultural area, and where farming plots counts as employment. The matter of registration, however, is a serious issue: differences in the threshold of what counts as a holding in various countries profoundly impedes comparison (cf. NIAE 2004).

Finally, in Hungary, the small-scale sector is much stronger than its counterparts in the Czech and Slovak Republics. The differences – the very weak but a little bit less fragmented Czech small-scale sector, the weak and fragmented Slovak plot farming, the fragmented but altogether rather well-positioned Hungarian small-scale farms – are reflected by data indicating the duality of farm systems of these countries as well, as the below table shows:

Table 5-3 Duality in the cultivation of agricultural land in the Czech and Slovak Republics and Hungary, 2001-2003

Farm size categories	**Czech Republic**		**Slovak Republic**		**Hungary**	
	Share of farms	Share in cultivation	Share of farms	Share in cultivation	Share of farms	Share in cultivation
Below 10 ha	72	3	94	4	94	15
10-50 ha	17	6	3	2	5	17
50-100 ha	3	4	1	2	1	8
over 100 ha	7	88	3	93	1	60
Total	100	100	100	100	100	100

Sources: Compiled from national census data

First, I have to highlight the most important peculiarity of Hungarian agricultural policy in the 1970s: the invention of a symbiosis of small-scale and large-scale production. The goods produced by small-scale entities within this symbiosis could be sold as commodities on external markets (other than local ones) as an integrated part of the produce traded within, or outside, the country. This is the most important structural characteristic of the Hungarian experience compared to the other former socialist countries, where household plots existed but were restricted either to household consumption or to local markets.

This major difference is evident in Torsello's (2003, 100) ethnographic description of a Slovak plot's farm operation. According to his description, the "plot-farmer" used the same resources as many of his Hungarian counterparts, used 3-4 household plots and got a large amount of feed from the co-operative, but the pigs raised on this basis were sold to the local butcher, not back to the co-operative. It could have happened in Hungary as well, but the vast majority of "family enterprise" produce was integrated by large-scale farms within various "schemes" tailored to the clients' homestead circumstances and the availability of family labour. The services of large-scale farms could either be restricted to selling the produce of plot-farms or to providing a whole package of inputs, transport and sales operations.

The chance to produce for broader markets generated a strong small-scale sector in Hungary by the late 1980s, when it accounted for roughly 38% of total agricultural production and contributed to the relative wealth of rural households in comparison to other socialist countries.

This principal advantage of Hungarian small-scale farming also determined the prospects for small-scale farm structures, explaining the quick increase of the sector's influence: within 5-6 years its share grew to 56% in spite of the nominal shrinkage of both large-scale and small-scale production. Swain differentiates the "Hungarian model", based on symbiosis, from the paths of countries like Romania and Albania, which started from a Stalinist model, and from the former Czechoslovakia, the GDR and Bulgaria, which operated according to a neo-Stalinist model, and from that of countries like Poland and Slovenia that abandoned collectivisation. According to Swain, the semi-market system of Hungary provided a good basis for a quick market-oriented transformation, whilst in countries like the successor states of the former Czechoslovakia, some common tendencies could be identified, such as "the resiliency of collective farms, the slow development of the private sector, and the tendency towards a 'second' transformation of the post-socialist co-operatives into private successor companies" (quoted by Torsello 2003, 106-107).

Two observations should be made here. A "second" transformation occurred in Hungary as well. Transformed co-operatives that were too indebted and/or overstaffed could not cope with the emerging capitalism of the mid-1990s, and either went bankrupt or was wound up or transformed into much smaller limited liability companies. In many cases, the so-called "holding co-operatives" nurtured would-be independent enterprises; this was the most common intermediate corporate form in cases when the pre-transformation co-operatives earned income from various agricultural and industrial production branches. (See Bihari et al. 1994.) As a matter of fact, most of the companies can be regarded as successors of the former collective sector in a way, because the bulk of the assets they began with had originated from former co-operatives and/or privatised state farms.

The other unique feature in Hungary was the socialist relations that characterized landownership: there was a vast amount of collective property under the control of co-operatives, and the state allowed a kind of land-distribution whereby pieces of land were allocated in favour of landless co-operative members (poor and/or young people) and employees. In the former Czechoslovakia, individual title deeds to landed property were formally maintained, and this excluded the application of similar solutions. Table 5-4 indicates the extent to which "land allotment" shaped property relations in Hungary: 61% of privatised land, or 3,459,870 hectares, were "distributed" to almost two million eligible claimants (landless co-operative members, and state-farm and co-operative employees), whilst 2,141,445 hectares of landed property, that is, 40% of the whole stock of privatised land, were sold at auctions to almost 760,000 bidders.

Table 5-4 Land Privatisation in Hungary, 2002

Categories	Assigned for eligible members/ employees	Resituated via land auctions
Assigned area (hectares)	3,615,173	
Settled claims (hectares)	3,459,870	2,141,445
Number of owners persons)	1,920,045	759,787
Average area/owner (hectares/persons)	2	3
Share form privatised land %	61	40

Source: Dorgai at al 2004, 25-26.

Of course, only a small proportion of the new landowners started to cultivate their newly acquired land. In any event, the fairly egalitarian land privatisation in Hungary safeguarded access to small-scale land cultivation for the majority of rural families, and many of them lived with this opportunity either voluntarily (entrepreneurs) or because of their circumstances (those who have been expelled from the labour market). This is another explanatory factor for the high share of small plots or small farms compared with the Czech Republic and Slovakia.

Still, small-scale farming in Hungary has witnessed as many challenges, and reacted to them as profoundly, as the large-scale sector. Immediately after the new, post-socialist farm structure had been installed in 1995-1996, very small farms began to be increasingly affected by the deep crisis in agricultural production in general and, indirectly, though just as strongly, by the successful transformation of large-scale farms in particular: processes such as getting rid of so-called "integrating" auxiliary farm products and all kinds of social allowances. This, notwithstanding the fact that many large-scale entities disappeared as a result of bankruptcy and winding up procedures at the very beginning of the new epoch in 1992-1995. In these new circumstances, the famous large-scale and small-scale symbiosis proved to be no longer sustainable, and this resulted in the disappearance of more than half a million small-scale producers (not the majority, but still sizeable number) in the last decade of the 20th century, which will be discussed later on. The small-scale undertakings that survived and were large enough to qualify as a holding, according to very generous statistical classification,[58] have been relying either on new networks developed by many foreign and domestic actors in the food sector and on trade, or, if they were lucky enough, on some surviving elements

[58] Just to provide the reader with an idea of the thresholds: 1500 m2 of garden or arable land, or 500 m2 of orchard or a single head of cattle or 50 poultry, etc represent some of the limits over which a household is classified as a holding.

of the old production chains. This has been typical of certain production fields, where multiple networks secured "integration", lessening the dependency of producers on large scale farms during the socialist era, in, for example the marketing of vegetables, 80% of which was produced by the small-scale sector[59]. Those small-scale entities which have fallen below the threshold of a "holding" since 1994, contributed to the increasing number of non-market agricultural units, which produce on a garden-scale primarily for self consumption with small sales of surplus produce on local markets. The ever quickening decline of the smallest holdings is the most important reflection of the above mentioned demise of the Hungarian dual farm system that had been based on the division of labour between small-scale plots and large-scale entities. In addition, the age structure of the farmers of small plots, namely, the dominance of the older generation, and the lack of willingness of the next generation to take over, have both contributed to the fast shrinkage of semi-subsistence farming. The demise of the smallest plots, however, is also part of a differentiation process reflected in various farm profiles from purely self sufficient, through semi subsistence to purely commercial farms indicated by the below table. It is telling about the changes, that the only growing farm type is that of business-oriented farm enterprise.

Highlighting the transitional peculiarities of small-scale farming in Hungary, the "service purchasing plots" have to be mentioned first. For some individual landowners, mainly for those possessing arable land, "farming" has become a relatively restricted activity of making a deal with agricultural service providers, that is, purchasing machinery and sales services.

The view is the same: large scale fields are owned by many share-proprietors and cultivated by one single corporate farm. However, some owners lease their land to the user and receive a rent according to the size of their property, whilst other owners pay for the machinery services provided and claim their share from the sales. The latter group of owners and "individual producers" are rightfully registered as such in statistics. Nevertheless, from a sociological and economic point of view, they are far from being ordinary producers, and are not like either the agricultural entrepreneur who operates a profit-oriented enterprise, or the farmer of a plot who produces for his own subsistence and to sell a small surplus. Sociologically speaking, the special concept of "farming based on service purchase", which was brought about by the unique circumstances of the post-socialist transformation, stands between ordinary leasing and individual farming, being closer to the former than the latter. So close, in fact, that land owners sometimes change status and opt for a simple renting scheme, generally for the purpose of increasing their income.

[59] For example, growers sold their products directly at the Budapest wholesale market, or worked with canning factories on a contractual or freelance basis.

Circumstances such as changes in the subsidy eligibility rules, taxation rates and the availability of land on the property and rental markets condition such decisions.

Table 5-5 Distribution of the population engaged in small-scale farming according to the goal of production in Hungary, 2000-2003

The goal of production	2000		2003		Index
	Number (thousands)	%	Number (thousands)	%	2003/2000
Only for self consumption	583,6	60,36	459,0	59,35	79%
Self consumption + sales of the surplus	304,1	31,45	224,1	28,97	74%
Primarily for sales	77,0	7,96	89,9	11,63	117%
Total	966,9	99,77	773,4	99,95	80%

Source: Magyar mezőgazdaság 2004. (Hungarian Agriculture 2004), Central Statistical Office, Budapest, 2005, 23. p

Farming in Hungary is to a high degree based on rented property, but far less so than in the successor states of the former Czechoslovakia. (Table 5-6) Reports from both the Czech Republic and Slovakia show that roughly 90% of the land is leased (Doucha et al. 2005; Blaas 2003). The relatively low proportion of rented land in Hungary is due to the fact that 37% of landed property is privately owned and 12% of the entire stock of agricultural land is used on the "basis of reciprocity"[60]. The former is the consequence of massive and continuous land purchases by entrepreneurs and managers: every producer who could afford to invested intensively in land and other assets. Most of these transactions served farm enlargement, thus increasing competitiveness and profitability and safeguarding the production base. In such cases, the ownership and use of agricultural land overlap. If a land owner was not directly involved in farming and a full range of agricultural services was available, cultivation on the basis of service provision might have been a feasible alternative to land leasing. This also contributed to the comparatively high degree of privately owned land within land use (see the above paragraph on "service purchases").

Twelve percent of agricultural land is managed on the basis of reciprocity. This practice is connected with tax-evasion strategies, mainly for small-scale land-users (this kind of transaction does not generate income, so it cannot be taxed) or with adaptation strategies aiming to overcome disadvantages caused by fragmented ownership. When a large-scale enterprise has to deal with

[60] It is a mutual assistance based on the exchange of goods or services.

hundreds of lease contracts, it may be easier to conclude a land-use deal with a neighbouring colleague, also renting hundreds of small parcels, and exchange lands semi-legally, than to convince owners to launch a real land consolidation scheme.

Table 5-6 Land-use titles in Hungary, 2002

Land-use by title in Hungary (on the basis of registered arable land, 2002 August)	
Area total (Ha)	3,168, 229
Own property %	37
Rented land %	51
Rented on reciprocal basis %	12
other %	1
The proportion of rented land in land-use	**%**
Co-operatives	85
Companies	61
Full time entrepreneurs	44
Part time entrepreneurs	36
Other small-scale farmers	25

Source: Dorgai et al 2004, 39.

As far as the reactions of post-socialist small-scale farmers to the challenges they have had to face during the last decade are concerned, we can summarise them as follows: the number of farmers of small plots has been shrinking dramatically due to the property accumulation and production specialisation (also "professionalization") that has been taking place amongst both small-scale and large-scale farming. Parallel to this process, non-market agriculture is growing due to the increasing number of very small plots that are falling below the statistical threshold that defines a holding.

Between 1994 and 2000 the number of holdings dropped by 20% (340,000 plots disappeared), which, however, still left a large number of producers, namely, 966,000. Between 2000 and 2003, half the above period, there was an equal drop of 20% in the number of small plots, reflecting the disappearance of almost 200,000 entities. This was a decline on an unexpected scale: some half million semi-subsistence dwarf holdings had disappeared within nine years! If we consider trends revealed by the last agricultural census and a recent farm structure assessment, it is clear that less and less small plots can continue:

decline is dominant in all categories under eight ESU sizes[61], while the number of larger individual farms is increasing.

What do these figures from the Hungarian case suggest? We see "professionalization", specialisation and property accumulation on one end of the spectrum, with a withdrawal from farming and a shift into non-market garden-scale cultivation on the other. These are all elements of the profound and overall change in the last decade that have shaped ownership and land use structures. It is important to highlight the fact that these changes do not seem to have weakened the small-scale sector as a whole. On the contrary, its ever growing share in land use proves that a differentiation process has been at work, which has been painful for the majority, but advantageous for the few who have survived. Future prospects are secure for small-scale commercial farms which manage to establish links with the new agri-food system in exchange for their former symbiotic relationship with now defunct large-scale socialist farms.

The role of small-scale farming: the Hungarian example

In the rest of the paper, I will continue my description of Hungarian agriculture. The most important change is *the end of the socialist model of farming*, characterized by a dual symbiotic system of large-scale and small-scale farms producing more or less for the same market. As far as the new situation is concerned, the role of small-scale agricultural activities is still very important.

It is much more important than in the successor states of the former Czechoslovakia. There is no doubt that it is extremely important because it provides both a supplementary and even the main source of income in rural areas, where the scarcity of on-farm and off-farm jobs confines large numbers of rural families to small-scale farm work. Statistical data and the empirical studies we conducted recently in some 50 villages belonging to five peripheral rural districts[62] confirm this. Nevertheless, small-scale farming no longer constitutes a secure means of accumulation in rural areas. Differentiations have been taking place reshaping both the large and small-scale sector of the farming system.

Data in Table 5-7 show the importance of agricultural activity in rural Hungary as well as its role in providing a supplementary income. Roughly one third of the population over 15 years of age performed agricultural work in 2001, and approximately a quarter of them, that is, 236,747 village residents worked more than 90 days in the year.

---

[61] 1 ESU=1,200 euros

[62] "For equal opportunities of small villages and villagers", a research project funded by the Hungarian National Research and Development Programme 2005-2007.

Table 5-7 Involvement of the population over 15 years of age in agricultural and occasional agricultural work in Hungary in 2001, in percent

Village population							
Denomination	**Total***	**Of which s/he pursued small-scale agricultural work**				**Occasional agricultural work**	
		No	**Yes**	**Less than 90 days**	**At least 90 days**	**Yes**	**No**
Age groups							
15–19	100	85,5	14,1	12,5	1,6	5,1	94,9
20–29	100	74,8	22,5	18	4,5	7,5	92,5
30–39	100	63,3	32,9	25,3	7,6	8,1	91,9
40–49	100	57,8	38	28,5	9,5	7,6	92,4
50–54	100	57,4	38,8	28,5	10,3	6,2	93,8
55–59	100	57	40,7	29	11,7	5,3	94,7
60–X	100	64,4	35,3	25,5	9,8	2,6	97,4
Total	100	65,3	32,3	24,3	8	5,9	94,1
Education							
Less than primary education	100	71,6	27,8	21,1	6,7	4,1	95,9
Primary education	100	63,2	34	24,9	9,1	6,8	93,2
Secondary + vocational	100	63,3	33,1	25,2	7,9	7,2	92,8
Final exam from secondary	100	65,8	32	24,7	7,3	4,6	95,4
Higher education	100	67,9	30,9	23,7	7,1	4	96
Economic activity							
Employed	100	60,3	33,4	26	7,4	5,2	94,8
Unemployed	100	66,7	33,3	24,4	8,9	19,5	80,5
On maternity leave	100	74,7	25,3	20,1	5,2	4,1	95,9
Retired	100	64,2	35,8	26,1	9,7	3,4	96,6
Relatives of retired persons	100	72,7	27,3	20,7	6,6	2	98
Other kinds of inactive earners	100	64,7	35,3	22,7	12,6	16,4	83,6
Without earnings	100	79	21	16,2	4,9	6,8	93,2

Source: Central Statistical Office 2004. Full time agricultural employment included. http://www.nepszamlalas.hu/hun/kotetek/kotetek.html

The importance of small-scale agricultural activity in supplementing income obtained from various kinds of social benefits is proved by the higher participation of the unemployed, elderly pensioners and people on early retirement schemes in agricultural work for more than 90 days. It is even more obvious as far as participation in occasional agricultural work is concerned: almost 20% of unemployed village residents and 16.4% of those with a regular income in the form of social benefits did occasional agricultural work in 2001, as opposed to 5.2% of those who were employed.

The attached figures (Fig. 5-1, 5-2, 5-3) indicate the overlap between, and discrepancies among, the following three indicators: (1) the proportion of households with no active wage earner; (2) the proportion of pensioners who retired early among the retired population as a whole; (3) the proportion of the population over 15 years of age engaged in small-scale farm operations. The first map shows the role and significance of the early retirement (disability) pension scheme as a commonly pursued "escape" strategy in rural crisis zones of high unemployment.

Fig. 5-1 Share of under age pensioners within the retired population. Deviation from the country average in Hungary, 2003

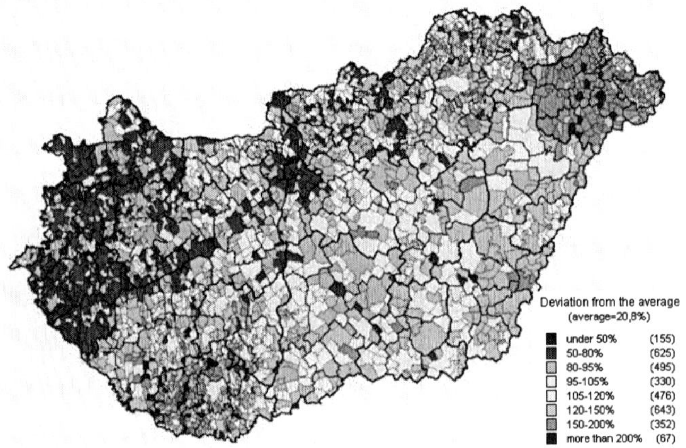

Fig. 5-2 Share of households without active employees. Deviation form the country average in Hungary, 2001.

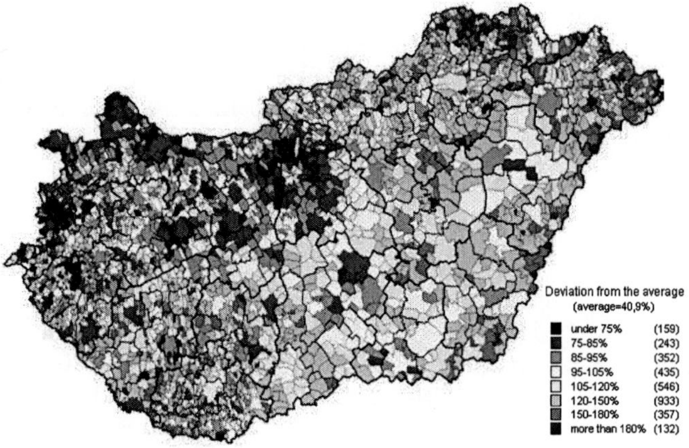

Fig. 5-3 Proportion of population over 15 years of age engaging in small-scale farming (small holdings and commercial farms together). Deviation from the country average in Hungary, 2000

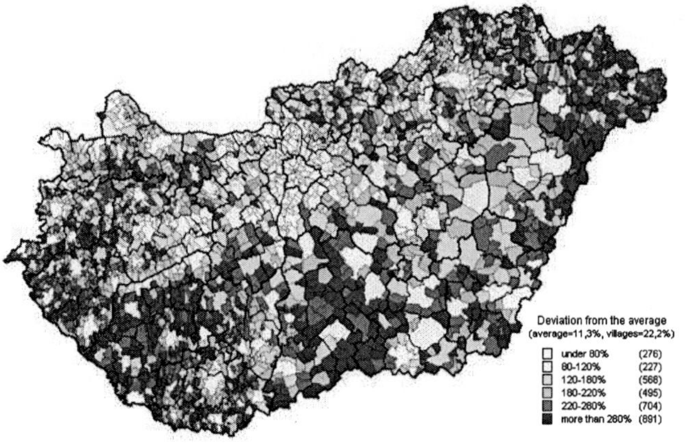

The second map shows the importance of small-scale individual farming activities in the lives of the adult population indicating a partial overlap with the first map. The explanation for this partial overlap of low employment districts and areas with a high density of small-scale agriculture lies in the peculiarities of agricultural structures in the Hungarian Great Plain, namely, the importance of small-scale agriculture in the more developed Southern Great Plain area, a traditional concentration zone of small-scale commercial farms.[63]

Livelihoods and small-scale farming

In the remaining part of this section, two short descriptions are provided about the new profile of agriculture and the state of transformation in two peripheral rural districts: one from the Western border region (Zala County), and the other from the opposite corner, the North-Eastern part of Hungary (Szabolcs-Szatmár-Bereg County).[64] The pictures that emerge from these descriptions do not have too much in common, except for the almost complete disappearance of large-scale successor co-operatives. They do demonstrate that there are different paths small-scale farming might follow within a country, which are determined not just by the agricultural but the wider context in which they are embedded. In Zala County, small-scale agriculture is increasingly loosing its importance and adopting new functions. It is becoming more a hobby than commercial farming: most of the inhabitants of working age find employment in nearby towns and are much less dependent on this kind of secondary income.

By contrast, in Szabolcs County, small-scale farming has a primary importance not only in terms of providing a supplementary income, but also as a major source of people's livelihood. Individual commercial farms cover 60-70% of the agricultural area; the rest is shared by a few companies, and thousands of farmers of small plots. In the villages we visited, local governments were also involved in production, as quasi-substitutes of the former co-operatives via a social assistance scheme called "social land program", providing many of the farmers with small plots (who were growing beans, cucumbers and tobacco, or

[63] Unfortunately the clarity of Hungarian statistics has deteriorated considerably in the last few decades. Therefore we cannot make a distinction between small-scale farms and commercial farms on the basis of statistical data.

[64] Both can be regarded as the first reports of our research on rural peripheries, in which endogenous resources, grassroots and top-down development policies aimed at preventing further decline are investigated. More than 800 interviews were conducted by the students of two universities located in the regional centres of peripheral rural regions. The work of processing the information systematically has been started but is far from being finished.

keeping beef cattle) and/or services such as organising inputs, marketing their products, etc. Primarily (although not exclusively) those families (many of whom are Roma) are eligible to this kind of social assistance, which have no other income than social benefits (such as unemployment benefit, maternity allowance, regular social benefit, etc.).

The profile and prospects of agricultural production in Western Hungary's peripheral districts: the Zala case[65]

In this area, consisting of ten villages and the town of Zalaszentgrót with 3,000 inhabitants, all of the agricultural co-operatives have disappeared. Even though they had been transformed into capitalist ventures in 1992-1993, they had gone bankrupt and had been sold off by the mid-1990s. Only one larger company survived: the former state farm of Zalaszentgrót was successfully privatized and became a joint-stock company owned by its former leaders, heads of production branches (which followed a short period, when it had been the joint property of the workers).

If we assess what has remained of the larger farm companies/co-operatives, the range of large-scale survivors is rather narrow. There is one single large, 2500 hectare farm managed by a joint-stock company, which hires most of its land from the state (with a contract valid for 25 years). There are also smaller but still relatively large-scale landed properties (farming few hundred hectares each), made up of lands from the former agricultural co-operatives, These lands are owned or hired by the former management of the co-operatives, and sometimes by other people who were somehow connected to the co-operatives.

Most of these farmers use assets that previously belonged to the co-operatives. Some of the land is owned by former land owners, some by never seen people who have bought land; most of them cultivate their own landed properties. The few family farms that have survived specialize in stock-raising (turkey and cattle, mostly beef cattle): some owners are former members of co-operatives, but some are entrepreneurs who brought in capital from elsewhere. Usually, they try to buy the lands they are hiring to keep stock. Renting land is more and more problematic for medium-sized companies: when renting land from owners who are not local – and often local owners let others use their land for free – they find that these owners ("strangers from cities", as locals call them) often ask for half, or all, of the rent to be paid at once. This caused an increase of rental prices because farmers have to rely on expensive bank loans. The larger companies work with large trading companies, called "integrators", who provide them with everything from seed-corn to counselling as well as

[65] The summary report was provided by Monika Váradi.

storage and marketing. However, it is the integrator who keeps most of the earnings and the subsidies, as it is the integrator that is eligible to subsidies and who dictates conditions via classical exploitation techniques, like: clients have to sell the product to the creditor on a price dictated by the latter. On the other hand, the smaller farms, although there are not many of them anyway, are left out of this system. There is a "black hole" with land informally owned and used by foreigners (German and Austrian owners). As foreign land ownership is illegal, we do not have data for this, only information received from interviews. And finally, there are the "frauds" (as locals call them): people who buy a few hundred hectares just for fun or to be able to join a shoot or for cultivation.

Auxiliary small-scale farms have disappeared. People used to keep dairy cattle, but they have stopped doing this. Our interviews show that most of those who do some gardening or keep animals, do not sell their products: they only produce food for their families. Among the small companies, are those that own vineyards and orchards – these can be found in most villages. People told us that they used to be able to sell their products to different dealers or at the local market but that today these no longer exist. At the same time, the inhabitants are getting older, and there are fewer and fewer family members who want to cultivate grapes and work in orchards. Vineyards are still cultivated by families in order to generate a supplementary income and/or for recreation. The families working these plots are in favour of retaining the traditional life of village. Other vineyards and other pieces of land are left uncultivated. And there are also people who use vineyards simply for recreation. They do not necessarily cultivate their plots but are interested in wine as a hobby and use them to entertain their friends. Some wineries have more financial resources, and their owners are also interested in the possibilities of tourism in Zala, but these are bigger enterprises, not the small companies we have been discussing.

At this stage of our research, we can only speculate as to why smaller companies have disappeared in this region. One reason might be that large companies have always been dominant in this region. Next to the manors, there were no wealthy peasants, poor agricultural labour overwhelmed in this region. These are mainly inhabited by small farmers. Another explanation might be that some villages in this region were involved in both mining and agriculture in the socialist period, and therefore the villages had at least two sources of income. There are also parts of the region where the quality of the soil is not very good. Even larger companies had difficulties because of this: most of their profits came from supplementary industrial factories, which also provided most of the jobs, too. This land is more suitable for rough grazing. Moreover, during the transformation of the co-operatives, most people did not want to work on separate farms (they wanted to keep their jobs in the successor co-operative instead), and, furthermore, even if they did want to farm they often had difficulties in obtaining tools. And finally, the traditional small farms have disappeared for the reasons mentioned above (people are getting older, there is no market for their produce).

The profile and prospects of Eastern Hungary's peripheral districts: the Szatmár case[66]

The region of Tiszahát consists of 13 settlements and lies in the north eastern corner of Hungary. There is little industrial activity and the region is economically underdeveloped. People from the region have always had to seek work elsewhere. Under the communist regime, thousands of workers commuted to distant industrial centres like Budapest, Székesfehérvár and Tatabánya: most of them were unskilled people working in heavy industry or the building trade. Most of those who stayed, worked in the larger agricultural plants: these were usually involved in raising cattle and producing fruit for the Eastern European markets. There were also supplementary plants (factories) making products for the co-operatives, like box factories, rag-sorting works and sewing shops: these played a fundamental role in employing mostly unskilled women. As salaries in the co-operatives were low, under communism people supplemented their earnings by working in their gardens (in a special symbiosis with the co-operative), growing cucumbers, beans and tobacco, and by raising beef cattle as well as producing milk.

After the structural transformation at the beginning of the 1990s, the most significant branch of the region's economy was still agriculture, even though the larger companies have ceased to function. Many of the former leaders and managers of the co-operatives, however, managed to become entrepreneurs. They run quite successful farms, which have a key role in organizing the production of smaller farms in the region, as well as selling their products.

Due to the process of structural transformation, the proportion of agricultural employees has dropped to 8% (that is, one third of the previous number), reflecting similar changes everywhere in the country, and the region concerned. At the same time, the number of those who supplement their income working in agriculture is remarkably high: according to the Agricultural Census in 2000, more than half of the population works in agriculture in one way or another. Eighty percent of the cultivated land is used by private farmers and 20% by companies. As for rearing stock, the difference is less pronounced: 60% of livestock is owned by individual farmers and 40% by companies. The significant role of individual farming, although it is partly rooted in the former peasant tradition, also reflects a new necessity: with the collapse of the

[66] The summary report was provided by Kata Rácz.

agricultural co-operatives, and with people unable to commute for the scarcity of jobs both in nearby urban centres and the surrounding rural area, there is no alternative.

Although only a few people are officially employed in agriculture, the "mini-region" is characterized by a peculiar black or grey economy: a number of people are employed seasonally. And they are not only locals, but also workers from Ukraine and Romania. Though most of the individual farmers in the region own less than five hectares, we can observe a process of concentration: however, even the stronger individual farms usually employ only the owners themselves or a few family members.

The local governments in the region play a significant role in organizing agriculture. Indeed, often they cannot afford the commitments they have undertaken. In many villages, they have been maintaining a special in kind form of social assistance called "social land programmes" for several years, using funds from tenders, or using their own resources, to give land and seed corn to those who cannot afford them, and to ensure that eligible people can use machinery owned by the local government. A key element of farming in the region has been gardening: people grow cucumbers, beans and tobacco, and this is a commonly accepted way of earning extra income for a large segment of society, including the Roma. Before the collapse of communism, these activities were coordinated by local co-operatives. After the breakdown of these larger companies, however, this role was assumed by local governments. In many villages, the local government plays key role in organising "social land programs". Depending on the concrete in kind schemes, it employs an advisor to improve the efficiency of production and the quality of products; and/or ensures market channels, and/or pays the rent for pastures, employs a shepherd, runs a milk collector, etc. The people using these services (which are very similar to those provided by the former co-operatives) are marginalized people who do not own land and who used to commute to cities as long distance commuters, and people who used to work in the co-operatives, supplementing their income by gardening at home. Earlier, these people earned quite good incomes, but they could not take advantage of the process of privatization.

A new development is the appearance of producer organizations in the vegetable and fruit sectors, which operate growing working according to EU norms. They should play a major role in organizing and finding markets. However, they are characterized by a lack of capital, and because of this, they cannot entirely fulfil these roles.

Conclusion

To start with some aspects of major importance related to the issues dealt with in the first part of this paper, when comparing various CEE countries especially the successor states of the former Czechoslovakia and Hungary, the profound nature of the changes that have taken place, the importance of path dependency, the decisive role of socialist and pre-socialist farming structures in shaping the new structures that have emerged all have to be underlined.

In contrast to the Western model, the bulk of small-scale agriculture in Central Europe is made up of semi-subsistence farms usually on small plots, not family farms or viable individual ventures run by agricultural entrepreneurs. The presence of peculiar farm management methods and unique rental and service schemes as transitory ways of farming have to be underlined as well. The real difference between the farming systems of the countries investigated here is the importance attached to farming small plots and the "nature" of the transformed large-scale sector in the three countries concerned.

To summarize the differences: Slovak agriculture has witnessed the least profound structural changes with the retention of a strong successor co-operative sector. In the Czech Republic and Hungary restructuring went far beyond the Slovak model, reshaping the large-scale farm sector. Here, private companies prevail, whilst small-scale commercial entities have become visible, but not dominant. Small-scale farms acquired about 12-14% of all agricultural land in both the Czech Republic and Hungary (and half of this, 7% in Slovakia). The peculiarity of the Hungarian case lies in the excessive changes that have taken place in the small-scale sector, which has ceased to exist as an easy and accessible means of accumulating and maintaining a degree of wealth for most rural families. The rapid disappearance of commodity-producing plots is painful in so far as it generates poverty if off farm employment opportunities are not available. The farming of plots is increasingly being replaced by farming as a hobby. Examples from the Western Hungarian border area prove this. However, in Eastern Hungary, small-scale farming still serves as a social buffer in areas of high unemployment providing the local population has retained its knowledge of, and has sufficient interest in, this kind of activity.

As far as future prospects are concerned, long-term and realistic strategies should be developed. A realistic approach to the rural question in Central and Eastern Europe will have to assume and expect that a further shrinkage of agricultural job-opportunities in Central and Eastern European countries, including the countries investigated here, is likely not only in the short term, but also in the medium term as a result of further restructuring of both large-scale and small-scale farming.

An expansion of investment and new job opportunities can be expected in the main urban and metropolitan areas and their immediate environs as well as, albeit sporadically, in rural centres. This suggests that increasing accessibility to urban areas and facilitating commuting by using the innovative experiences of Europe and beyond, must become major priorities within development policies. The same applies to the promotion of Internet access in rural areas in terms of both IT infrastructure and knowledge, as a condition of distance-working and life-long learning. Promoting the quality of primary education in rural areas is increasingly becoming a major issue in Central and Eastern Europe.

The promotion of small-scale production by encouraging co-operation amongst producers as well as developing market-based linkages to the food chain in a way that prevents exploitation by large-scale trading companies ("integrators") is of major importance, as is the support of encouraging pluri-active production on small-scale farms (such as food procession, develop services, etc.)[67]. Any small-scale activity that increases the main, or supplementary, income of rural households deserves attention, because rural restructuring is going to be a long-lasting exercise during which the social buffer role of pluri-active small-scale farming will remain inevitable and crucial. The farming of plots is usually mentioned as a major source of supplementary income in rural areas and this is how it has been described above. Beyond this major role, its integrative potential is also considerable, as some Hungarian examples prove, in terms of reintegrating families that suffer from social exclusion. (Such as the so-called "social land programmes" favouring the rural poor, primarily the Roma). The potential of small-scale agricultural activity, however, cannot be developed everywhere, in each context. It cannot be expected to bring rapid results or provide remedies for massive spatial segregation of the rural poor, mostly but not only Romany in the Hungarian and Slovak context that is always connected with social exclusion. Therefore, a Europe-wide, integrated cohesion policy targeting rural peripheries should be developed until – to quote Alan Pouliquen (2001, 84) – "migration towards urban jobs … will establish itself as a major way of reducing agricultural over-employment, as everywhere else in the past", a rule that applies to the reduction of mass unemployment as well.

References

Alanen, I. (1998) The effects of internal struggles within collective farms on emerging enterprise structures. The case of Estonia. *Replika*, Special issue, 145-161.

[67] Multifunctional farm activities see Heinonen 2007.

Begg B. & M. Mieke (2001) Rural Change in Bulgarian Transition, in *Europe's Green Ring* ed. by L. Granberg, I. Kovács & H. Tovey. Ashgate, London, 107-26.

Bihari, Z., K. Kovács & M. Váradi (1994) Restructuring Hungarian agriculture. The case of The Golden Age, in *Agricultural Restructuring and Rural Change in Europe* ed. by D. Symes & A. Jansen. Agricultural University, Wageningen, 136-52.

Bihari, Z. & K. Kovács (2005) Slopes and Slides: Spatial Inequalities in Employment Opportunities in the Turn of the Millennium, in *Hungarian Spaces and Places: Patterns of Transition* ed. by G. Barta et al. Pécs, Centre for Regional Studies, 360-77.

Blaas, G. (1997) *Restructuring Agriculture in Slovakia* (final report). Soros Foundation, RSS project number 481/1994.

—. (2003) Food and Agriculture in the Slovak Republic, in *The Challenges of EU Accession* ed. by C. Csaba et al. The International Bank for Reconstruction and Development. Washington, 41-55.

Blaas, G. & K. Kovács (1997) *Intermediate Ownership and Farming Structures.* Research Report Scheme of the Soros Foundation, RSS project number 481/1994.

Dorgai, L. et al (2004) *A magyarországi birtokstruktúra, a birtokrendezési stratégia megalapozása* [Hungary's Holding Structure; Laying the Foundations of a Land Consolidation Strategy]. Agrárgazdasági Kutató Intézet, Budapest.

Doucha, T., E. Divila & M. Fischer (2005) Land Use and Ownership and the Czech Farm Development, in *Rural Development Capacity in Carpathian Europe* ed. by Z. Florianczyk & K. Czapiewski. Warsaw, 39-151.

Fertő, I. (1999) *A magyar mezőgazdaság strukturális problémái* ... [The Structural Problems of Hungarian Agriculture]. MTA Közgazdasági kutatóközpont, Műhelytanulmányok no 2.

Hann, C. & M. Sárkány (2003) The Great Transformation in Rural Hungary, in *The Post Socialist Agrarian Question* ed by C. Hann & Property Relation Group. LIT verlag Münster, 117-43.

Heinonen, M. (2007) Multifunctional Farm Activities in the New Member States, in *Reflecting Transformation in Post-socialist Rural Areas*, ed. by M. Heinonen et al. Cambridge Scholars Publishing, Newcastle, 137-62.

Kovách, I. (2001) De-pesentisation of Hungarian Rurality, in *Europe's Green Ring* ed. by L. Granberg, I. Kovács & H. Tovey. Ashgate, London, 66-88.

Kovács, K. (1998a) Elfújja a szél? [Blown by the Wind?] *Replika* 33-34 (December), 137-50.

—. (1998b) Strengths, Controversies and a Show Case of a Failure … the Hollóföldje Case. *Replika* Special issue (December), 173-90.

Central Statistical Office (2005) Magyar mezőgazdaság 2004. [Hungarian Agriculture 2004] Budapest.

—. (2004) Magyarország mezőgazdasága, gazdaságtipológia 2000, 2003 [Agriculture in Hungary, Farm Typology 2000, 2003] Budapest.

—. (2001) A mezőgazdasági tevékenység jelentősége a foglalkoztatásban. KSH Népszámlálási kötetek 2001 [The Importance of Agricultural Activity in Employment 2001]. Budapest.

Námerová, I. & N. Swain (1998) Co-operative Transformation and Co-operative Survival in Slovakia. *Replika* Special issue, 207-22.

NIAE (Network of Independent Agricultural Experts in the CEE Candidate Countries) (2004) *The Future of Rural Areas in the CEE New Member States.* IAMO (Institut für Agrarentwicklung in Mittel und Osteuropa), Halle.

Pouliquen, A. (2001) *Competitiveness and Farm Incomes in the CEEC Agri-Food Sectors*. INRA publication. http://europa.eu.int/comm/agriculture/publi/reports/ceeccomp/index_en.htm

Rácz, K. (2004) Karikási munkások, kutatási zárójelentés, Egy rendszerváltó mezőváros, Nagykőrös [Karikás working class. Final report of the OTKA research no TO 32295.]

Report on Agriculture and Food Sector in the Slovak Republic (2004) MoA, Bratislava.

Swain, N. (1994) *The Ethics of Agricultural Transformation.* Centre for Central European Studies, University of Liverpool. Working Papers. Rural Transformation Series No. 31.

Kaneff, D. (1998) Private Co-operatives and Local property Relations in Rural Bulgaria. *Replika*, Special issue, 161-72.

—. (1998a) Küzdelmes életutak egy változó világban. 'Nemesfalu' és az 'Aranyszőlő RT' [Harsh Life Histories in a Changing Society: Nemesfalu and the Aranyszőlő Company]. *Replika* 33-34 (December), 151-62.

—. (1998b) *Central European Agricultural Structures in Transition.* University of Liverpool, Centre for Central and Eastern European Studies, Working Papers Rural Transition Series, No. 53.

Torsello, D. (2003) Trust and Property in Historical Perspective, in *The Post Socialist Agrarian Question* ed. by C. Hann and the Property Relation Group. LIT verlag, Münster, 93-116.

Váradi, M. M. (1998) Keskeny az ösvény. Esettanulmány a 'Harmónia' Mgtsz átalakulásáról. *Replika* 33-34 (December), 121-36.

Wolf, R. Eric (1973) Parasztok in *Vadászok, törzsek, parasztok* ed. by E. R. Service, M. D. Sahlings & E. R. Wolf. Kossuth, Budapest 319-449.

CHAPTER SIX

THE EUROPEAN MODEL OF AGRICULTURE AND RURAL DEVELOPMENT POLICY CHOICES IN THE NEW MEMBER STATES

IRINA RÂMNICEANU & ROBERT ACKRILL

Introduction

In recent years, the Common Agricultural Policy (CAP) of the European Union (EU) has undergone enormous change. In particular, for most commodities prices and trade are distorted much less than before 1992. Budget costs have, however, remained very high. It is in this light that the development of the European Model of Agriculture (EMA) can be seen. In seeking to promote a multifunctional role for agriculture, broadening the scope of the CAP beyond commodity-based income support, the new focus is drawing attention to the idea that whilst spending may not have fallen, the range of economic outputs being supported is now not only much wider, but also more in line with public concerns – over the environment, food quality and so on. This found its clearest expression with the creation, in 1999, of a second "pillar" of CAP support: Rural Development. Recently, the EU enlargement has seen ten New Member States (NMS) implementing a CAP which has evolved in response to the negative consequences of the original scope and instruments of the policy in the EU15. This raises questions about the relevance for the NMS of the CAP and whether or not the CAP can accommodate the considerable regional variation – and hence local needs – across the NMS.

This paper focuses on the first step taken by the NMS in the implementation of EU Rural Development policy: the choices these countries have made from the long menu of policy measures available to them. Both the pre-accession SAPARD programme (Special Accession Programme for Agriculture and Rural Development) and post-accession "full" Rural Development policy are analysed.[68] The policy choices made are examined to see if they reveal a willingness to promote a multifunctional role for agriculture. This will, in turn, indicate the extent to which the EMA is being supported in the NMS. In contrast to much recent work on Rural Development, this paper looks at the full range of policy measures, contained in all relevant documentation, not just Rural Development Plans, as a result of which the analysis of multifunctionality covers more than just environmental measures. This avoids any artificial truncation of the post-accession analysis.

The paper proceeds as follows. First we review the ideas behind the European Model of Agriculture and Multifunctionality and consider how this has been translated into rural policy options. Then we present the pre-accession policy choices made by the NMS under the SAPARD. After reviewing the countries' post-accession documentation (Rural Development Plans and either the Single Programming Documents or the Operational Programmes) we present the findings and outlines the findings of an initial analysis to ascertain why certain policy choices may or may not have been made.

The European Model of Agriculture, multifunctionality and New Member States

The CAP has undergone considerable change in the last two decades. Whilst spending on the CAP has been maintained, the instruments of support have changed, making the policy much less trade-distorting. Furthermore, a wider range of policy goals and policy instruments has been brought under the umbrella of the CAP, accompanied by notable additions to the lexicon of the CAP.

Politically, attempts have been made both to justify continued budget outlays and to raise support for the aforementioned reforms. Difficulties arise because these arguments are, in effect, directed at quite different constituencies who, on the face of it, have irreconcilable views – those who want the CAP reformed (a position often allied with a desire to cut spending) and those who want the policy – and the associated expenditure – left intact. The principle of support has thus remained, but a key part of the reform process has been to shift the emphasis from the production of commodity outputs to the producers of a wide range of commodity and non-commodity outputs. Herein lays the basis for the new framing of the CAP and the support it provides.

The key concept over-arching the new policy is the EMA. Although there is no single accepted definition of the EMA, one of the simplest and clearest

[68] Cyprus and Malta are excluded from this paper. As well as having very different recent economic histories, these countries did not participate in SAPARD.

comes from ex-Commissioner, Dr Franz Fischler (2001), who captured its essence as "Competitiveness, Sustainability, Multifunctionality". Fischler argues that "Competitiveness" has been developed in the CAP through the progressive de-coupling of support and, for most commodities, reductions in price support and associated trade barriers. "Sustainability" is seen to have three elements: economic, social and ecological. Support payments have helped keep farmers on the land and thus in rural communities (underpinning economic and social sustainability), whilst ecological sustainability has been promoted by the progressive de-coupling of, and imposition of environmental cross-compliance conditions on, those payments.

Third, there is "Multifunctionality", like the EMA a recent entry into the CAP lexicon and one also lacking a universally-accepted definition. It is this component of the EMA which is at once its distinguishing and most controversial element. The OECD (2001) argues multifunctionality can be seen in two ways. A "positive" reading of multifunctionality (the view adopted by the OECD) sees it as a characteristic of farming. As an economic activity, farming produces jointly a range of commodity and non-commodity outputs. A "normative" reading, however, gives multifunctionality a value in itself, a goal pursued in accordance with societal demands. Whilst the OECD may wish to avoid considering "the functions and objectives assigned to agriculture by society… [t]his is…the core of the European debate on multifunctionality" (Garzon 2005, 5). Indeed, it is a recurring theme in this paper that the normative reading is essential, in the context of the CAP, to go from understanding the concept to identifying and analysing the policy instruments that arise from it. These instruments operationalise not only multifunctionality but, ultimately, the EMA.

The CAP was traditionally a sectoral policy, seeking primarily to support farmers' incomes in accordance with Article 39 of the Treaty of Rome. Transfers were centred on commodity-specific Common Market Organisations (CMOs) with, for most sectors, support linked to production via price support. Since 1992, three CAP reforms have changed the CAP fundamentally. First, the nature of income support has been transformed. Second, in 1999 a new strand of support instruments was created, establishing what has become known as Pillar II of the CAP (Pillar I being income support).

In Fischler (2001), the Commissioner who drove the 1999 and 2003 reforms aligns "Competitiveness" with the policy instruments within Pillar I of the CAP, reforms to which have progressively de-coupled support from production. Fischler also aligns "Sustainability" with Pillar I policy instruments, with new policy goals incorporated both directly, via de-coupling and indirectly via, for example, environmental cross-compliance.

Within this reform process, multifunctionality found its clearest expression in 1999, with the creation of Pillar II of the CAP and the label "Rural Development". This had been preceded, in 1996, by the Cork Declaration for A Living Countryside. The preamble (see, *inter alia*, European Commission 1997) stated the conference was "persuaded that the concept of public financial support for rural development [...] is increasingly gaining acceptance." This conference followed the conclusion of the Uruguay Round of GATT talks, Article 20 of the Final Act acknowledging that further reform and liberalisation of agricultural policies was needed. These talks should take into account, *inter alia*, "non-trade concerns" including, according to the Preamble to the URAA, "the need to protect the environment".

In terms of understanding the new CAP framework, van der Ploeg and Roep (2003, 37) argue that

> Multifunctionality and Rural development may be the key unifying concept of [the EMA] and response to the many expressions of the crisis [in European agriculture] which are more and more perceived as outcomes of the previously dominant model of *agricultural modernization* [emphasis in the original – K.K.].

The sequence here is clear: the previous CAP policy instruments generated a "crisis" to which the EMA – and its associated policy instruments – are the response.

In this paper, the focus is on the (Pillar II) policy choices faced by and made by the NMS. Pillar I policies and policy instruments are implemented across all EU member states and where there are differences in implementation between the EU15 and NMS (most notably the phased introduction of direct payments), this is conducted in a uniform manner agreed in advance within a common framework. Pillar II policies, however, are implemented differentially across all member states, each of whom faces an extensive policy menu and makes choices based on the match-up between policy options and domestic needs. Crucially, however, (and in contrast to the *sequence* of events suggested by van der Ploeg and Roep for the EU15) the NMS are seeking *simultaneously* to modernise their agricultural sectors and implement the Rural Development policies that operationalise multifunctionality and, ultimately, the EMA.

In order to analyse the Pillar II policy choices made by the NMS, a framework is needed within which the measures available and chosen can be located. This paper divides the individual components of the Rural Development policy menu into two categories: measures that are either principally Competitiveness-oriented ("C" policies) or principally Multifunctionality-oriented ("M" policies). This maintains a sharp distinction between those elements of Rural Development that complement Pillar I policies (reforms to which were associated by Fischler with the promotion of "Competitiveness" within the EMA) and those elements that promote the "Multifunctionality" agenda, including non-agricultural measures. The present paper, by taking a normative view of multifunctionality, thus looks not only at environmental elements of Rural Development but at these other measures, M and C, which address wider rural concerns. A positive approach, on the other hand, would focus principally on agri-environmental measures (AEMs), reflecting their "jointness" with agricultural activity (see OECD 2001).

One problem in assigning Rural Development measures as principally C or M oriented is the lack of a clear structure in the Community's Rural Development menu (see also Râmniceanu 2004). In assigning a particular orientation to individual measures in this paper, reference has been made to the structure of policy measures used by the European Commission. The European Commission (2003c) indicates a structure for the current (2000-2006) programming period. Of particular help, however, was the European Commission (2004), which sets out the much clearer structure of the Rural Development policy in the next (2007-2013) programming period. Where there is not an exact mapping of policy measures, especially with the SAPARD, a judgement has been made as to the closest reasonable match.

This two-axis approach contrasts with the three-axis classification of Rural Development measures presented by the European Commission. As it will be seen below, the two-axis approach simplifies and clarifies the policy analysis. Importantly it remains consistent with the normative view of multifunctionality taken in this paper. This can be seen by considering the three-axis structure of Rural Development measures to be introduced from 2007 (see European Commission 2004).

In that structure, Axis 1 measures address "Competitiveness" which, as indicated above, are aligned with Pillar I policies and thus reflect the "traditional" focus of the CAP. Axes 2 (land management) and 3 (diversification of the rural economy and the quality of life in rural areas) divide the other policies neatly into the agricultural and non-agricultural elements that are embodied in the normative approach to multifunctionality, consistent with the EMA. In other words, it is the normative view that unifies non-commodity agricultural elements and non-agricultural elements of Rural Development under "Multifunctionality".

SAPARD: Policy choices prior to EU accession[69]

The SAPARD was established in 1999[70], with the express aims (Article 1(2)) of:

> (a) contributing to the implementation of the *acquis communautaire* concerning the common agricultural policy and related policies;
> (b) solving propriety and specific problems for the sustainable adaptation of the agricultural sector and rural areas in the applicant countries.

The applicant countries faced a foreshortened (see Dwyer et al. 2003, 9) menu of 15 (Pillar II) measures they could draw upon. These are shown in Table 5-1, along with their assignment as either C or M oriented.

Article 4(3) then gave further guidance as to the choices the applicants should make:

> In their plans, applicant countries shall ensure that priority is given to measures to improve market efficiency, quality and health standards and measures to create new employment in rural areas, in compliance with the provisions on the protection of the environment.

Whilst Article 1(2) of the SAPARD Regulation refers to the CAP in general, Pillar I concerns are not mentioned in Article 4(3) – and are addressed indirectly only insofar as preparation to implement the acquis will include countries preparing their administrations to implement CAP support instruments, such as managing direct payments and intervention storage. The factors influencing each country's (Pillar II) policy choices between C and M measures are discussed in the section of general findings and policy implications. It is, however, clear from both Article 1(2)b and Article 4(3) that the EU15 wished the applicant countries to emphasise C measures in implementing the SAPARD. Fig. 6-1 confirms the applicants respected this.

From the list of 15 policy options shown in Table 6-1, three measures were chosen by no country: setting up farm relief and farm management services; establishment and updating of land registers; and agricultural water resources management. On the other hand, four of the other 12 measures were chosen by all eight countries, with another three measures chosen by six or seven countries. One stand-out feature is the difference in spending allocation between

---

[69] The focus of this paper is the policy *choices* made by the applicants from the policy menu faced. For details on the *implementation* of SAPARD see, *inter alia*, European Commission (2003a).

[70] Council Regulation (EC) No 1268/1999 of 21 June 1999, Official Journal of the European Communities, L161, pages 87-93.

the various measures. Seven countries may have chosen to implement the measure supporting environmentally friendly agricultural practices, but this received only 2.1% of public funds (and just 1.2% of total funds).[71]

Table 6-1The SAPARD policy options available to applicant countries

Competitiveness-oriented measures	Multifunctionality-oriented measures
Investment in agricultural holdings	Agricultural production methods designed to protect the environment and maintain the countryside
Improving the processing and marketing of agricultural and fisheries products	Forestry, including afforestation of agricultural areas, investments in forest holdings owned by private forest owners and processing and marketing of forestry products
Improving the structures for quality, veterinary and plant-health controls, for the quality of foodstuffs and for consumer protection	Development and diversification of economic activities, providing for multiple activities and alternative income
Improvement of vocational training	Renovation and development of villages and the protection and conservation of the rural heritage
Setting up producer groups	
Development and improvement of rural infrastructure	
Establishment and updating of land registers	
Agricultural water resources management	
Setting up farm relief and farm management services	
Land improvement and reparcelling	

Notes: Technical Assistance is omitted. Available for all C and M measures, it included studies to assist with the preparation and monitoring of SAPARD, information and publicity campaigns. In this paper, the sums available under this heading are split between C and M totals in proportion to the total sums assigned to each by the NMS in implementing the measures in table.
Source: Council Regulation (EC) No 1268/1999, page 89.

[71] Slovenia chose not to utilise this policy option, partly because of the limited budget, partly because it had chosen to implement an agri-environmental programme funded entirely nationally (see Network of Independent Experts 2004, 151-152; Konečný 2004, 71).

Fig. 6-1 Take-up of Competitiveness-Oriented and Multifunctionality-Oriented Policy Measures under SAPARD in the New Member States (shares of public funding)

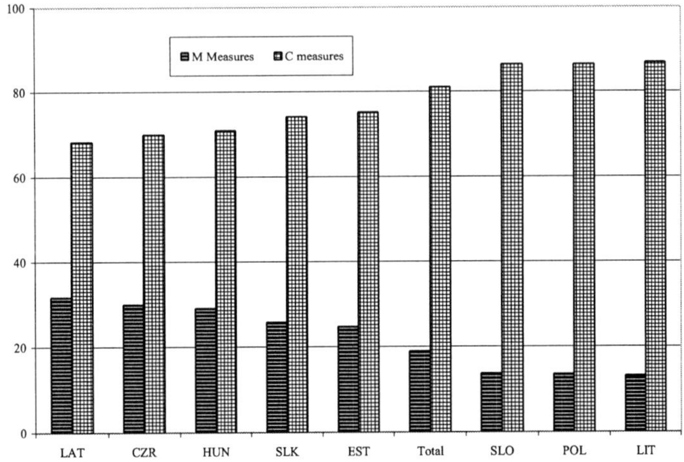

Source: own calculations, using data from national SAPARD Programming documents.

In contrast to the limited funds for M measures, investment in agricultural holdings and processing took over 50% of total resources in every country except the Czech Republic. This drives the pattern in Fig. 6-1, where C measures dominate. Furthermore, under SAPARD the M measures are dominated not by environmentally-oriented policy options, but by measures promoting economic diversification, the one M measure referred to in Article 4(3) of Regulation (EC) No 1268/1999. This emphasises the importance of the normative approach to understanding and analysing the EU Rural Development policy. Note also that of the NMS8 Poland, by far the largest country[72], assigned the largest share of spending to developing rural infrastructures.

Despite the clear pointers on implementation provided by Article 4(3) of Regulation (EC) 1268/1999, the distribution of adoption was uneven. Investment in holdings, a key measure designed to "improve the efficiency of agriculture" was utilised heavily in all countries, but only three countries employed "land improvement and reparcelling" (and only the Czech Republic did so to a significant degree), whilst no country pursued the "establishment and updating of land registers", which would have further facilitated this process.

---

[72] For example, Poland's utilised agricultural area is 94% of total utilised agricultural area in the other seven NMS.

"Quality and health standards", referred to explicitly in Article 4(3), was taken up only in the Czech Republic.

The one M measure Article 4(3) refers to, "Development and diversification of economic activities, providing for multiple activities and alternative income" was taken up by all eight countries. Although Article 4(3) does not refer explicitly to non-agricultural employment, a necessary consequence of improving the structure and efficiency of agriculture will be labour-shedding. A sustainable rural economy will thus need new non-agricultural jobs, as well as additional non-agricultural activities that can generate a second income for farmers.[73]

One feature of Article 4(3) is that it refers to environmental policy only indirectly. There are, moreover, only small sums devoted to such measures. That said, the agri-environmental measures under the SAPARD were intended only as pilot projects, with "the objective of developing practical experience of agri-environment implementation at both the administrative and farm levels"[74] (see also Network of Independent Experts, 2004, Chapter 7). There were also fears that this inexperience could lead to implementation problems. Such concerns are, though, in no way an indicator of a lack of funding under the post-accession programmes – as shall now be seen.

Implementing Rural Development Policy as full members, 2004-2006

The current structure for implementing the EU Rural Development policies is very complex. First, for the NMS, 31 measures (see Table 6-2) have been accumulated across several Regulations.[75] 27 of these measures are

---

[73] Whether economic diversification under the EU Rural Development policy is capable by itself of delivering such employment is, however, less clear (see Chaplin et al, 2004).

[74] Article 4 of Commission Regulation (EC) No 2759/1999 of 22 December 1999, laying down the rules for implementing Council Regulation (EC) No 1268/1999.

[75] The "core" Regulation is "Council Regulation (EC) No 1257/1999 of 17 May 1999 on support for rural development from the European Agricultural Guidance and Guarantee Fund (EAGGF) and amending and repealing certain Regulations" (OJ L 160, 26.6.1999, p. 80), amended by Council Regulations: 1783/2003 (OJ L 270, 21.10.2003), 567/2004 (OJ L 90, 27.3.2004) and 583/2004 (OJ L 91, 30.3.2004). Rules applying Rural Development in the NMS are set out in Commission Regulation 141/2004 (OJ L 24, 29.1.2004), detailed by Commission Regulation 27/2004 (OJ L 005, 9.1.2004) and amended by Commission Regulation 740/2004 (OJ L 116, 22.4.2004). Detailed rules for applying 1257/1999 are provided by Commission Regulation 817/2004 (OJ L 153, 30.4.2004). A consolidated version of Regulation 1257/1999 is available via the EUR-LEX website.

implemented across the EU25 – although measure "w"[76], "management of integrated rural development strategies by local partners", is not applicable in the NMS as such: in the EU15, local LEADER+ measures are implemented separately from the "mainstream programmes" (Preamble to Council Regulation 583/2004). Measure"w" thus provides the option of implementing local measures through these programmes. In the NMS, the addition of Articles 33f and 47a to Council Regulation 1257/1999 allows them to implement LEADER-type measures directly through the "mainstream programmes" (via Objective 1 documentation), rendering measure "w" redundant for them.

Other measures from the EU15 Rural Development menu are also linked with specific provisions for the NMS as laid down in the Treaty of Accession. Measure "l" ("setting up farm advisory services, farm relief services and farm management services") corresponds with "farm advisory and extension services", provided for in Article 33g. Similarly, measure"x" ("implementing demanding standards") is reflected in "support for compliance with Community standards", provided for in Article 33c.

Four[77] further measures were introduced specifically for the NMS via the Act of Accession addressing, to an extent, possible problems with the top-down Europeanization of NMS Rural Development policy. Two of these measures, "ab" and "ac", are shown in Table 6-2. A third, "technical assistance" ("ad"), is treated in the same way as such funding under SAPARD. The sums are shown in Fig. 6-2, assigned to C and M in proportion to the sums utilised under measures "a"-"ac" (see also the note to Table 6-1). The fourth measure ("ae") is "complements to direct payments". In the early years of membership, the NMS can "reverse-modulate" Rural Development money, using some Pillar II funds to top-up Pillar I direct payments. This measure is excluded from the main analysis because the funds are used on Pillar I measures.

Another complication arises from the different types of documentation and programme used to implement the EU Rural Development policy.

[76] The letters identifying each Rural Development policy measures – see also Table 6-2 – are laid down by the EU in the relevant Regulations.

[77] Excluding Malta from the analysis excludes two country-specific measures laid down in the Treaty of Accession – "complements to state aid in Malta" (af) and "full-time farmers in Malta" (ag).

Table 6-2 Rural Development policy measures, document type and policy orientation

		Competitiveness-oriented measures		Multifunctionality-oriented measures
RDPs	d	Early retirement	e	Less-favoured areas
	x	Compliance with Community standards	f	Agri-environment and animal welfare
	ab	Semi-subsistence farming	h	Afforestation of agricultural land
	ac	Setting up producer groups		
OPs/ SPDs*	a	Investment in farms	i	Other forestry measures
	b	Start-up assistance for young farmers	n	Basic services for the rural economy
	c	Training	o	Renovation and development of villages
	g	Improving processing and marketing of agricultural products	p	Diversifying agricultural activities
	j	Land improvement	s	Encouragement for tourist and craft activities
	k	Reparcelling	t	Protecting the environment
	l	Setting up farm advisory services	v	Financial engineering
	m	Marketing of quality agricultural products	w**	Management of integrated rural development strategies
	q	Agricultural water resource management		
	r	Development of infrastructure		
	u	Restoring agricultural production		
	y	Use of farm advisory services		
	z	Farmers' voluntary participation in food quality schemes		
	aa	Producer group activities related to food quality		

Notes: *Some of these measures may, in the case of Objective 2 regions, also be included in RDPs (see text for details). ** LEADER-type measures in the NMS (see text for details).For details of omitted measures 'ad' (technical assistance) and 'ae' (complement to direct payments), see the text.

Sources: Council Regulation (EC) 1257/1999, detailed by Commission Regulation (EC) 817/2004 and Commission Regulation (EC) 141/2004.

Rural Development Plans (RDPs) cover measures funded through the EAGGF Guarantee Section. Guidance Section-funded measures in Objective 1 regions are, however, coordinated through Community Support Frameworks and transposed into either Operational Programmes (OPs) or Single Programming Documents (SPDs).[78]

As a general rule, SPDs are used when Community funding is less than €1 billion (see Regulation 1260/1999, Article 15(1)). Note that whilst SPDs are indeed presented as single documents, OPs are presented in a series of thematic documents. This paper is concerned with the policies presented in the OP dealing with agriculture and rural development.

OPs have been submitted by the Czech Republic, Hungary, Poland and Slovakia, whilst SPDs have been used by Estonia, Latvia, Lithuania and Slovenia. Six countries are classified entirely as Objective 1, but the Prague region in the Czech Republic and Bratislava in Slovakia are Objective 2. In these regions, some measures are funded through the Guarantee Section and presented through the RDP, which in Objective 1 regions are presented through OPs or SPDs. The Czech Republic chose not to submit Prague region into any rural development programme. This leaves Slovakia uniquely submitting such measures through its RDP.

National Rural Development Plans

Table 6-2 shows seven measures are implemented through RDPs, plus "technical assistance". Note, however, that in the NMS about two-thirds of public funding for Rural Development measures comes from the EAGGF Guarantee Section and is channelled through the national RDPs. As described above, the RDP for Slovakia also includes some measures implemented in the country's one Objective 2 region, Bratislava that in Objective 1 regions are funded through the Guidance Section and are, therefore, implemented through the OP/SPD.

Compared with SAPARD policy choices, it is clear from Fig. 6-2 that the national RDPs offer greater scope for adopting and implementing M measures. Of the seven Objective 1 measures taken up (excluding technical assistance and transfers to Pillar I), over one third of available funding is to be devoted to less favoured areas, with another quarter supporting agri-environmental and animal welfare measures. Note that the NMS are obliged to implement agri-environmental policies, although the extent of uptake varies considerably (from 66% of total public funding on M measures in Hungary, down to 12% in

---

[78] The basis for RDPs is Regulation 1257/1999; for OPs/SPDs it is Regulation (EC) No 1260/1999 of 21 June 1999 laying down general provisions on the Structural Funds (OJ L 161, 26.6.1999).

Latvia). Given the emphasis on efficiency and restructuring, noted earlier, it is curious that less than one-eighth of funds are to be devoted to measures related to early retirement.

Comparing the C/M balance for Slovakia with and without Bratislava, it is clear from Fig. 6-2 that the overall impact of the sums spent on the six (Objective 2) measures implemented in the capital region are modest – less than 10% of total public spending in Slovakia and only about one-half of one percent of total public spending incurred through the RDPs. Overall, Slovakia's ranking amongst the eight countries is unchanged whether Bratislava is included or excluded, being second only to the Czech Republic in adopting a pro-multifunctionality policy mix through the RDPs.

Fig. 6-2 Take-up of Competitiveness-Oriented and Multifunctionality-Oriented Policy Measures under RDPs in the New Member States (shares of public funding)

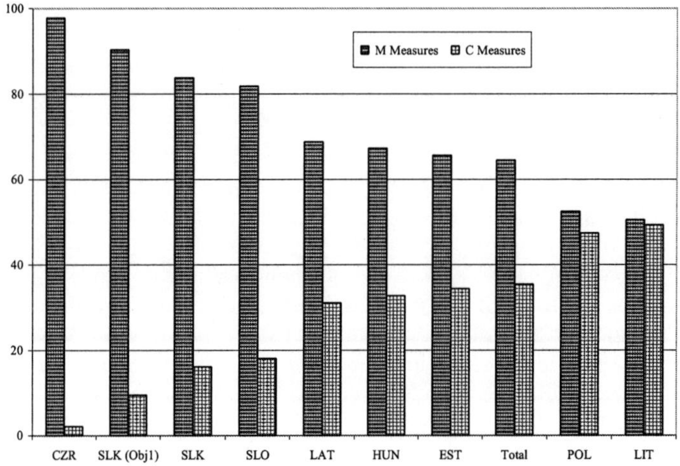

Source: own calculations, using data from national Rural Development Plans.

Single Programming Documents and Operational Programmes

Support from the EAGGF Guidance Section, although the minority share of total Pillar II funding in the NMS, is channelled through either SPDs or OPs towards what Table 6-2 shows is not just the majority of measures but, within which, there is a notable majority of C measures. This is shown in Fig. 6-3. Moreover, the two principal measures in funding terms – investment in farms and the processing and marketing of agricultural products – are the same as under the SAPARD. Post-accession, only in the Czech Republic are these two measures not still the two most well publicly-funded measures adopted. The most significant change in the funding of C measures between the SAPARD and the OPs/SPDs is rural infrastructure. The take-up of the measure is much lower post-accession, although this is driven largely by the policy decision of just one country, Poland, for whom previously, rural infrastructure was the second most well-funded measure adopted.

The question of goodness of fit of Rural Development Policy measures to countries' needs cannot be judged solely on policy uptake, because there may be other measures needed by some or all NMS that are not available. That said it is still interesting to note the range of combinations of measures taken up by the different NMS. Only three measures are taken up by all eight countries. Two measures, setting up farm advisory services and the marketing of quality agricultural products, are each taken up by only two countries whilst restoring agricultural production, the use of farm advisory services and environmental protection are each taken up by just one country.

"Basic services for the rural economy" is a measure taken up in three countries, but not in any of the larger, OP-submitting NMS. Support for tourist and craft activities is taken up in the three Baltic States, but is otherwise adopted only by Hungary. There are, furthermore, some measures (farmers' participation in food quality schemes, producer group activities related to food quality, protecting the environment and financial engineering) that no country has pursued.

As for whether there is a difference in policy adoption between the four "OP" countries and four "SPD" countries, Fig. 6-3 suggests a clear difference in the C/M balance. Whilst all eight countries have a bias towards adopting C measures over M measures, the balance is skewed more for the OP than SPD countries. As a result, the four SPD countries lie to the left of the overall average, whilst the four OP countries lie to the right. Simply in terms of measures adopted (recall Fig. 6-3 shows money allocated) the four smaller SPD countries have pursued relatively more M measures (compared with C measures) than have the four OP countries.

Fig. 6-3 Take-up of Competitiveness-Oriented and Multifunctionality-Oriented Policy Measures under OPs and SPDs in the New Members States (shares of public funding)

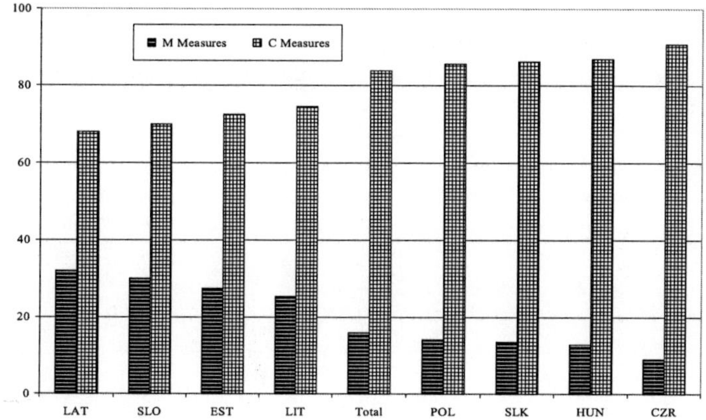

Source: own calculations, using data from national Operational Programmes or Single Programming documents.

A key point from the foregoing discussion is that individual documents direct the NMS more towards either M policies (RDPs) or C policies (OPs/SPDs). The next section draws this information together, to analyse the overall picture and see how the Rural Development policy as a whole is being implemented in the NMS. The next section also considers briefly some possible reasons why the NMS may have made the Rural Development policy choices they did. This will allow us to offer preliminary suggestions as to how the design of policy variables can influence policy outcomes.

Overview of general findings and policy implications

Fig. 6-4 draws together the data from Fig. 6-2 and 6-3 to show the uptake of M and C measures across all post-accession Rural Development programmes. This shows that, overall, there is a largely balanced take-up of M and C measures, albeit with five out of eight countries assigning more public funding to M than C measures. The average is pulled to the right because of the weight of Polish spending – which is allocated 50% of total public funds (EU and national) assigned for Rural Development measures in the NMS8.

In order to distinguish more formally between the policy mix in each country, the following distinction is made, based on spending quintiles allocated to M and C oriented policy measures. If a country allocates more than 80% of public Rural Development funds to M measures, that country is described as exhibiting a Strong M-Preference. If the M-allocation is between 60% and 80%, this is referred to as Moderate M-Preference; for an M-allocation between 40% and 60%, a Balanced Approach; between 20% and 40%, a Moderate C-Preference; and below 20%, a Strong C-Preference. From this, the following observations can be made.

Fig. 6-4 Take-up of Competitiveness-Oriented and Multifunctionality-Oriented Policy Measures under all post-accession policies in the New Member States (shares of public funding)

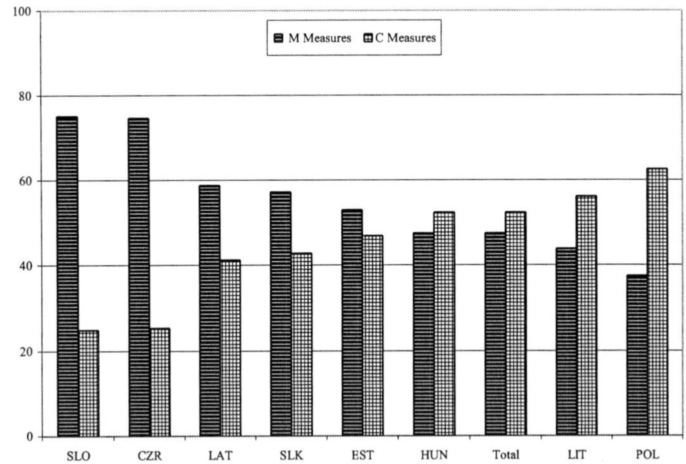

The pre-accession picture under the SAPARD saw C-measures dominate. Five countries exhibited a moderate C-preference, the other three a strong C-preference. Given that Poland was one of the latter, the extra weight of this largest of the SAPARD countries meant the overall C/M balance across the eight countries was for a strong C-preference. In contrast to this pre-accession picture, the Rural Development Plans post-accession provided much more support (absolutely and relatively) for M measures. Three countries (Slovenia, the Czech Republic and Slovakia) exhibited a strong M-preference, whilst three more (Latvia, Estonia and Hungary) adopted measures representing a moderate M-preference. Lithuania and Poland chose to pursue a balanced approach. The overall situation across the eight was for a moderate M-preference.

As seen in Fig. 6-3, the policy choices made under the Operational Programmes or Single Programming Documents reflected much more closely the balance of measures adopted pre-accession under SAPARD. The split was four-four between a moderate and strong C-preference. That said, only Poland (strong C-preference) and Estonia and Latvia (moderate C-preference), had the same degree of C-preference as under SAPARD. As with pre-accession policy adoption, the weight of Poland results in the overall C/M balance under OPs and SPDs being strongly for a C-preference. The overall post-accession picture, however, shown in Fig. 6-4 (and implied by the foregoing discussion) is one of balance between C and M measures. Two countries (Slovenia and the Czech Republic) exhibit a moderate M-preference, whilst Poland exhibits a moderate C-preference. The other five countries (and the overall eight-country average) are pursuing a balanced approach. Of the latter five countries, three have a policy mix that results in over 50% of funding assigned to M measures.

The next issue to consider is the extent to which this outcome was pre-determined by the way in which the legislation was set down. The SAPARD policy mix confirms the intentions of the EU15, as described in earlier. Also we argued that the introduction and subsequent development of Rural Development policy as an explicit arm of the CAP is linked inextricably to the European Model of Agriculture, via multifunctionality. That RDPs should have a bias towards M measures is, therefore, not surprising. Indeed, Article 43(2) of Council Regulation 1257/1999 makes it clear in the second indent that the member states must "ensure the necessary balance is kept between the different support measures", whilst the first indent demands that the Member States shall in their RDPs "provide for agri-environment measures throughout their territories and in accordance with their specific needs". The emphasis on M measures is thus consistent with the view of Rural Development (and RDPs) being aligned with the promotion of multifunctionality, within a two-Pillar CAP.

In contrast, OPs and SPDs are aligned with EU regional policy. Paragraph 1 of the preamble to Council Regulation 1260/1999 links the policies covered therein to

> Article 158 of the Treaty [which] states that, in order to strengthen its economic and social cohesion, the Community shall aim at reducing disparities between the levels of development of the various regions and the backwardness of the least-favoured regions or islands, *including rural areas* (emphasis added).

Article 1 then identifies three policy objectives: promoting economic development in lagging regions, supporting the economic and social conversion of areas facing structural difficulties and supporting the adaptation and modernisation of policies and systems of education, training and employment.

There is thus a clear link between economic development goals and the C-measure orientation of the OPs and SPDs. It is important to bear in mind, however, that it is a question of emphasis rather than exclusivity towards C or M measures. Thus, for example, the economic conversion of rural areas facing structural difficulties might include diversification out of agriculture – an M oriented measure and one consistent with the broad normative reading of multifunctionality adopted in this paper.

At this stage, an outline can be provided of the ongoing element of the work presented in this paper. Whilst an investigation into the policy choices made by the eight countries is, of itself, worth reporting as a way of identifying the broad thrust of policy being implemented under the broadened CAP, the present work is being taken one stage further. The question being asked is whether economic factors and/or specific policy factors are influencing the policy choices being made. The economic variables being considered are GDP per capita and agriculture's share of total output (respectively, a general variable and a sectoral variable). The key policy variable being considered is the rate of co-funding available for the different measures. This is, in turn, split into two – the EU share of public (national plus EU) funding and the private share of total (private plus public) funding.

Initial results suggest the following. Pre-accession, none of the variables identified above appear to have had a significant positive influence on the take-up of M measures. Given the legislative emphasis and constraints described earlier, however, this is as expected, a priori. That, in itself, indicates the influence that legislation can have on policy uptake and, therefore, the importance of the detailed framing of such legislation should EU member states have particular policy outcomes they wish to pursue. Post-accession, initial results suggest that the uptake of M measures is significantly correlated with the indicators of economic need – GDP per capita and agriculture's share of total output. Both correlation coefficients have the appropriate sign. This suggests that, post-accession, the new member states are adopting policy measures broadly appropriate to their domestic need and circumstance. On the other hand, co-funding rates appear not to be statistically significantly correlated with post-accession policy take-up. This provides both good and not so good news for policy-makers. On the one hand, private co-financing requirement appear not to have a negative effect on policy take-up. On the other, EU contributions appear not to have a positive effect on policy take-up.

Overall, however, these tentative first results suggest that how the legislation is drawn up can have a powerful effect on policy take-up; that the range of measures available appears to allow considerable national variation in policy take-up – in such a way, moreover, that reflects different national economic circumstances and needs; and that co-funding appears not to influence policy take-up. Across the full range of post-accession rural development measures available to them, the new member states are adopting a balanced mix of competitiveness-oriented and multifunctionality-oriented measures, thus reflecting the greater breadth of CAP policy outcomes expressed through the "European Model of Agriculture". To the extent that Pillar I spending still constitutes the majority of CAP funding, even in the new member states, multifunctionality remains something of the Cinderella arm of the CAP. That said, given how recently Pillar II was established as a means for promoting multifunctionality and, ultimately, the European Model of Agriculture, the evidence presented here suggests she is going to the ball.

Conclusion

Recent CAP reforms have introduced a new term into the policy lexicon: the European Model of Agriculture (EMA). This has been used as a way of framing the EU response to crises faced by European agriculture. One, concise, definition states that the EMA promotes competitiveness, sustainability and multifunctionality in European agriculture; goals pursued to different degrees across the two pillars of the CAP. The second pillar, rural development, has been the principal channel for measures aligned with multifunctionality and promoting the EMA. To accommodate rural diversity in the EU, moreover, rural development policy implementation is based on member states making policy choices from a long list of individual measures.

This paper has focused on rural development programming, as the start of the policy process for the (Central and Eastern European) NMS. It has examined which measures these countries chose to adopt, both before and after accession. It has also classified the elements of the rural development menu as competitiveness-oriented (C) or multifunctionality-oriented (M), comparing the balance between the two to consider the extent to which the NMS are promoting the EMA. Moreover, the paper has investigated the factors that have underpinned the rural development options, with a view to determining whether domestic economic needs and/or measure accessibility impacted on the promotion of the EMA. The wide scope of the current analysis (i.e. the entire set of the rural programming documents as well as the full range of the rural development measures) underscores the novel approach of this paper.

Under the pre-accession SAPARD programme, the applicants chose predominantly C-oriented measures. There were, however, a number of legislative constraints on policy adoption that ensured this outcome. With the post-accession policies, these constraints were removed. Each NMS had two sets of documents through which Rural Development measures were to be implemented, one funded from the Guarantee section of the EAGGF (Rural Development Plans, RDPs), and the other from the Guidance Section (either Operational Programmes, OPs; or Single Programming Documents, SPDs).

Policy adoption through the former was shown to have an M-orientation, whilst the latter had a C-orientation.

When funding for all post-accession measures was drawn together, it was found that most countries allocated equal or greater shares to M measures. To help categorise policy choices more formally, this paper establishes a classification of C and M orientation based on quintile shares of total funding going to each category. Using this, five of the eight countries were shown to favour a balanced adoption of M and C measures in implementing Rural Development Policy, whilst two countries showed a moderate M-preference and one a moderate C-preference. This contrasts starkly with the adoption of SAPARD measures, where all countries exhibited strong or moderate C-preferences. These results were shown to be consistent with the wider goals of related EU policies: Guidance-funded measures are aligned with structural policies, consistent with a competitiveness orientation. With M measures, however, there is a clear lineage back from RDPs to the establishment of Pillar II of the CAP and the EMA, hence the multifunctionality-orientation.

Further, at this stage tentative, investigation of possible factors underpinning policy choice suggested that whilst pre-accession SAPARD policy choices were dominated by legislative imperatives, post accession multifunctionality choices were significantly correlated with measures of economic need. On the other hand, co-financing rates appeared not to have a significant effect on policy choice – either positively or negatively. There are also other policy factors affecting the promotion of the EMA in the NMS. In these countries there will be no compulsory modulation of Pillar I direct payments into Rural Development before 2013. Moreover, the NMS can reverse-modulate – take some Rural Development funds and use them to boost Pillar I payments to farmers. The NMS have chosen to allocate 15% of available RDP funds for reverse modulation. Overall, whilst many measures have been adopted that promote multifunctionality in the rural economic space, these policies on modulation have constrained the extent to which multifunctionality is being promoted via Rural Development programmes (note, however, that the EMA also covers competitiveness, which is aligned with Pillar I support: thus reverse modulation switches resources to a different facet of the EMA). That said, on balance the NMS have allocated substantial shares of available funds to M measures, which not only suggests they are promoting the EMA – it would appear that policies arising from the multifunctionality component of the EMA are appropriate for their needs.

References

Extensive use was made of all eight countries' SAPARD Plans, Rural Development Plans, Single Programming Documents, SPD Complements, Operational Programming Documents and OP Complements. All documents were obtained from the websites of the national governments.

Ackrill, R. W. (2005) Romania's EU Accession Negotiations: The Significance of the EU Budget. *Romanian Journal of European Affairs* 5(1), 5-21.

Baldock, D., J. Dwyer, P. Lowe, J.-E. Petersen & N. Ward (2001) *The Nature of Rural Development: Towards a sustainable integrated rural policy in Europe.* A ten-nation scoping study for WWF and the GB Countryside Agencies, Institute for European Environmental Policy, London.

Chaplin, H., S. Davidova & M. Gorton (2004) Agricultural Adjustment and the Diversification of Farm Households and Corporate Farms in Central Europe. *Journal of Rural Studies* 20(1), 61-77.

Dwyer, J., D. Baldock, G. Beaufoy, H. Bennett, P. Lowe & N. Ward (2003) *Europe's Rural Futures – The Nature of Rural Development II: Rural Development in an Enlarging European Union, revised edition.* Report for WWF and Land Use Policy Group, Institute for European Environmental Policy, London.

European Commission (1997) *The Agricultural Situation in the European Union: 1996 Report.* OOPEC, Luxembourg.

—. (2003a) *Report from the Commission to the European Parliament, the Council, the European Economic and Social Committee and the Committee of the Regions: SAPARD Annual Report – year 2002.* COM(2003)582 final, Brussels, 7.10.2003.

—. (2003b) *Fact Sheet: Rural Development in the European Union*, Office for Official Publications of the European Communities, Luxembourg.

—. (2003c) *Fact Sheet: Overview of the Implementation of Rural Development Policy 2000-2006.* Office for Official Publications of the European Communities, Luxembourg.

—. (2004) *Proposal for a Council Regulation on Support for Rural Development by the European Agricultural Fund for Rural Development (EAFRD).*COM(2004)490 final, {SEC(2004)931}, Brussels, 17.7.2004.

—. (2005) *Agri-environment Measures: Overview on General Principles, Types of Measures, and Application.* Directorate General for Agriculture and Rural Development, Unit G-4 – Evaluation of measures applied to Agriculture, Studies.

European Environment Agency (2004) *Agriculture and the environment in the EU accession countries: Implications of Applying the EU Common Agricultural Policy*. Environmental issue report No. 37, EEA, Copenhagen.

Fischler, F. (2001) *The European and Indian Models of Agriculture: What we Share, Where we Differ*. Speech to the Confederation of Indian Food Trade and Industry, New Delhi, 17 April. Speech/01/168. (This is no longer available on the Europa website).

Garzon, I. (2005) *Multifunctionality of Agriculture in the European Union: Is there Substance behind the Discourse's Smoke?* Center on Institutions and Governance Presentation Paper No. 20, Institute of Governmental Studies, University of California, Berkeley.

Konečný, M. (2004) *EU Enlargement and Agriculture: Risks and Opportunities*. Friends of the Earth Europe, Brussels.

Network of Independent Agricultural Experts in the CEE Candidate Countries (2004) *The Future of Rural Areas in the CEE New Member States*. Institut für Agrarentwicklung in Mittel-und Osteuropa (IAMO), Halle.

OECD (2001) *Multifunctionality: Towards an Analytical Framework*. OECD, Paris.

van der Ploeg, J. D. & D. Roep (2003) Multifunctionality and Rural Development: The Actual Situation in Europe, in *Multifunctional Agriculture: A New Paradigm for European Agriculture and Rural Development*. Ed. b G. van Huylenbroeck & G. Durand. Ashgate, Aldershot, 37-53.

Râmniceanu, I. (2004) *Questioning Rural Development in an Enlarging EU: The Case of Romania*. Working Papers Series No. 9, European Institute of Romania.

Saraceno, E. (2004) *Rural Development Policies and the Second Pillar of the Common Agricultural Policy*. Paper presented to 87th EAAE Seminar, Vienna.

CHAPTER SEVEN

MULTIFUNCTIONAL FARM ACTIVITIES IN THE NEW MEMBER STATES

MAARIT HEINONEN

Introduction

The accession of eight Central and Eastern European countries (CEECs) to the EU on 1 May 2004 has diversified the picture of EU agriculture and rural areas. The farming sector in the new Member States is characterised by the existence of a large number of farms: approximately 4 million farms with 39 million hectares of utilized agricultural land. There are considerable differences in farm size, farm ownership, labour productivity, yield per hectare and distribution of capital between the old and new member states. Such factors challenge EU agricultural policies, and structural policies are also influenced because the restructuring of agriculture has an impact on rural areas in general.

Since the 1980s, EU agricultural policy has supported multifunctionality in agriculture and rural areas (see e.g. Chaplin, Davidova & Gorton 2004; Râmniceanu & Ackrill 2006). It has, for example, provided financial support for activities which aim to diversify income opportunities in rural areas, such as agri-tourism and organic farming. The increased recognition of multifunctionality has resulted in changing expectations of wider society of the role of agriculture in rural development in Europe. Agriculture is now expected not only to provide food and fibre at a reasonable cost, but also to contribute to other functions or goals important to society, such as environmental management, preservation of landscape and biodiversity, food quality and the social viability of rural areas. Partly in response to this, but also as a result of the failure of productivist models in Western Europe to provide increasing numbers of farmers with viable and sustainable livelihoods, a range of new multifunctional farm strategies is emerging. They include strategies aimed at increasing the quality and added value of food products at farm and regional level (such as organic farming, on-farm processing, direct sales, and quality production) and introducing new systems that combine primary production with a range of activities not traditionally associated with agriculture (such as agri-tourism, landscape management, and energy production).

While the use of the concept multifunctionality was initially driven mainly by debates in international policy arenas, especially those concerning the legitimacy of public support to agriculture (WTO, OECD) and the potential role of agriculture in attaining environmentally and economically sustainable development (FAO, EU),[79] the concept has also increasingly received attention from a range of natural and social-science disciplines. Multifunctionality in the agriculture and rural areas of the EU 15 has by now been fairly well documented and researched. However, much less is known about their relevance, the degree to which they are taken up by farm households and rural policies, and their contribution to economically, ecologically, and socially sustainable rural development in the new Member States of Central and Eastern Europe. The CEEC project, a part of the EU-funded research project called MultAgri,[80] has started to fill this gap with the available data from the eight Central and Eastern European countries[81]: Estonia, Latvia, Lithuania, Poland, Czech Republic, Slovakia, Slovenia and Hungary. [82]

---

[79] See Chapter Six (Râmniceanu & Ackrill 2007) for a detailed description of the concept of multifunctionality in Europe. Here we use the same understanding of multifunctionality as found in Chapter Six.

[80] MultAgri was a "Specific Support Action" undertaken within the Sixth Framework Research Programme of the European Commission (Proposal/Contract no. 505297). With a partnership of 26 research organisations from 15 countries the project provided a comprehensive overview of existing research, particularly in Europe, on different aspects of the multifunctionality of agriculture and rural areas. The Aleksanteri Institute (The Finnish Center for Russian and East European Studies) participated from May 2004 to September 2005 in one of the thematic axes of the project: "Multifunctionality of activities, plurality of identities and new institutional arrangements (WP4)". The reports are available at www.multagri.net

[81] The other two new Member States, Cyprus and Malta, were excluded from the CEEC-project, because they don't share the same history as the other new member states and are not located in Central or Eastern Europe.

[82] The participants of the CEEC project: (1) *Estonia*: Anne Põder, Helvi Põder &Tiiu Ohvril (Estonian Agricultural University); (2) *Latvia*: Sandra Šūmane, Ilze Lāce & Anita Kalniņa (Institute of Philosophy and Sociology); (3) *Lithuania*: Arunas Poviliunas, Kristina Rybakova & Jurgita Abromaviciute (Vilnius University); (4) *Poland*: Anna Pluskota-Lewandowska, Jolanta Maciag & Beata Blok (Nicolas Copernicus University); (5) *The Czech Republic*: Michal Lostak, Lukas Zakata & Helena Hudeckova (Czech University of Agriculture in Prague) (6) *Slovakia*: Gejza Blaas, Martina Brodová, Daniela Cimborova & Anna Zemanova (Research Institute of Agricultural and Food Economics); (7) *Hungary*: Gyöngyi Schwarcz & Katalin Rácz (Centre for Regional Studies; Institute of Ethnology); and (8) *Slovenia*: Barbara Leder (Marboro University);

In this paper, the focus will be on analysing multifunctional farm strategies in CEECs based on the findings of the CEEC project (Heinonen & Granberg 2005). Analytically, attention will be paid to the different paths, or ways, of diversifying activities in CEE farm units.

Conceptualising multifunctional farm activities

The Impact project[83] and certain other studies (Van der Ploeg et al. 2000; Van der Ploeg, Long & Banks 2002; Van der Ploeg & Roep 2003; Râmniceanu & Ackrill 2007) have conceptualised multifunctional agriculture within the wider process of rural development which is becoming increasingly multifaceted. Multifunctional activities aim to secure better social, environmental and economic conditions for a more sustainable rural development. Agriculture produces not only food, fibre and timber, but also other benefits or non-commodity outputs valued by society such as preserving landscape and biodiversity. Parallel to the evolution of demand, many farmers have engaged in new (economic) activities not usually associated with conventional agriculture, through new strategies such as diversification. These new strategies are seen to arise from the basic elements of a farm.

Fig. 7-1 illustrates three basic aspects of a farm – (a) the agro-food supply side (or chain); (b) rural area; and (c) the mobilisation and use of resources – and the new directions of farm strategies (Van der Ploeg & Roep 2003). As part of the agro-food supply chain, a farm produces commodities, such as milk and potatoes. The second aspect of a farm is its location in, or relationship with, a rural area. A rural area has two dimensions: the natural environment and local society. Located in a rural area, a farm helps both to maintain and to change the rural landscape. A farm is also part of a local, and regional economy, and culture. The third aspect of a farm concerns the mobilisation and use of farm-related resources. Resources such as labour, knowledge, animals, plant material, capital, land, water, machines and commercial networks are essential for the production of farm commodities.

---

(9) *Coordinating unit*: Maarit Heinonen and Leo Granberg (Aleksanteri Institute, University of Helsinki, Finland).

[83] The Impact project (The socio-economic impact of rural development practices and policies: realities and potentials) was a transnational survey in six European countries (Ireland, the United Kingdom, the Netherlands, Germany, Italy and Spain) of 3,200 professional farmers in 2001. One central task was to obtain information on farmers' experiences of and activities regarding rural development.

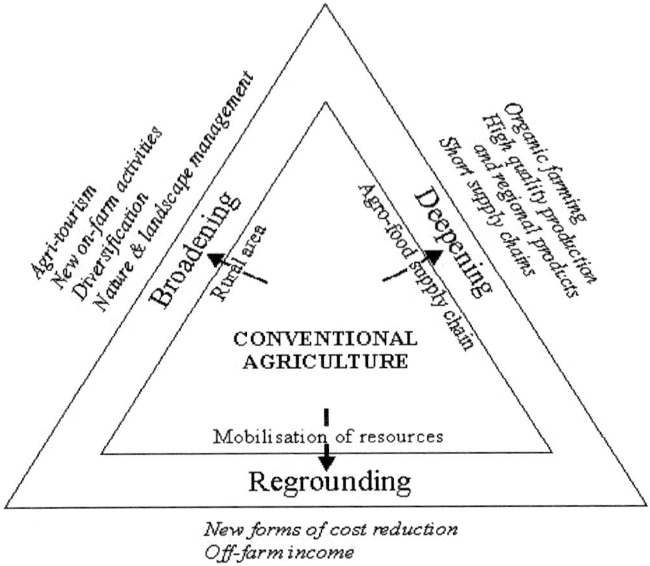

Fig 7-1 Structure of rural development at the farm enterprise level (van der Ploeg & Roep 2003)

Rural development operates at all three aspects or levels of a farm and re-organises farm strategies. Through recent rural development, the agro-food supply side is *deepening*. Deepening refers to the process whereby farm units seek new or revive old activities in order to respond to food chain developments and changing consumer demands. Conventional agricultural activities are transformed and expanded in order to deliver products that provide more value for both farmers and consumers. Typical deepening activities are organic farming; the production of high quality (local and regional) products; and reducing the gap between production and consumption, such as different ways of selling farm produce directly to consumers.

New farm strategies can also be created by reorganising and developing rural areas. Fields and other farm land can be used not only for food or fibre production but also for other activities, namely for recreation. By *broadening* their activities farm units try to response to changing societal demands on rural areas. These broadening activities include agri-tourism; nature conservation and landscape management; the development of on-farm activities such as care farms, school farms, different kinds of contract work; and new forms of agricultural production for non-food use, such as the production of income crops for energy and plants for medical use.

As for the mobilisation and use of resources, a development is termed *re-grounding.* One important type of re-grounding is pluriactivity which refers to the adoption of alternative use and valorisation of internal farm resources. Typically this takes a form of an off-farm income mainly salaried work, but also different social transfers such as pensions) through which a farm is partly maintained.

Taken together, *deepening, broadening* and *re-grounding* activities are conceptualised to reshape a farm into a multifunctional enterprise that delivers a broader range of products and services than a conventional farm. With this theoretical framework, a farm is enlarged into a more complex rural enterprise, which is involved not just in more markets but in different types of markets, such as tourism, services and energy. This will increase overall income and reduce dependency on any one market and will secure the long-term survival of a farm.

This kind of rural development with new multifunctional elements has occurred at farm level in Western Europe. In the CEEC project, the aim was to analyse the present situation in CEECs.

Methodology

The CEEC project for the MultAgri project was conducted as a "desk-study" with co-operation of research teams in the target countries.[84] The aim of the CEEC project was to obtain a general view of the role of multifunctionality in agriculture: what does it mean, and to what extent is it playing a role in agriculture and rural areas. An additional task was to discover whether Central and Eastern Europe is a special case, in that its farm structures differ

---

[84] A research team typically consisted of three members with a senior researcher as team coordinator and PhD students and/or master degree students in the fields of rural sociology or rural economy. In October and November 2004, the teams collected and reviewed state-of-the art of research and government documents, and evaluated various national agricultural and rural statistics concerning multifunctional agriculture. Some interviews with the spokesmen of support systems, agricultural policy, advisory services and farmers' unions were conducted. With the help of discussions at a two-day feedback seminar (held after the data collection)between the representatives of the CEE teams, the coordinator of the work package, the coordinators of the CEEC project and some other researchers in the field of multifunctional agriculture, the CEEC teams finalized their country reports. Each team produced a 40-60-page long country report. The comparative CEEC report (Heinonen & Granberg 2005) was produced on the basis of the country reports, utilizing additional information and discussions of the feedback seminar.

considerably from those in other EU countries. The data consisted of (a) the state-of-the art research and government documents concerning multifunctional agriculture in agricultural policy, support systems, different multifunctional activities at farm level, and role of small- and medium-sized enterprises in supplying multifunctionality in rural areas; and (b) national agricultural statistics.[85] In addition to reviewing documents and statistics, we also created a reference list and listed the main researchers and research teams on the various topics concerned ad an aid to further research in this field[86].

Another task of the CEEC project was to get an overview of multifunctional activities and strategies currently employed on CEE farms. We classified the various (economic) activities currently in use on farms other than those associated with conventional farming in terms of the Impact project[87] by reviewing documents (in total 319 different documents), national agricultural statistics and some other core quantitative sources (e.g. databases from the various ministries of agriculture). In the search for documents, we used multifunctionality, multifunctional agriculture, multiple functions of agriculture and related terms or words as our primary search. We also searched under the

---

[85] We also analyzed to what extent the main agricultural statistics have taken multifunctionality into account especially which multifunctional activities were covered and to what extent (which variables were used).

[86] The reference list consists of 319 references and there are 197 researchers or researcher teams in the researcher list. The lists are available at www.multagri.net →

[87] The farm activities regarded as multifunctional (and their definitions) by the CEEC project:

(1) *Organic agriculture*: Farms registered and certified as organic (or ecological or biological depending on national terminology), including farms in the process of conversion to organic

(2) *Quality production*: Agricultural and food production other than organic where the specification of quality results in price premiums. This may include food products and other products which are registered and certified under public/private labels. On-farm processing of food products (certified or not)

(3) *Direct marketing*: Different forms of directly marketing farm produce to consumers by farmers

(4) *Agri-tourism*: Farmer-operated on-farm accommodation and other leisure services for tourists

(5) *Agricultural production for non-food use*: Various forms of agricultural production those are orientated at non-food use. Also forestry included

(6) *On-farm activities*: Farmer oriented or farm-based activities that are not related to food, agricultural production or tourism

(7) *Nature conservation and environment management*: Paid activities to protecting nature, the environment, and the landscape

(8) *Off-farm activities*: Income from part-time farming, salaried work of the farm manager or spouse off the farm, pensions and other social transfers.

headings of specific multifunctional activities (organic farming, food processing, direct sales, agri-tourism, production for non-food use, different on-farm activities and income from off-farm activities) and under keywords like farm diversification, rural development, sustainable agriculture, part-time farming, and pluriactivity.

Interpretations of multifunctionality in CEECs

The interpretations of multifunctionality in CEECs are summarized in Table 7-1. The concept of multifunctionality is acknowledged in all the target countries but there are some differences between countries in interpretation. Since the accession process to the EU in the late 1990s, the ideas of the multifunctionality of agriculture and rural areas has been incorporated into the relevant government documents in all CEECs with the exception of Poland. Since the early 1990s, there have been academic and political discussions on multifunctionality in rural areas with the development of a Polish concept of "multifunctional villages" which refers to promoting rural entrepreneurship as a central way on solving rural poverty. Polish family farms in particular have a long tradition of pluriactivity, and in that sense multifunctional agriculture is a new term for an old set of farm practices.

Multifunctional agriculture is often cited and generally accepted in recent government documents (during and after accession to the EU) concerning both agricultural and rural policy even if definitions of it vary and alternative concepts are also used. The notion of multifunctionality as such is not very widely used. Academic, political and non-governmental organisations and other actors have employed concepts such as organic farming, agri-tourism, craft work, which can be regarded as multifunctional activities. Several categories instead of multifunctionality are also found, such as supplementary farm activities, non-agricultural production, economic activities, other profit-making activities and alternative agricultural activities. They are used to signify different multifunctional farm activities.

Several (mainly economic and policy) studies concerning certain multifunctional farm activities have been carried out in CEECs. They typically concentrate on a specific activity (especially organic farming and agro-turism) with little, if any, reference to the general or theoretical discussions of multifunctionality. Here once again Poland is an exception with many studies focused on rural entrepreneurship.

Table 7-1 The concept of multifunctional agriculture (MFA) CEECs

Country	Is the concept MFA used explicitly?	When MFA acknowledged / driving forces?	Which MFA functions receive most attention?	Is MFA addressed in research?	Alternative concepts
Estonia	No	EU Accession	Economic Social	Very little	Economic diversification; Sustainable development; Alternative economic activities
Latvia	No	EU Accession	Environmental Economic	Indirectly, not very well	Rural or Sustainable development
Lithuania	Yes	EU Accession	Economic Social	Yes, but ambiguous	Agricultural diversification; Farm restructuring; Alternative activities
Poland	Yes	Early 1990s Employment	Economic Social	Yes	Multifunctional countryside; Employment generation; Entrepreneurship
Czech Republic	Yes	EU Accession	Economic Environmental Social	Yes, but in general level	Landscape maintenance; Sustainability; Non-market functions
Slovakia	Yes	EU Accession	Economic; Social; Environmental	Little, mostly technical	Agricultural diversification; Non-commodity outputs; Regional viability
Hungary	No	EU Accession	Economic; Social; Environmental	Little, fragmented	Eco-social agriculture; Rural development; Territorial balance
Slovenia	Yes	EU Accession	Economic; Social; Environmental	Little, indirectly and fragmented	Rural development; Supplementary activities

Source: Heinonen & Granberg 2005.

Before analysing the main conclusions of the CEEC project concerning multifunctional farm activities, we need to examine briefly what is arguably the most important feature of CEECs' farm structure, namely, the dual farm structure.

Dual farm structure[88]

The most crucial difference in the agriculture of the CEECs compared to that of the EU15 is related to the dual farm structure. On the one hand, CEECs have very large agricultural enterprises owned and operated by a public (state, municipal) or private (limited company, limited partnership etc) economic unit. A large-scale farm of this kind may have hundreds or even thousands of hectares of agricultural land and hundreds of farm animals. On the other hand, there are a huge number of small farms which are more or less part-time oriented, family owned and operated farms with some piece of farmland and woodland and a few farm animals. There are two kinds of small-scale farms. In the first kind, a private farmer (called family farmer, individual farmer or self-employed farmer depending on the country) owns or operates (the leasing of land is common especially in the Czech Republic and Hungary) more than one

[88] The statistical classifications of farm units differ between CEECs and in some cases the farm categories within a country's statistical records are blurred. These discrepancies make comparisons difficult; hence the numbers of farm in different categories presented here are only estimates. Moreover, agricultural reform has affected national agricultural censuses in the form of redefinitions, which makes comparison between CEECs even more complex. For example, the definitions of agricultural units in the Estonian Agricultural Census were changed in 2001. The new definitions are as follows. *An agricultural holding* is a production unit where there is at least one hectare of agricultural land and where agricultural products are produced mainly for sale. Agricultural holdings are divided into (a) operating holdings (holdings where agricultural products are produced), and (b) non-operating holdings (holdings where agricultural products are not produced and where agricultural land is unutilised and where there are no farm animals). *An agricultural household plot* is a production unit where there is less than one hectare of agricultural land, but where there are at least three fruit trees or six berry bushes, or ten rabbits, ten domestic fowls or other farm animals or at least three beehives, and where agricultural products are produced mainly for the owner's own consumption. *A holder of the holding* is a person on whose account and in whose name the holding is operated and who is economically and legally responsible for the holding. Holders are (a) a legal person (public or private economic unit; namely a general partnership, limited partnership, private limited company, public limited company, commercial association or non-profit organisation), and (b) a natural person (*sole proprietor*; namely, a sole holder of a holding which is not a legal person and not linked to any holdings of other holders; or partners who manage their individual holdings as if they were one holding) (Põder & Põder 2005).

hectare of land (or more than five hectares, depending on the country) which is registered in a land cadastre or similar system. Its agricultural products are used mainly for sale. The second kind of farm is called an agricultural household plot or semi-subsistence farm depending on the country. The household plot differs from the private farm in using most of the agricultural produce for its own consumption. Moreover, household plots are not usually listed in the farm register (although in some countries, like Estonia, they are).

CEECs differ considerably when it comes to farm structure, as can be seen in Table 7-2.

The high proportion of land that is cultivated by co-operatives and commercial companies is especially characteristic of Slovakian (89%) and Czech (71%) agriculture. Slovenia, Poland, Lithuania and Latvia represent the opposite end of the spectrum where a high proportion of land is cultivated by family farms; namely, 94%, 85%, 87% and 80% respectively. Estonia and Hungary can be placed in a middle category, but still with the dominance of family farms (they operate approximately 60% of total agricultural land). The proportion of household plots in the total number of farms is high in all these countries, ranging from 39% in Latvia to 94% in Hungary.

The dual farm structure has inevitably created a dual agricultural policy. The European Model of Agriculture, to some extent, both strengthens and obscures this division (see Râmniceanu & Ackrill 2007). Basically, CEE agricultural policy has two main aims. On the one hand, the goal is to increase the competitiveness of agricultural production. This goal supports large-scale farming and large family farms (helping them to get larger) in conventional crop and livestock production with intensive production methods. On the other hand, rural and agricultural policy face the challenge of finding answers to the livelihood (and other) problems of the huge number of small family farms and the even bigger number of tiny household plots which have the status of a farm.

Table 7-2 Farm types, their share of farmland and average farm size in CEECs

	Legal type	Nr of farms	Share of farmland	Average farm size (ha)
Estonia (2001)	State farms	76	1	
	Co-operatives	-		
	Commercial companies	927	37	
	Individual farms/operating farms	67,984	62	
				13
Latvia (2001)	State farms	127	1	
	Co-operatives	-	-	
	Commercial companies	477	9	
	Individual farms/operating farms	37,618	49	
	Household plots/semi-subsistence farms	96,525	39	
				12
Lithuania (2003)	State and municipal farms	80	3	
	Co-operatives	50	1	
	Commercial companies	463	9	
	Individual farms/operating farms	277,970	84	
	Household plots/semi-subsistence farms	331,980	3	
				5
Poland (2002)	State farms	-	-	
	Co-operatives	314	1	
	Commercial companies	550	11	
	Individual farms/operating family farms	1,971,700	83	
	Household plots/semi-subsistence farms	976.900	2	
				8
Czech Republic (2000)	State farms	-	-	
	Co-operatives	746	29	
	Commercial companies	2,281	42	
	Individual farms/operating farms	35,219	26	
	Other (semi-subsistence)	21,739	3	
				68
Slovakia (2001)	State farms	-	-	
	Co-operatives	715	54	
	Commercial companies	721	35	
	Individual farms/operating farms	5,473	10	
	Household plots/semi-subsistence farms	62,213	2	
				31

Table 7-2 Continued

	Legal type	Nr of farms	Share of farmland	Average farm size (ha)
Hungary (2001)	State farms	12		
	Commercial companies*	8,382	60	
	Individual farms/operating farms	924,788	40	
	Household plots/semi-subsistence farms	835,616		
				4
Slovenia (2001)	State farms	-	-	
	Co-operatives	-	-	
	Commercial companies	103	5	
	Individual farms/operating farms	86,324	94	
				6

* Includes some co-operatives.
Sources: CEE Country Reports, author's calculations

In countries where small farm units dominate the farm structure, multifunctional farm activities may offer viable development strategies for farming families by offering opportunities to obtain (extra) income. In countries with a strong large-scale farming system, like the Czech Republic and Slovakia, these diversified activities are important for both large-scale corporate farms and small family operated farm holdings but not necessarily in the same way. The Czech professional union of large-scale farmers and the union of family farmers have different interpretation of multifunctionality. The union of large-scale farmers supports multifunctionality in the sense of diversifying their activities by adopting intensive production methods. They base their argument partly on the fact that large-scale farms had experience of diverse farm activities from the era of the collective farm before the 1990s when many large-scale farms received more than 50% of their income from non-agricultural activities. Their vision is that intensive farming should be concentrated in the most favourable areas (near cities with good soil) and that large-scale farms are the most suitable for this kind of agriculture. Meanwhile in less-favourable areas (such as mountainous areas) farms should be oriented to non-productive functions, such as maintaining the landscape. The latter multifunctional task could be left to small family farms. Whereas large-scale farmers prefer to operate in the productive sector (both agricultural and non-agricultural production), family farmers stress not only production but other values, such as the right to farm, the viability of a village and tradition. The multifunctionality of family farms (small-scale farms) is best understood in a normative interpretation of multifunctionality (see Râmniceanu & Ackrill 2007).

Multifunctional CEE farms

After classifying the income activities of farms using the national agricultural statistics, we can state that a remarkable proportion of CEE farms have one or more multifunctional activities. In practice, small-scale farms depend largely on off-farm income and the smallest ones, ie. all household plots are semi-subsistence farms with off-farm income. Leaving regrounding activities aside, we find that a quite remarkable proportion of CEE farms engage in several deepening and broadening activities.

A typical multifunctional farm concentrates on one multifunctional activity. According to the statistical data of four countries (Table 7-3), 70-90% of multifunctional farms are involved in one multifunctional activity. However, there are a number of farms with many multifunctional activities. Statistics on combining of different multifunctional activities are only indicative, because they do not cover all the activities regarded as multifunctional; the common multifunctional activities, such as the important actitivities, namely, organic farming and off-farm activities (off-farm income, pensions) are not always included in national agricultural statistics conserning the combining of multifunctional activities. There is also a lack of data on the type of multifunctional activities that are interconnected. Hence, if these activities are taken into account, the proportion of the farms with more than one activity will definitely rise. According to many national documents (CEE country reports), organic farmers are especially active in combining multifunctional activities, such as food processing (processing organic raw materials to products on the farm), direct marketing (e.g. selling organic products at a farm shop) and agri-tourism.

Table 7-3 Percentage of farms by number of multifunctional activities (MFA) in some CEECs*

	Farms with	
	1 MFA activity	**2 or more MFA activities**
Slovakia (2001)	79.5	20.5
Latvia (2001)	84.7	15.3
Czech Republic (2000)	72.9	27.1
Poland (2002)	93.2	6.8

* Organic farms and off-farm occupation are not involved.
Source: CEE country reports

Apart from family farms, large-scale corporate farms are also involved in multifunctional activities. In the Czech Republic, the latter are very multifunctional. A single Czech large-scale farm has more multifunctional activities than a multifunctional family farm. Almost two thirds of the private or state operated large-scale farms which have multifunctional activities, have more than one such activity (Lostak & Zakata 2005). These multifunctional large-scale farms seem to be the reason why the Czech Republic has a higher proportion of farms with more than one non-agricultural activity than any other countries (see Table 7-3).

Although the differences of the multifunctional farm activities among CEECs, there are some common characteristics that are shared by all CEECs.

Re-grounding of resource base

According to recent research on agricultural diversification[89] in three Central European (the Czech Republic, Slovakia and Hungary) farms the off-farm activities (occupations, pensions) is a common way to diversify the farm income (Chaplin et al 2004). Also the CEEC project indicated that off-farm activities play a very important role not only in Central European farms but in farms across the whole of CEE. It is the most typical single multifunctional activity, and is especially characteristic of the strategies of farming families.. In addition to off-farm occupations (salaried work), social transfers is a typical source of income. A pension is a common source of income as are other social transfers and unemployment benefits. In practice, all household plots have other sources of income outside the farm. Furthermore, from one half to three-quarters (depending on the country) of family farms currently operating receive off-farm income.

The importance of off-farm income is especially noticeable in Poland where the farm structure is dominated by small-scale farms. In 2002, only 30% of the family farms received their main income from agricultural production whilst for plots the figure was 15%. For as many as 60-65% of family farms (see Table 7-4), the primary income was off-farm income (other occupations, pensions, other social payments). The situation regarding farm incomes in Estonia differs from that in Poland: 87% of operating farms received their income totally or almost totally from the conventional farming in 2001 (Põder & Põder 2005).[90]

---

[89] Chaplin et al. (2004) uses the concept of agricultural diversification for farm income from non-conventional farming activities.

[90] More than 75% of farm income is received from conventional farming.

Table 7-4 Main income sources of private farms in Poland 2002, in percent

Main source of income	Family farms*	Small plots**
Income from agriculture	30	15.2***
Non-agricultural activities on farm	5.6	2.8
Off-farm occupation	23.6	19.7
Pensions	24.9	18.1
Social care payments	3.9	5.6
Mixed (above mentioned)	4.7	
Living from others' income (not agricultural income)		37.9
Other (e.g. renting land and equipment)	7.3	

*Family farms with more than 1 ha agricultural land (1,971,700 farms in 2002).
**Small household plots with less then 1 ha agricultural land (976,900 farms in 2002).
*** Land is the only source of income for 1.7% of plot owners, the main source for 0.2% and an additional source for 12.4%. In total, for 15.2% of plot owners it is a meaningful source of income.
Note: Here used the Polish terminology for small-scale farms.
Sources: Maciąg & Pluskota-Lewandowska 2005; Heinonen & Granberg 2005

While for many Western European family farmers, part-time farming has increasingly represented a new form of wealth – combining the opportunity to live in the countryside, maintain a farm and simultaneously have an off-farm job with all the associated income security and social contacts – it seems for the most part to still be considered an expression of rural poverty in CEECs. The high share of retired farm owners reflects a more general problem, namely, the unfavourable age structure of the farming population in CEECs.

Chaplin et al (2004) argued that there are relatively few ways to diversify in Central Europe except by off-farm activities. However, our study revealed that there is a range of non-agricultural activities, which are rather extent and have an obvious importance for farms as sources of extra income.

Broadening of relations with rural area

In general in the CEECs, broadening activities are more common and multiple than deepening ones. A wide range of on-farm activities constitute the most important category among multifunctional farm activities beside off-farm activities. Various contractual services imparticular (e.g. services with tractor and other machinery to other farmers), together with construction and transport activities were typical for all the CEECs. Various craft activities (e.g. pottery; and modern craft activities) were also important in some countries, especially Estonia, Poland, Slovakia and Slovenia). Various trading activities were rather common in the Czech Republic and Slovakia. Certain forms of production for non-food use were very important especially forestry and wood processing in the Baltic countries. Some new tree planting activities (such as Christmas tree plantations) were also taking place. Moreover, generating and distributing renewable energy provided extra income for some farms.

Many of the broadening activities mentioned have a rather long tradition in the most of the CEECs. Agri-tourism, on the other hand, is a newer form of a broadening activity; it has only developed since the 1990s. The number of tourist farms has been increasing especially since the mid-1990s when several non-governmental organizations were established to promote both agri- and rural tourism. The main service offered by tourist farms is still accommodation. Other services are increasingly being provided in response to increasing number of tourists and resultant demand for holidays in the countryside. For example, Lithuanian tourist farms advertise a range of services designed to appeal to businessmen, fishermen, cyclists, children, walkers, winter sportsmen, and horse-riders (Poviliunas 2005). Typically tourist farms are family operated, but some large-scale corporate farms also provide tourist services. For example, in the Czech Republic there were 18 legal entities (9% of tourist farms) operating in agri-tourism in 2000 (Lostak & Zakata 2005).

Documents reviewed for this study revealed high expectations that tourism would become a significant business sector in rural areas in CEE. Tourism in rural areas is certainly a dynamic and growing sector. The needs and the potential of rural tourism for new rural development have also been acknowledged in recent years at the official level: they are one of the most important branches in national rural development plans. However, to some extent, expectations concerning rural tourism are evidently unrealistic. Rurality as such is not enough to generate tourism. Tourism might be a good option in areas that can offer real attractions (such as a special landscape, architecture and services). In addition, the development of the necessary basic infrastructure and institutions to support tourism is hampered by the lack of capital. Only in certain rural areas with favourable conditions can tourism play an important role in rural livelihoods.

Deepening activities and food supply chains

Compared to many broadening activities, deepening activities are relatively new in CEECs. However, Central European countries (the Czech Republic, Slovakia, Slovenia, and Hungary) have long traditions of quality production and direct selling, at least, in some products, (especially wine).

As with agri-tourism, organic farming is also a new business branch in CEECs, in the late 1980s and early 1990s; thatis, during the beginning of the period of the decollectivisation and privatisation process of agriculture. Hungary is an exception is Hungary as organic farmind started here already in the early 1980s from a strong grassroot movement of eco-activists. Despite organic farming's recent arrival on the scene, it is the single most studied and surveyed multifunctional activity in CEECs. The reason for this is that organic farming is (unlike many other activities) controlled and subsidised.

Table 7-5 Number of organic farms and acreage of organic land* in CEECs, 2003

Country	Nr of farms	Acreage (ha)	% of farmland	Average size (ha)
Estonia**	810	48.000	5.3	59
Latvia	352	24.480	0.9	48
Lithuania	700	23.289	0.7	33
Poland	2.304	49.928	0.3	n.a.
Czech Republic	810	254.995	6.0	315
Slovakia	100	60.000	2.4	667
Hungary	239	113.816	2.0	476
Slovenia	1.451	20.018	2.6	14

* Includes both farms certified as organic farms and farms in transition to organic status.
** In 2004.
Sources: CEE country reports; www.organic-europe.net/country_reports; Heinonen & Granberg 2005

Although the number of organic farms and the acreage of ecologically cultivated land have both increased especially in the recent years,[91] organic farming is still only a small part of the total agricultural sector. The state of organic agriculture differs considerably among CEECs. It is relatively strong and well-established in the Czech Republic, where organically operated land represents around 6% of the all agricultural land, whereas the average in the EU was 3.4% in 2003. However, organic land in the Czech Republic is mainly for permanent grass and for landscape maintenance. In other Central European countries and in Estonia, organic farms account for a notable proportion of the total agricultural land and have done so for several years. Despite having a large number of organic farms (very small units); Poland has a weak organic agricultural sector, as do Latvia and Lithuania (see Table 7-5).

[91] It is obvious that government support has increased farmers' interest in organic farming.

Large-scale corporate organic farms, export-orientatedness, and weak domestic markets characterise the organic sector in CEECs. This is especially true in Slovakia, where corporate farms dominate the organic sector. In 2004, a total of 62 Slovakian organic farms were registered, of which only 14% were operated by family farms (Brodová 2005). In the Czech Republic and Hungary the average size of organic farms is also relatively high because of the many large-scale farms that operate in the organic sector. In Estonia 6% of organic farms were operated by the legal entities, but their share of the total amount of organically cultivated land was as high as 48% in 2001. In Latvia, Lithuania, Slovenia and Poland organic farms are mainly operated by small-scale farms, namely farming households.

Central European countries' organic food sector is highly export-orientated. Early interest in organic agriculture was largely based on the thought of export opportunities to Western Europe. Today, most Hungarian and Slovakian organic products (approx. 95%) are exported to Germany, Austria and the Netherlands. The domestic market for organic products is relatively small in every CEEC. The underdeveloped state of these markets is evident in the fact that most organic produce is sold as conventional (non-organic) produce, without being labelled. There is a twofold problem: the marginal consumer interest (because of the high price of organic products and the lack of information about the organic sector) in organic products and the poor functioning of systems for the processing, packaging and marketing of organic foodstuffs. There is also a lack of a variety of organic products, and supply and demand do not always meet. Furthermore, organic food is still seen more as healthy food (many organic food products are sold at health food shops) rather than the produce that is environmentally friendly. In other words, organic food is still limited to certain well-defined consumer groups and has not become part of the shopping habits of the average consumer.

Although each CEEC handles the processing, handling and packaging of its own farm produce, there is a larger variety of farm processed produce and food processing as a multifunctional activity is more important in Central European countries than in the rest of the CEECs. Meat, milk and wine are the core products of quality food production and processing. Fruit, vegetable and potato processing are also important activities. Furthermore, several farms produce bakery products, and there are also farm-based abattoirs. In Slovakia, wine production and bottling is mainly located in the south which has a very long viticultural tradition. Hungary and Slovenia are also known for their wines. However, in general, the processing of raw material is not very developed compared to many Western European countries, such as France and Italy.

The direct selling of farm products is the least studied multifunctional activity in CEECs, and there was very little statistical data on it. Direct selling takes various forms: from farm shops, farmers' markets and selling at farm gates to direct supplies to local shops, restaurants and schools. Every CEEC has some direct marketing channels, but the volume differs. The amounts range from a bottle of milk sold to a neighbour from a family farm or household plot to direct supplies of milk products to local schools and shops from a large-scale farm. Only Slovakia and Slovenia have nation-wide data on farms with direct sales of farm products. There are some statistics on the direct sales of organic farms at least for the Czech Republic). Direct sales seem to have more importance as an income source in Central European countries than in the other CEECs. Direct selling is the most important multifunctional activity (if we exclude off-farm activities) in Slovakia in terms of the number of farms: 1,808 farms sold their products at their own farm shop or at premises, in 2001 (Brodová 2005). As much as three-quarters of Slovakian farms have diversified their activities (that is, other than conventional and organic agriculture).

Different paths of diversification

Farms in CEECs adopt multifunctionality in different ways. However, farms seem to diversify their economic activities by following two or three main paths.

The first path is essencially a somewhat continuation of the traditional diversification of functions characteristic of state farms in the era of central-planning before the 1990s. During that period, state farms were typically involved in many other activities along with conventional agricultural production. They had, for instance, local shops, restaurants, food processing facilities, slaughterhouses, and engaged in various trading activities. State farms were also engaged in construction and transport activities, and even manufacturing and other industrial concerns. They also supported many other local services, such as cultural facilities and schools. With the transformation of the socialist economies this kind of multifunctionality or multiactivity was greatly reduced because many state farms were privatised which led to the separating land and communal activities in rural areas in general. Now however, many (now mainly company owned) large-scale farms do have diverse activities. Agricultural statistics for the Czech Republic (Lostak & Zakata 2005), for instance, reveal that up to half the large-scale farms owned by enterprises or by the state are involved in at least one activity which can be regarded as multifunctional. Food processing and different on-farm activities, typically services, are common activities on company or publicly owned farms. However, they are not very involved in the field of agri-tourism (See Table 7-6). To what extent the diversified activities of today's large-scale farms are the legacy of the era of centrally planned economies or newly adopted activities (new activities or new ways of organising old activities) is a question still to be answered.

Table 7-6 Number of Czech farms* with activities other than farming**, 2000

	Natural persons* **	**Legal entities******
Food processing	332	206
Agri-tourism	188	18
On-farm activities	3.173	2.399
Product diversification	59	111
Other (not classified) activities	4.436	2.716

* Includes farms whose main activity is farming

** We have classified the activities "other than farming activities" mentioned in the Czech agro-census of 2000 into five groups. *Quality production* includes the processing of meat, fruit, vegetables, potatoes and milk; and the production of beverages, flour, bread, candies, pasta etc. *On-farm activities* include services for farming, construction and building activities, trading activities and transport services. *Product diversification* includes the hunting and breeding of wild animals, the production of a vegetable and animal fat and oils, and the production of animal feed. Organic farming is not included in the category "other than farming activities". Forestry and wood processing were not included in the agro-census.

*** *Natural persons* include the Czech farm categories of unregistered family farm, a natural person not on the business register, a natural person on the business register, a private farmer not on the business register, a private farmer on the business register, a freelancer and a foreign farmer.

*****Legal entities* include the Czech farm categories of public trading company, limited company, joint-stock company, cooperative, state farm, etc.

Sources: Lostak & Zakata 2005; Heinonen & Granberg 2005.

Farming households (family farms and household plots) have followed a different path in diversifying their activities on the farm. As we have learned, CEE family farms and household plots are more or less part-time concerns. One of the main consequences of the agricultural reforms undertaken since the 1990s was the reduction in agricultural incomes, which has drastically affected the livelihood of farming households. For example in Poland, which has a strong family farm structure, the decline in farmers' incomes has in many cases been as much as 60%. Farming households have been forced to look for other sources of income. Most of them have turned to part-time farming with off-farm occupations. The income derived from various social benefits has also increased especially among the smaller farms. In the late 1990s, Polish farms with less than five hectares received almost 40% of their income in the form of social benefits (see Table 7-4). Set against this background, it is not surprising that multifunctional activities have become a core feature of small Polish farms: 73% of all multifunctional farms have less than five hectares (see Table 7-7). Having multifunctional activities is not a new phenomenon for family farms. Agricultural censuses and the documents reviewed in our study show that Polish farmers in particular have diversified their non-agricultural activities, mainly various services, for decades. However, the transition period since the 1990s and the EU accession at the turn of the twenty-first century have seen an increase in the number of farms involved in multifunctional activities. In 1996, a total of 249,000 Polish farms were engaged in non-agricultural activities but by 2002 the number had risen by 46% to 346,400 farms (Maciąg & Pluskota-Lewandowska 2005).

Table 7-7 Multifunctional activities* by farm size in Poland, 2002

Ha	< 1	1-5	5-10	10-15	15-20	20-50	50-	
%	29.8	43.5	14.0	5.5	2.5	3.2	1.5	100

* The Polish agro-cencus uses the concept of multifunctional activities and the activities listed largely correspond to those definitions used in our CEEC project.
Sources: Maciąg & Pluskota-Lewandowska 2005; Heinonen & Granberg 2005.

The third path involves farming households which operate or have the potential to operate in new kinds of multifunctional activities, such as organic farming, agri-tourism and other new on-farm activities (such as care farms). Such farm units need to have sufficient social, educational and economic resources to diversify. One example of the large amount of social and educational human capital required comes from the Czech Republic, where a farmer has started a renewable energy production business, producing bio-gas from corn. He has a PhD degree in molecular chemistry, and is able to find all necessary information to be "on the top of the development" (Lostak & Zakata 2005).

Conclusion

The multifunctionality of agriculture is a relatively new concept in the new EU Member States of Central and Eastern Europe. Nevertheless, since the accession to the EU, the concept of the multifunctionality of agriculture and rural areas has become incorporated into the relevant government documents. The concept of multifunctionality is not widely used. Instead, governments tend to use related concepts, such as alternative economic activities, agricultural diversification and non-agricultural production. The emphasis in national rural development plans and their implementation is on income diversification for farms and rural areas. Other aspects of multifunctionality, such as environmental and social issues, are subordinated to this.

Although the emphasis given to various forms of multifunctional farm activities differs from country to country, there are common characteristics among CEE countries. The central characteristic is the dual farm structure (to some extent even in Poland and Slovenia where agriculture is based on family farms) with large-scale farm units on one side and more or less part-time small family farms and even smaller household plots on the other. Each farm unit adopts multifunctionality in its own way. Farming households typically have off-farm income either from another occupation or pension. Many multifunctional family farms provide services using their own farm equipment and practise forestry. A number of family farms are also involved in organic farming and agri-tourism. Characteristically, large-scale farms are involved in several multifunctional activities at the same time.

Several studies on the alternative economic activities of farms have been carried out in CEECs. They typically concentrate on a specific activity and its characteristics (such as organic farmers and tourist farms) with little reference to the general discussion of multifunctionality. Furthermore, a focus on economic and to some extent political issues dominates these studies. Theoretical and more general studies are rarer. Although basic national statistics on many multifunctional farm activities exist in every target country, they are rather narrow and lack detail. Since the early 1990s, the multifunctionality of rural areas as a topic has features in Polish academic and political discource. The focus of the multifunctionality of villages is on entrepreneurship as a central way to solve the poverty of rural and peasant populations.

To understand the different contexts of multifunctional agriculture and rural development various CEE countries and to be able to make comparison with the EU15, it is necessary to use broad disciplinary approaches and methods to study rural societies in general and the complex inter-relationship between social, cultural, economic and geographical factors. Generally speaking, it would be more fruitful to make comparions between some, rather than all, CEECs, because each country is different and has issues specific to it even though there share some crucial common characteristics. In addition to empirical studies on different multifunctional activities, there is a need for a more general approach, or inquiry, in to how multifunctionality is working at the policy level (especially local ways of governance) and among different professional bodies.

One of the most important research tasks is to better define and operationalise the concept of the multifunctional farm in the CEE context. Obviously the presence of a multifunctional activity does not necessarily mean that a farm acts in a multifunctional way. What elements make diversified activities on farms multifunctional? The necessity for additional income is, however, an obvious factor in the adoption of multifunctional activities. There is a need for a more detailed analysis of the driving forces behind multifunctionality using a more socio-cultural approache alongside the currently dominant economic viewpoint. The different social, economic and cultural (the "spirit"of entrepreneurship) resources of farmers and rural populations are crucial in diversifying farm activities. Moreover, the farmer identity has changed since the collapse of communism and certainly this certainly is reflected in farm strategies.

A dual farm structure implicates to the different strategies to diversity on. Large-scale farms, family farms and household plots diversify differently. It will be especially interesting to study the multifunctionality of large-scale farms. Are their activities just the legacy o the era of the central plan or something new? To what extent do privately owned large-scale farms take responsibility for local development in times of recession? Do they continue on farming and providing other activities that are important to villages? Futhermore, differences in the understanding multifunctionality between farm units (large-scale farmers vs. farming households) and their repective interest groups (such as farmers' unions), and the implications of these for agricultural policy and support systems would be another fruitful topic of research. Land tenure also has effects on multifunctionality. What kind of influences do the leasing of agricultural land and foreign investments have on multifunctionality in rural areas? Another important topic is the functioning of local governance in connection with farmers, non-governmental organisations and other local actors, because it has a key role in the framing of multifunctionality and rural development in general (see Macken Walsh 2007).

Although the accession process to the EU with its publicly funded measures and programmes (esp. for organic farming and agri-environmental measures) has definitely encouraged farms to take up multifunctional activities, some of these , activities have longer traditions (e.g. off-farm occupations, wine processing and many on-farm activities). We may conclude that multifunctionality in agriculture and rural areas does indeed have many roots in long-established practice and is not merely a political concept. This is the case not only in the EU15 but also in the CEECs.

References

CEE country reports:

Brodová, M. (2005) *Country Report of Slovakia.* CEEc project. Multifunctionality of activities plurality of identities and new institutional arrangements. Unpublished report. 39 p.

Leder, B (2005) *Country Report of Slovenia*. CEE-research. Multifunctionality of activities plurality of identities and new institutional arrangements. Unpublished report. 62 p.

Lostak, M. & L. Zakata (2005) *Country Report of the Czech Republic*. CEEC project. Multifunctionality of activities plurality of identities and new institutional arrangements. Unpublished report. 44 p.

Maciąg, J. & A. Pluskota-Lewandowska (2005) *Country Report of Poland*. CEEC project. Multifunctionality of activities plurality of identities and new institutional arrangements. Unpublished report. 65 p.

Poviliunas, A (2005) Country Report of Lithuania. CEEC project. Multifunctionality of activities plurality of identities and new institutional arrangements. Unpublished report. 44 p.

Põder, A. & H. Põder (2005) Country Report of Estonia. CEEC project. Multifunctionality of activities plurality of identities and new institutional arrangements. Unpublished report. 59 p.

Schwarcz, G. & K. Rácz (2005) Country Report of Hungary. CEEC project. Multifunctionality of activities plurality of identities and new institutional arrangements. Unpublished report. 49 p.

Šūmane, S., I. Lāce, A. Kalniņa (2005) Country Report of Latvia. CEEC project. Multifunctionality of activities plurality of identities and new institutional arrangements. Unpublished report. 59 p.

Other references:

Chaplin, H., S. Davidova & M. Gorton (2004) Agricultural adjustment and the diversification of farm households and corporate farms in Central Europe. *Journal of Rural Studies*, 20, 61-77.

Heinonen, M. & L. Granberg (2005) Regional Report for Central & Eastern European Countries. WP4: Multifunctionality of activities, plurality of identities and new institutional arrangements. MultAgri Project. D4.2. www.multagri.net/section/deliverable/index.php?section=5

Macken Walsh, A. (2007) Community Action in Post-socialist Lithuania: a Comparative Case-study of Two Rural Villages. In *Reflecting Transformation in Post-socialist Rural Areas*, ed. by M. Heinonen et al., Cambridge Scholars Publishing, Newcastle, 185-214.

Râmniceanu, I & R. Ackrill (2007) The European Model of Agriculture and Rural Development Policy Choices in the New Member States. In *Reflecting Transformation in Post-socialist Rural Areas*, ed. by M. Heinonen et al. Cambridge Scholars Publishing, Newcastle, 115-36.

van der Ploeg, J.D., A. Long & J. Banks (eds.) (2002) *Living Countrysides. Rural Development Processes in Europe: The State of the Art.* Elsevier. Doetinchem, The Netherlands.

van der Ploeg, J.D., H. Renting, G. Brunori, K. Knickel, J. Mannion, T. Marsden, K. de Roest, E. Sevilla-Guzmán & F. Ventura (2000) Rural Development: From Practices and Policies towards Theory. *Sociologia Ruralis* 40 (4), 391-408.

van der Ploeg, J.D. & D. Roep (2003) Multifunctionality and rural development: The actual situation in Europe, in *Multifunctional Agriculture: A New Paradigm for European Agriculture and Rural Development* ed. by G. Van Huylenbroeck & G. Durand. Ashgate, Hampshire, England, 37-53.

PART II

TRANSFORMATION OF RURAL COMMUNITIES

CHAPTER EIGHT

LITHUANIAN LOCAL COMMUNITY MOVEMENT AS A RESISTANCE TO RURAL EXCLUSION

ARUNAS POVILIUNAS

Introduction

Among EU members Lithuania belongs to a group of countries with a comparatively large rural population. In 2005 out of a total population of 3.43 million about 33.4% lived in rural areas. There are 21.5 thousand villages in Lithuania. The majority of them (66.7%) are small settlements with 50 residents or less (Statistikos Departamentas 2002, 56). Over the past three years, more than one thousand local community centres have been established in rural areas, and over the last two years 33 Local Action Groups (LAG), within the framework of the LEADER+[92] programme have begun to function. By the beginning of 2006, 27 LAGs had presented their strategies for local development. The realization of the LEADER+ programme has encouraged national and local governments to put rural and local development issues onto the agenda. Fig. 8-1 reveals the fast growth in the number of rural community organizations. These organizations are initiated by local people in order to deal with social, cultural, political and economic problems in rural areas.

Research into rural community centres has revealed that the leaders of rural communities treat this growth as a form of resistance on the part of the rural population to the processes of rural exclusion (ALF 2005). This article aims to examine Lithuania's rural community centres and attempts to describe their key features.

[92] The EU programmes LEADER, LEADER II and LEADER+ stand for **L**iason **E**ntre **A**ctions pour le **D**éveloppement de L'**E**conomie **R**urale (links between actions for the development of the rural economy) and were designed to help rural actors develop the long-term potential of their local area by implementing integrated, high-quality, original strategies for sustainable development. LEADER+ has a strong focus on partnership and networks for exchanging experiences.

Fig. 8-1 Increase in rural community centres in Lithuania

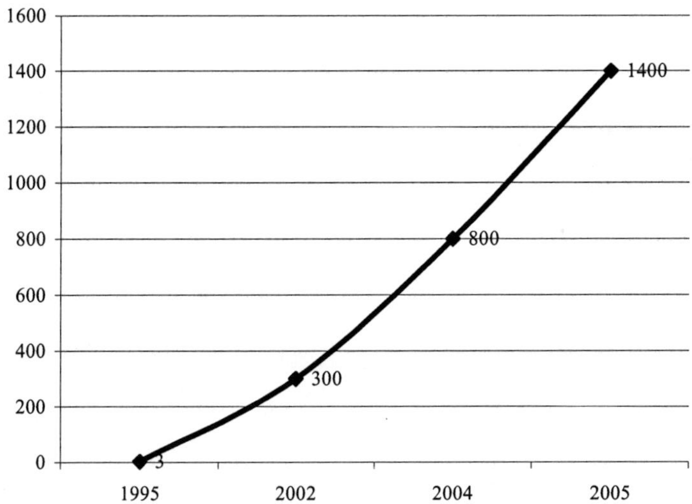

Source: ALF 2005, 6 and The State Enterprise Centre of Registers (http://www.registrucentras.lt/jar)

These aims include several tasks: (a) a discussion of the concept of rural exclusion; (b) the elaboration of a toolkit for an analysis of rural exclusion; (c) an investigation into the different aspects of rural exclusion; (d) an analysis of cases of social innovations.

The article is partly based on the personal experience of the author with rural development processes on different levels. The starting point was a four-year period of participatory action research collaborating with local communities at the grassroots level. Since rural communities are an integral part of the county administration, the recognition and acceptance of local community initiatives by the municipal administration creates favourable conditions for local initiatives. Therefore, the next step was close cooperation at the municipal level with one LAG that is a social partnership of different stakeholders interested in local development. These experiences are reflected in the analysis of concrete cases of social innovations.

Retarding the Lithuanian countryside

The economy of Lithuania is improving. The high rates of economic development recorded from 2001 to 2004 point to an improvement in the economic situation of the country. Lithuania's GDP grew at a rate of 6.4% in 2001, and 6.8% in 2002. In 2003, GDP growth accelerated to 10.5% (Kazlauskas & Misiunas 2005, 4). Despite some decline in GDP in 2004 and 2005 compared with the growth rate recorded in 2003, other indicators (i.e. average monthly gross earnings, the unemployment rate) testify to Lithuania's success in maintaining macroeconomic stability and pursuing structural reforms.

The structural reforms have stimulated a rapid growth in labour productivity. Labour productivity in the economy grew by 22% in 2000 as compared to 2003 and by 4.9% in 2004 as compared to 2003. The fastest growth of productivity and added value was observed in the production and consumption sectors. Productivity growth rates were higher in industry, construction, and productive services than in the economy as a whole. The growth in productivity in the past three years exceeded the growth in wages thus enabling the economy to maintain competitiveness in conditions which saw an appreciation of the nominal LTL exchange rate: during 2001-2003 wages grew by 11.5%, and labour productivity grew by over 20% (Ibid, 6). Lithuania has, in recent years, witnessed a fall in unemployment. The average annual level of unemployment fell from 13.8% in 2002 to 7.2% in 2005 (Statistikos departamentas 2006). A particularly high rise in employment was recorded in the construction sector.

Social statistics record small but positive changes in the field of social provision which facilitates access to resources, rights, goods, and services for all. The increasing amount of per capita social transfers demonstrates the influence of economic growth as well as changes in social policy. The increases in 2005 of social transfers for the elderly by 8.5%, for the family and children by 18.6% as compared to 2004 indicates the success of social policy measures; the decline of social transfers to the unemployed indicates the growth of the economy and an increase in the emigration of the labour force.

Some national experts have claimed that social policy reforms have not succeeded in profiting from the high rate of economic development but have lagged behind it (Lazutka 2006, Gylys 2006). But the electorate only partly "shares" this evaluation of the experts. The political leaders responsible for social policy reforms are popular and have high ratings in public opinion polls. This means that the politicians have been successful in their public relations campaigns in presenting the changes in social policy as significant or at least satisfactory. For example, according to public opinion polls, the Minister of Social Security and Labour was for a long time one of the most popular politicians.

But these positive trends in the economy are linked mainly with the urban sector. Official statistics do not present such a rosy picture when it comes to rural issues. On the contrary, official statistics reveal no sign of, let alone a trend in, improvement in the rural sector. Rurality was treated as a metaphor for poverty.

Rural statistics highlight the issues of poverty. For example, statistics for the relative poverty rate[93] demonstrate that the rural population is living in less favourable conditions than the urban population. In 2005, on the average the rural population suffered from poverty almost two times more than the inhabitants of the Lithuanian towns and almost four times more as the inhabitants of the five largest cities (Fig. 8-2).

Fig. 8-2 Relative poverty level by place of residence in Lithuania, in procent

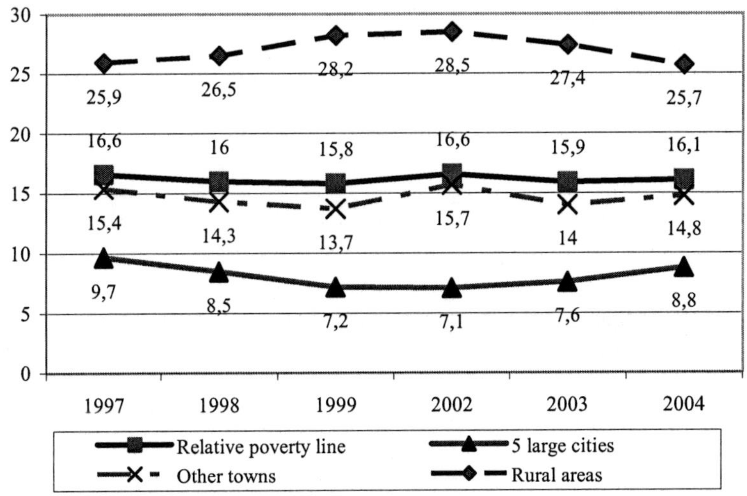

Source: Katsiaouni et al. 2000, 71; Statistikos departamentas 2005

The core group of the rural poor are farmers, particularly small scale farmers and one third of farmers are living below the relative poverty line (Fig. 8-3).

[93] The relative poverty rate is the proportion of people whose consumption expenditure falls below the relative poverty line. The relative poverty line, estimated as 50% of average consumption expenditure, is used for analysing the degree of poverty and for planning social and economic policy.

Fig. 8-3 Relative poverty level by socio-economic group in Lithuania, in procent

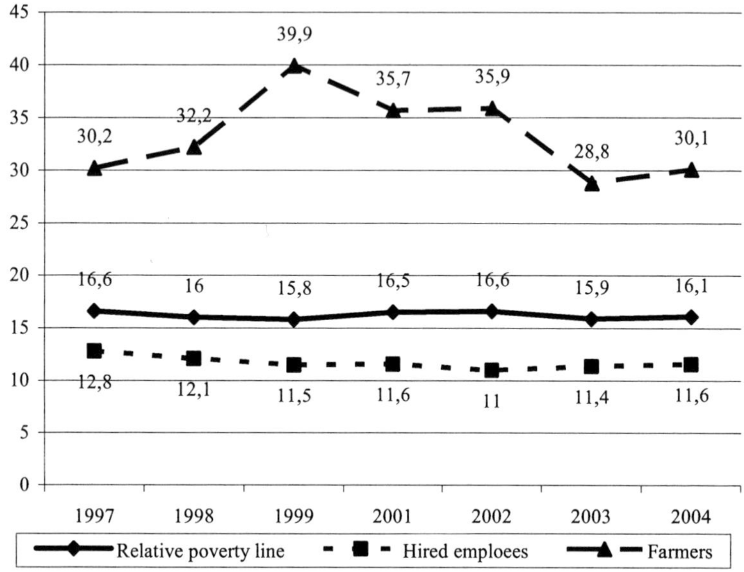

Source: Katsiaouni et al. 2000, 71; Statistikos departamentas 2005

In March 2005 there were more than 320,000 registered farmers with an average farm size of 8.84 ha. Seventy-eight percent of farms had less than 10 ha. Most of the farms were registered as family farms, which were the key-stone of the agricultural reform after Lithuania's declaration of independence in 1991.

At the beginning of 2004, there were 190,992 working family farms in Lithuania. However, during 2004 the number of family farms declined by 18%. The shrinking number of family farms is associated with the declining role of family farms in gross agricultural production. If agricultural companies and enterprises are gaining noticeable momentum, family farms are loosing it.

Summarizing this snapshot of the general situation of the economy with the accent on issues of rurality, the following conclusions may be drawn. The growth of the economy is recording comparatively high rates but it is mostly linked with the urban sector. One third of farmers live below the relative poverty line. The public discourse warns that small family farms, which were the corner stone of the Lithuanian agricultural reform in the 1990s enforced by the World Bank (Alanen 2004, 51), have no future.

Political discourse concentrates on the prospects for, and problems of, agriculture and "has forgotten" the rest of the rural population that does not participate and is not likely to participate in competitive agricultural production. The final accent of this snapshot could be as follows: the inner logic of data presentation in official statistics does not reflect the rural situation as it is, but the stance and configuration of power that is producing the dominant official discourse on rurality.

Interpretation of rural exclusion

For the deconstruction of the dominating discourse on rurality that are shaping public policy measures, a conceptual approach, a relevant methodology and a toolkit are needed. An analysis of the data presented in Table 8-2 is a good starting point for a discussion of the theoretical approach and methodology to be chosen for this research.

In table 8-2, one's attention is attracted by the change that has taken place between 2003 and 2004 in the numbers receiving social assistance in two of the groups listed; namely, the group of children from families at risk and the group of persons and families at risk. These groups, unlike the other four (the groups with disabilities and the elderly), lack tangible and measurable indicators. The label "families at risk" originated as an attempt to destigmatize the previous label "asocial families". The Department of Statistics (Statistikos departamentas 2002) used the following definition of an "asocial family" and subsequently of "families at risk":

> Asocial families (or "families at risk") are families that are registered by the municipal agencies for the protection of children's rights for excessive drinking, drug or other toxic material abuse, immoral behaviour, a lifestyle that is unacceptable to society, the bad care of their children, the neglect of their children's health, and for being deemed unable to guarantee the harmonious and well-rounded development of their children.

All these qualitative and fuzzy indicators of "asocial behaviour" were transferred from the definition of an "asocial family" to the definition of "families at risk" and depend on the value judgements and social interaction between potential clients of the social protection system and personnel of social protection agencies of social control institutions.

In rural areas the number of children from families at risk receiving social assistance at home is increasing (in 2004 it increased by 57.1% as compared to 2003), whilst in urban areas, on the contrary, the number is falling (in 2004 it fell by 58.3% as compared to 2003) (Table 8-1). Do these changes or "facts" reflect objective processes of further "rural decline" or are they indicators of a shift in the practice of social control institutions, in this case, the social care services? What is the logic of the praxis of social control institutions and how can it be revealed and understood?

Table 8-1 People receiving social assistance at home in Lithuania, in absolute numbers

	In urban areas			In rural areas		
	2003	**2004**	**Change (%)**	**2003**	**2004**	**Change (%)**
People who receive social assistance at home (in total)	5,509	5,522	+0.2	3,461	4,081	+17.9
The elderly	1,832	2,004	+9.4	1,611	1,638	+1.2
Disabled elderly	2,520	2,647	+5.0	916	1,102	+20.3
Disabled of working age	432	369	-14.6	111	177	+59.5
Disabled children	69	77	+11.6	28	32	+14.3
Children from families at risk	336	140	-58.3	385	605	+57.1
People and families at risk (excessive drinking, drug abuse, etc.)	262	221	-15.6	403	510	+26.6
0ther	58	64	+10.3	7	17	+142.9

Source: Socialines apsaugos ir … 2006.

A discussion of the concept of rural exclusion

If social exclusion is understood as the exclusion of less integrated social groups from participation in the mainstream of societal development at least two different concepts of social exclusion are possible.

The structural or positivist approach delineates the norms and values of society that are treated as objectively given, focuses on the characteristics of excluded social groups and analyses conditions that provoke behaviour which does not conform to those norms of society accepted by the majority. This approach is based on psychological and sociological forms of determinism and treats a social agency as the function of various so-called objective structures. The major questions raised by the structural or positivist approach towards exclusion as objectively given are as follows: (a) what social, economic, political, legal, and cultural conditions are most likely to exclude some social groups from the mainstream of societal development? (b) What are the characteristics of excluded social groups? (c) How can social exclusion best be minimized? (Rubington &Weinberg 1987, 3)

The interactive approach focuses on the definitions and actions both of the socially excluded groups themselves and of the groups who label and treat them as socially excluded, and the interaction between the two. The major questions raised by the interactive concept of social exclusion are as follows: (a) what are the reactions of social groups labelled as socially excluded? (b) How do these labels influence the social relations? (c) How do the self-perception and identity of labelled groups change? (Ibid, 4)

The elaboration of a toolkit for the analysis of rural exclusion

Representatives of the constructivist approach on social exclusion are more inclined to stress activities that are directed towards the empowering of the disadvantaged. The improvement of social interaction in public policy processes is associated with, for example, destigmatization campaigns, social advertising, and neighbourhood campaigns.

Insofar as public policy is a process of social construction, public policy analysis could include discourse analysis. Discourse analysis can reveal power configurations and the ways in which opinions, beliefs, language, values and other tools of social construction are deployed to orchestrate societal change and provide interpretations of social exclusion and inclusion policies. What are the political and ideological priorities in the area of social inclusion? What kinds of interpretations of social exclusion/inclusion prevail in approaching rural life? How is the societal fabric of social exclusion/inclusion understood and how is it interpreted? What is the interpretation of the relation between policy and outcomes? These and similar questions could be answered using the method of discourse analysis, that is, the critical evaluation of social "texts" or narratives in order to reveal their concealed constraints and contradictions.

A good analytical tool for the analysis of discourses informing policies aimed at tackling social exclusion/inclusion issues was elaborated by Ruth Levitas (1998). She has distinguished three discourses that in different modes construct interpretations of social exclusion/inclusion.

The Moral Underclass Discourse (MUD) "presents the underclass or socially excluded as culturally distinct from the 'mainstream" (Ibid, 21). It merges the concept of social exclusion with that of the "underclass". The term "underclass" refers to a group at the bottom of the socio-economic structure, but one that has also developed its own lifestyle, which in effect separates it from the rest of the population. MUD stresses an economic dependence on welfare benefits which in turn result from and create a wider deviant culture. The moral underclass discourse is rooted in neo-conservatism. This form of discourse invariably highlights the pathology of the poor, the creation of "pathological communities" and a culture of "dependency". The policy implications are "not the extension of citizenship rights, but their greater conditionality, reduction, or removal" (Ibid, 18).

The Social Integrationist Discourse (SID) emphasizes on the significance of paid work and employment for social inclusion. It narrows social exclusion/inclusion to participation in paid work and emphasizes the way in which paid employment fosters both social bonds and social responsibilities. "Social integrationist discourse ignores inequalities between those in paid employment as well as the significance of non-paid work, such as child-care, usually by women, for social inclusion" (Watt 2000, 16). SID represents European influences and social exclusion is understood as the "break down of the structural, cultural and moral ties, which bind the individual to society" (Levitas 1998, 21).

The Redistributionist Discourse (RED) identifies relative poverty and discrimination as the main sources of exclusion from the full rights of citizenship in civil, political and social spheres. Certain groups of people lack the material resources necessary to participate in activities which are the norm for most members of society, or are denied full citizenship rights. Social exclusion is viewed as a dynamic process which arises out of inequalities along the lines of ethnicity, gender and social class. The RED on social exclusion is embedded in the social democratic tradition.

"RED, SID and MUD differ in what the excluded are seen as lacking. In RED they have no money, in SID they have no work, and in MUD they have no morals." (Ibid. 7)

Stephen Pavis, Gill Hubbard and Stephen Platt claim that within SID the emphasis is upon the achievement of consensus, engaging all members of society in civic participation and the avoidance of social disharmony. The redistributive discourse highlights power relationships, structural disadvantage and the limited resources available to certain groups. The dependency/underclass discourse warns of the possibility of the transmission of a deviant culture and values from the underclass to mainstream society (Pavis et al. 2001).

The toolkit chosen for the analysis of rural social exclusion is a combination of the constructivist conceptual approach with elements of discourse analysis. This combination is relevant for the conceptualization of rural social exclusion issues and for attempting to understand the rise of the rural community movement. Whilst adopting the constructivist approach one needs to be aware of certain limitations. The means of constructing reality or mental constructs (e.g. treatments, myths, stigmas, labels, narratives) are dependent on power configurations that are embedded in institutionalized narratives.

The investigation of the different aspects of rural exclusion

An analysis of public policy discourse reveals that the agricultural development policy does not treat rural development policy as a separate issue and that strategic priorities are linked to the development of agriculture (Poviliunas 2003, 9). Rural communities were not considered as social and political agents capable of participating in rural development. This "political" exclusion of rural communities leads to a decline in investment in the rural social infrastructure (e.g. schools, medical service and cultural institutions) and supports a long term increase of social transfers (Ibid. 13).

Living in rural areas is closely connected to land cultivation. However, the petty production currently prevalent in Lithuania has the character of self-subsistent farming, that is, production for one's own needs. Farmers are the most impoverished group in Lithuania. While petty production dominates the country's agriculture, it is considered marginal and written off by national policy makers. When agricultural policies are discussed, issues such as structural funds, production quotas, EU requirements, the size of the commercially viable farms and new technologies are raised. However, these issues are at best marginal to the interests and concerns of an overwhelming majority of the country's "farmers", as officially defined (Poviliunas 2003, 10).

"The impact of these negative attitudes is directly expressed in the lack of applications submitted by the rural population to the EU for projects directed at rural social infrastructure improvements" (Ibid. 11). Even when funds are available, there is relatively little interest among the rural population in developing proposals to acquire badly needed funding. In other words, if you are not a farmer satisfying EU standards or do not own a successful rural tourism business, there is no future for you in rural areas.

In a situation where, in political discourse, agricultural development is substituted for rural development, where the most important criterion of the success of rural policies is the growth in the percentage of commercially viable farmers, and where such farming is considered the only viable future for rural life, the majority of the village and township population see their lives as lacking any prospects or future.

Unless agricultural development and rural population are differentiated, EU structural funds for the development of agriculture will only increase rural marginalization. When the mass media is advertising successful EU projects as the most important form of rural development, the majority of the rural population is forced to believe that they cannot be full fledged participants of rural development (Ibid. 2003, 14).

Instead of increasing financial, social and cultural investments in rural areas, rural productivist policies construct and facilitate even more pronounced rural marginalization in the country and the devolution of rural areas to the realm of social welfare. For example, from 1996 to 2004 welfare payments to the rural population increased by 30%. In comparison, in the largest cities, there was a slight decline in the relative weight of welfare payments in overall income of urban population.

When welfare accounts for such a large proportion of rural income, this encourages the rural population not to look for employment, but to look for ways to qualify for welfare. This demoralizes both the employed and the unemployed rural population. It does not make much sense to work when doing so provides only a minimally higher income than welfare payments. In turn, receiving wages reduces one's entitlement to social welfare.

Thus, the rural population is increasingly becoming a 'burden' for more enterprising social groups and an object of paternalistic care. In turn, patronage coordinated and carried out by various state agencies stigmatizes the rural population. Social policy is transformed into social patronage, which in turn contributes to the formation and reproduction of a subculture of dependency.

Therefore, the 'rural underclass' is not only an objective social fact, but is also a social construct of the MUD, which constructs rurality as a subordinated object, dependent on paternalistic policies directed at various forms of social care. Such policies not only help the disadvantaged, but also construct them as objects of social care, as the alter ego of those providing social welfare and support.

When rural policies become subsumed under agricultural policies, then aspects of life that are not considered important from the point of view of commercially viable and competitive agriculture loose value, become insignificant and are marginalized. The political marginalization of the countryside is one of the most significant obstacles to rural development. The way to overcome this is to separate agricultural and rural development.

When rural development is substituted for agricultural development, then, from the point of view of the Ministry of Agriculture, rural communities as socio-cultural entities cease to exist. Instead of rural communities, the institutions of social control subdivide the rural population into potential agricultural producers, and the rest which, from the point of view of commercial agriculture, are a burden. Since the non-agricultural rural population does not have "productivist" value from the viewpoint of agricultural production, it is designated as the recipient of social welfare and the subject of the corresponding state agencies which administer and supervise welfare provisions to the rural poor. Welfare payments are not only a monetary provision to the needy, but also symbolic acts that signify relationships of dominance, subordination and social control.

The differences between agricultural and rural development are presented in Table 8-2.

Table 8-2 Dimensions of agricultural and rural development

Dimensions \ Cases	**Agricultural development**	**Rural development**
Approach	Market economy	Social economy
Operating agent	Farmers, entrepreneurs, agricultural corporations	Rural communities, community groups, social partnerships, LAGs
Goals	Competitive and profitable agriculture	Reduction of social exclusion and poverty or promotion of social inclusion and local empowerment in rural areas
Prevailing types of capital	Financial capital	Social capital
Basis for receiving investments	Business plan	Strategic plans for the development of rural communities
Means	Effective investments	Social initiatives and innovations (formation of partnership groups, social entrepreneurship, local community participation)
Supporters	Banks, business partners	Charity organizations, national and foreign donor groups, LEADER+

The differences between a market economy and a social economy can be seen in the given dimensions and in terms of the following questions: who is the main operator, what are the main goals, what type of capital prevails, what is the basis for receiving support, what are the means to achieve the goal, and who are the supporters and partners? The differences in these dimensions clearly demonstrate that if agricultural development is largely seen in terms of production and market oriented enterprises, rural development is mainly a social affair, a matter for the social economy[94].

[94] "The social economy entities are, by nature, parts of a stakeholder economy, whose enterprises are created by and for those with common needs, and accountable to those they are meant to serve. Their primary purpose is not to obtain a return on capital. They are generally managed in accordance with the principle of "one member, one vote". They are flexible and innovative – Social Economy enterprises are being created to meet changing social and economic circumstances. Most are based on voluntary participation,

Social innovations as public policy tools for rural social inclusion

The social economy approach starts as a means of satisfying the needs of members and users which have been ignored or inadequately fulfilled by the market or the state and gives these people an opportunity to organise their production and consumption patterns through independent, democratic forms of expression. A social economy is closely linked with social innovations that ought to replace the practices of social policy that are reproducing social exclusion. “The term ‘social innovation’ is used to denote the development and application of new or improved activities, initiatives, services, processes, or products designed to address social and economic challenges faced by individuals and communities” (Goldenberg 2004, iv).

In the last part of this article I will discuss two cases where different methodologies of social inclusion have been applied (participatory action research and social partnership approach).

Participatory action research: The case of Balninkai Community

Balninkai village (population 469) is located in Moletai County, in Eastern Lithuania. Moletai County is a quite typical poor rural county, with a per capita GDP that is about 20% below the national average. In 2001 the county’s population was 25,248; of these 71% lived in villages, and the unemployment rate was 12%. Dairy farming was the most significant economic activity. Poor soil quality restricts other forms of farming. The farms in Moletai tend to be small by national standards: on average 13.2 hectares per farm compared to a national average of 17.2 hectares (Juska et al. 2005).

The method of participatory action research was applied in the project that has started *Part II: Transformation of Rural Communities* in Balninkai village in 1999. It was the mayor of Moletai County who proposed including Balninkai village in the project. The project, which aimed at the elaboration and realization of a local community development model, includes six different communities. A strong leader and a well-liked catholic priest guaranteed a good start for the activities of the PAR project in Balninkai.

PAR attempts to create an interaction between practice and theoretical research. In order to reveal the potential of sociology as a methodology of social innovation and social inclusion, local community analysis from the very

---

membership and commitment.” (European Commission, Enterprise and Industry Directorate-General).

beginning strives to include the interests and experience of the people in all its research and theorizing activities. Cooperation, participation, and reflection create favourable conditions for societal change. Inclusion is at the same time empowerment, and PAR procedures provide an opportunity to realize both.

The active representatives of the community of Balninkai village who later established the Balninkai Community Centre from the very beginning actively cooperated with the sociologists. In the case of Balninkai, as in the majority of cases of rural development, activity was initiated and led by a group of local activists. Usually these groups include between 5 and 15 representatives of local elites (ALF 2005).

The cooperation between the community members of Balninkai village and the sociologists reveals that it is possible to participate in the process of community development and simultaneously to analyse it. The aim of the analysis was twofold: to assist the local action group in the process of initiating societal change and to analyse the procedure of social innovation.

In the first stage of the initiation process, generative themes in a Freirerian sense were used (Juska et al. 2006, 15-17). Generative themes or concepts are codifications of complex experiences and are able to generate considerable discussion and analysis. A codification is a concrete representation of day-to-day situations. In Freirerian methodology, it could be a photograph, a drawing, or even a word. As a representation, a photograph or word is an abstraction, or metaphor, which permits a dialogue that leads to an analysis of the concrete reality represented (Freire 2000).

In the first meetings with the community activists, the concepts of poverty, social exclusion, rural exclusion, "asocial family", local community, and rural development were used as generative words. At the following meetings, the local action group discussed social demographic indicators, the designing of a questionnaire, and interpreted the results of the survey. Representatives of Balninkai community during these intensive discussions began to analyse critically the relationship between the public discourse and their day-to-day experiences. Using Freirerian terminology, this process could be defined as decodification, that is, an analysis which takes place through dialogue, which reveals previously unperceived meanings of the power relations represented by that codification. Decodification is the principal work of a local action group in rural development. The aim of these introductory meetings was to engage, activate and empower representatives of the local community. These discussions not only generated conceptual changes in the interpretation of rurality, but were also a place for accumulating power and strength to initiate changes.

In the five years since its creation, the Balninkai Community Centre has become one of the most important institutions in the village significantly enhancing the social and cultural life of its population. The Centre was awarded more than twenty grants totalling about LTL 140,000 (about € 45,000). These funds enabled the Centre not only to offer different educational and cultural activities for local people, but also to rent, repair and adjust for the elderly the premises of closed kindergarten. Several computers were acquired, an antenna for wireless communication was built for connection to the Internet, and basic computer training was provided. The Centre now has its own website[95]. The next target is a former *kolkhoz* building used as a Cultural Centre. The Balninkai Community Centre has drawn up a plan for its transformation into a multifunctional Community Centre.

During the reflection sessions, members of the Balninkai Community Centre identified several clusters of success factors. The first cluster includes the effective leadership and management of the Community Centre; the support of the Church and the participation of the priest in the activities of the Balninkai Community Centre; the recognition of the Balninkai Community Centre by the Balninkai community; the support of the municipality and the mayor; and the success of the early stages of the process. The second cluster encompasses factors linked with the public relations campaign, that is, an effective and intensive public relations campaign lead by the Balninkai Community Centre inside Balninkai Community (visiting every household with questionnaires, the constant dissemination of information about events during Church services, the blessing by the priest of flower seeds[96], a conference for the whole of Balninkai community, and various education programmes on ecological agriculture, computer literacy, etc.); an effective public relations campaign on a regional, national and even international level (a lot of publications in local and national newspapers, an informative website, broadcasts on Lithuanian Radio, a broadcast about Balninkai on the Euronews channel, active participation in various seminars, conferences, etc.); and an effective use of ICT for accessing and disseminating relevant information. Last but not least, the cluster is associated with the commitment of Balninkai Community Centre members to ongoing training and capacity building, and their ability to initiate appropriate structures and involve new members at various stages of community development.

Community organizations are important actors in rural development. However, the example of the Balninkai Community Centre also reveals that such centres cannot solve by themselves acute problems like unemployment and

---

[95] http://www.balninkai.com

[96] Balninkai Community Centre and the priest have elaborated the excellent idea how to decorate the village and to consolidate the community of the village. During the Feast Day the priest has blessed sufficient amount of flower seed and after celebration of the Mass disseminated among the parish. This initial public action of the Balninkai Community Centre was strong foundation stone for the future activities.

poverty, although they see this as one of their main goals. Community centres cannot control many of the factors that are crucial for bringing about desirable changes. Rural development in Lithuania so far has been hindered by "the absence of comprehensive national and regional rural development policies, underdeveloped rural infrastructure, lack of access to fiscal and other resources, declining agricultural employment, growing migration from rural areas to the cities, declining rural birth rates and aging" (Juska et al. 2005, 5). For overcoming these obstacles, the formation of social partnerships at the local and regional level is essential.

The social partnership approach: The case of Moletai County

Moletai County is a prime example of regional and rural development based on the cooperation of local governmental institutions, the private sector and NGOs (among which the leading role is played by community centres).[97]

Success in Balninkai encouraged other villages. However, the municipal administration did not have sufficient administrative skills and knowledge to operate in a completely new situation when, at the grassroots level, village communities started to engage in social activity. This public policy challenge led to a constructive decision at the Moletai municipal level. The local administration together with community leaders decided to establish a social partnership and delegated to it the responsibility for elaborating a rural development policy for Moletai County.

The first steps in the development of social partnerships in Moletai County were made in 2002 when Moletai municipality together with the leaders of local communities implemented a project called "Creation and Implementation of Effective Rural Development Policy Model". One of the main tasks defined in the rural development policy model was the active involvement and empowerment of stakeholders as social partners. These stakeholders include representatives from governmental and public institutions, the private sector and non-governmental organizations. As a result of the implementation of the project, rural communities have become the partners of local government in the creation of rural development policy.

In 2002 social partnership groups were already at work. At the local community level, eleven "Small Local Action Groups" (SLAGs) that were

[97] The crucial importance of social partnership as a basis for implementing a policy of rural development was only recently recognized in the national programmes dealing with regional development: Lithuania's Rural Development Programme for 2006-2008 has already defined means of dealing with poverty and social exclusion in rural areas of Lithuania, based on the close cooperation of governmental institutions, private enterprises and NGOs.

comprised of active representatives of community centres, the leaders of NGOs, local entrepreneurs and representatives of local government were established. As a result of the cooperation between local communities centres, Moletai municipality and other public institutions, a Local Action Group of Moletai County was established in 2003, which prepared a Plan of Moletai County Rural Development 2004-2006 (Molėtų rajono vietos … 2003). The plan defined the vision and goals of rural development, namely, the further improvement of social partnership in the county (the development of partnership skills), the fostering of social integration in rural communities (dealing with problems of socially vulnerable groups), the fostering of social activity of local inhabitants (promoting the trends of alternative rural activities, encouraging new businesses), and improving the infrastructure of rural areas. Fighting against rural social exclusion was identified in the plan as one of the main goals of rural development. According to the plan, problems in rural areas are to be solved not by national or regional governments alone, but through the cooperation of social partners. For example, the centres of rural communities are included in implementing the optimization of the network of social and public services in the county, the renovation of buildings for public use, the organization of cultural life in the community, and the organization of youth and children leisure time activities.

And yet, in Lithuania, the potential of social partnership has been used in rural development processes to a comparatively small degree. A large number of rural community organisations and local action groups are still weak, and their members lack the knowledge, skills and resources necessary for effective work. There is no effective training system for specialists in rural development. Hopefully, the successful realization of the LEADER+ programme will increase the role of local communities and social partnerships in rural development.

Notwithstanding specific objectives and activities, each successful case of rural development and realization of social innovation is based on a number of principles. These include (1) the organisation of a social partnership at the grassroots level with the participation of a permanent team of practitioners and representatives of the target group; (2) the involvement of relevant stakeholders; (3) successful attempts at empowerment of representatives of the target group from the initial stages of actions designed for social inclusion; (4) a targeted public relations campaign aimed at the destigmatization and social advertising of the target group; (5) a multidimensional approach and a systematic search for links between actions, as part of an integrated strategy.

Conclusion

A critical analysis of the political discourse reveals that it does not treat rural development policy and agricultural policy as separate issues and policy priorities are linked with the development of agriculture. Therefore, rural communities are not considered as social and political agents capable of participating in rural development. The exclusion of rural communities from the mainstream of societal development supports the permanent increase of subsidies for a "paternalistic" system of social care, when, at the same time, there is an obvious lack of investment in programmes for rural community development. Even official statistics are inclined to treat rural residents who are not engaged in competitive agriculture as part of an underclass.

An effective rural inclusion policy is based on an interactive interpretation of social exclusion therefore empowerment and destigmatization are necessary preconditions of effective strategies of social inclusion.

The successful cases mentioned above prove that there has been a shift in social inclusion policy towards communicative policy-making, towards the notion that improving decision making involves improving communication, understanding, trust, open discussion and cooperation between those involved in social inclusion policy areas. Successful strategies of rural inclusion include (a) a decentralised approach and the conversion of common objectives of social inclusion into concrete policies at the regional and local level; (b) mutual learning, by actively communicating social innovations in the field of social policy; (c) and the active participation of all stakeholders in the development and implementation of the processes of decision making and in the implementation of decisions.

References

Alanen, I. (2004) The Transformation of Agriculture Systems in the Baltic Countries, in *Mapping the Rural Problem in the Baltic Countryside: Transition Processes in the Rural Areas of Estonia, Latvia and Lithuania*, ed. by I. Alanen. Ashgate, Aldershot, 5-58.

ALF (2002) Atviros Lietuvos fondas [Open Society Foundation – Lithuania] *Pilietinių iniciatyvų ir viešojo administravimo programos ataskaita* [The Report of the Civil Initiatives and Public Administration Program] http://lark.osf.lt/OSF/Ataskaita2002/PilietineViesasisAdministravimas2002.doc

—. (2005) Atviros Lietuvos fondo iniciatyvos "Skaitmeninių bendruomenių link" grupė, Vilniaus universiteto Socialinių studijų centras [The Initiative of the Open Society Foundation "Toward Digital Communities"; The

Centre for Social Research of Vilnius University] *Kaimiškųjų bendruomenių organizacijos: Tyrimo rezultatų apžvalga* [The Organizations of Rural Communities: The Research Report].
http://www.bendruomenes.lt/downloads/structure//AtaskaitaKaimoBendruomeniuOrganizacijos.pdf

Bowring, F. (2000) Social Exclusion: Limitations of the Debate. *Critical Social Policy*, Aug 2000, 20, 307-30.

European Commission, Directorate-General for Employment, Social Affairs and Equal Opportunities, Unit E2 (2005) *Report on Social Inclusion 2005: An Analysis of the National Action Plans on Social Inclusion (2004-2006) Submitted by the 10 New Member States.*
http://europa.eu.int/comm/employment_social/social_inclusion/docs/sec256printed_en.pdf

European Commission, Enterprise and Industry Directorate-General (2005) *Importance of Social Economy Enterprises.*
http://europa.eu.int/comm/enterprise/entrepreneurship/coop/index.htm

Freire, P. (2000) *Pedagogy of the Oppressed.* Continuum, New York.

Government of Lithuania (2004) *National Action Plan Against Poverty and Social Exclusion in 2004-2006.*
http://europa.eu.int/comm/employment_social/social_inclusion/docs/nap_incl_2004_lt_en_version.pdf

Gylys, P. (2006) *Socialinė demokratija Lietuvoje: praeitis, dabartis, ateitis* [Social Democracy in Lithuania: Past, Present, Future].
http://www.bernardinai.lt/index.php?543515114

Goldenberg, M. (2004) *Social Innovation in Canada.* Canadian Policy Research Networks Inc. (CPRN) http://www.cprn.org/en/doc.cfm?doc=1128

Juska, A., A. Poviliunas & R. Pozzuto (2005) Resisting Marginalisation: The Rise of the Rural Community Movement in Lithuania. *Sociologia Ruralis* 45 (1/2), 3-21.

—. (2006) Rural Grass-roots Organizing in Eastern Europe: the Experience from Lithuania. *Community Development Journal* 41 (2), 174-188.

Katsiaouni, O., J. Gorniak & R. Lazutka (2000) *Poverty in Lithuania: Capacity Building for Rural Poverty Reduction.* UNDP, Vilnius.

Kazlauskas, A. & A. Misiunas (2005) General Indicators of the Economic Development. *The Survey of the Lithuanian Economy, n*o. 1.
http://www.std.lt/uploads/apzvalga_e/2005-1/Contents.htm

Lazutka, R. (2006) *Patriotizmo praradimas* [The Loss of Patriotism].
http://www.politika.lt/index.php?cid=9322&new_id=11401

Levitas, R. (1998) *The Inclusive Society? Social Exclusion and New Labour.* Macmillan, Basingstoke.

Lietuvos darbo birža [Lithuanian Labour Exchange] (2005) *Lietuvos darbo biržos ataskaita 2004* [Report of Lithuanian Labour Exchange 2004]. http://www.ldb.lt/LDB_Site/index.htm

Lietuvos Respublikos socialinės apsaugos ir darbo ministerija [Republic of Lithuania Ministry of Social Security and Labour] (2005) *Konsoliduotas Lietuvos Respublikos 2004–2006 metų nacionalinio kovos su skurdu ir socialine atskirtimi veiksmų plano įgyvendinimo priemonių 2005–2006 metams sąrašas* [The Consolidated Nomenclature of the Measures for 2005-2006 for the Implementation of the National Action Plan against Poverty and Social Exclusion of Republic of Lithuania].

Ministry of Social Security and Labour (2004) *Social Report 2003.* http://www.socmin.lt/index.php?299157638

Molėtų darbo birža [Labour Exchange of Moletai] (2005) *2004 metų veiklos ataskaita* [The Report of 2004]. http://www.ldb.lt/moletai/fr_ataskaitos.html

Molėtų rajono vietos veiklos grupė [Local Action Group of Moletai County] (2003) *Keisdamiesi keičiame: Molėtų rajono kaimo plėtros planas 2004-2006* [Rural Development Plan of Moletai County for 2005-2006] http://www.sav.moletai.lt/index.php?-835747331

Pavis, S., G. Hubbard & S. Platt (2001) Young People in Rural Areas: Socially Excluded or Not? *Work Employment Society*, Jun 2001, 15, 291-309.

Poviliunas, A. (2003) *Kaimo atskirties profiliai* [Profiles of Rural Exclusion]. Kronta, Vilnius.

Rubington, E., & M.S. Weinberg (1987) *Deviance: the Interactionist Perspective.* (6th edition) Allyn & Bacon, Boston.

Socialines apsaugos ir darbo ministerija [Republic of Lithuania Ministry of Social Security and Labour] (2006) *Socialinės paslaugos ir socialinis darbas.* [Social Services and Social Work] http://www.socmin.lt/index.php?-2086129439

Statistikos departamentas [Department of Statistics] (2006a) *Business tendency survey results in manufacturing, construction, retail trade and services.* http://www.std.lt/uploads/docs/versl_tend_060131_e.doc

—. (2006b) *Main indicators of activity of the population in 2005.* http://www.std.lt/en/pages/view/?id=1405

—. (2006c) *Namų ūkių biudžetų tyrimo rezultatai.* [Results of Household Survey] http://www.std.lt/lt/pages/view/?id=1335

—. (2005) Gyvenimo lygis ir skurdas [Living Standart and Poverty]. Statistikos departamentas prie Lietuvos Respublikos Vyriausybės, Vilnius.

—. (2003) *Darbo jėga, užimtumas ir nedarbas 2003/IV* [Work Force, Employment and Unemployment. The Fourth Quarter of 2003]. Statistikos departamentas prie Lietuvos Respublikos Vyriausybės, Vilnius.

—. (2002) *Lietuvos gyventojų 2001 m. surašymas.* [Lithuanian Population Census of 2001] Statistikos departamentas prie Lietuvos Respublikos Vyriausybės, Vilnius.

Watt, P. (2000) Discourses of Social Exclusion Housing: An Analysis of Bringing Britain Together: a National Strategy for Neighbourhood Renewal. *Housing, Theory and Society* 17 (1), 14-26.

CHAPTER NINE

COMMUNITY ACTION IN POST-SOCIALIST LITHUANIA: A COMPARATIVE CASE-STUDY OF TWO RURAL VILLAGES

AINE MACKEN WALSH

Introduction

Post-socialist EU member states joined at a time when local actors, in the form of voluntary rural community organisations, have increased decision-making power in the rural development process (see Nemes 1999). Given the particular heritage of rural collective action in post-socialist states, EU expansion provides new basis for researching into how these rural societies will embrace and give emergence to the idea of "community", and how newly established community organisations in post-socialist Europe will operate. Nuances in approaches to community action, influenced by post-socialist experiences as well as present rural conditions in recently acceded EU member states, provide a new opportunity to profile case-specific variations within the context of an enlarged EU.

This paper focuses on the Ukmerge district of Lithuania, where a Rural Partnership Programme (RPP) was implemented from 2000 to 2003. The programme set out to mobilise villagers in the district, with a view to encouraging the establishment of community organisations and the implementation of community development projects, funded by the RPP itself. This paper adopts a comparative approach, focussing on the formation and action of two neighbouring villages, and asks why community action spurred by a RPP-funded project in each case had different outcomes. Local determinants influencing each of the respective communities are identified — historical and current social, economic, and cultural factors as well as the influence of key actors in the locality. The villages' different historical experiences of collective farming are identified as crucial to the social and economic condition of the villages today. The formation processes of the community organisations within each village, and the process of community development project creation and implementation, and the end results are all followed through in order to reveal who defined its parameters; the actors who did and did not become involved in implementation; how the project worked in practice; and the outcome with respect to the consolidation of 'community'. What the term came to mean to villagers, and the issues it inspired in local discussion and action, is discussed with respect to each of the two cases with a view to identifying the nuances of the concept of collective voluntary action in practice, as influenced by different local experiences, and the attitudes generated, under socialism.

The paper has five sections. The first presents the key tenets of the rural governance debate followed by a descriptive summary of the Ukmerge district and the main aims and objectives of the RPP. Case studies of community action in two villages are presented in sections three and four. Section five asks why there were different reactions to the establishment and operation of the community organisations in the two villages and puts forward some possible explanations.

Key tenets of the rural governance debate in the EU context

Over the life-span of the EU Common Agricultural Policy (CAP), there have been tendencies towards different conceptions of rurality and, consequently, of the policy's engagement with the broader rural civil society. There has been a notable transition from the productivist approach, the failures of which, in part, heralded the landmark "Future of Rural Society" document in 1988 (CEC 1988) (see Gray 2000). The LEADER (*Liaisons Entre Actions de Development de l'Economie Rurale*) programme, in 1991, marked the unprecedented incorporation of principles of governance into EU-led rural development. The programme is described as "a sustained and sustainable process of economic, social, cultural and environmental change designed to enhance the long-term well-being of the whole community" (Moseley 2003a). The LEADER programme's references to "community" illustrate the goals of the programme, which re-orientate the approach to rural development on the basis of two principles: namely, decision-making to take place as close as possible to the site of implementation (the principle of subsidiarity); and hierarchical decision-making structures being replaced by mechanisms involving representatives from a wide range of governmental and non-governmental organisations (the principle of partnership) (Osti 2000, 172). The non-statutory organisations that have been involved in LEADER and other rural governance programmes are often called community organisations: interest groups, which in this case, are intended to represent a territorial unit. How these organisations operate in practice, both at the territorial level and in partnership with other sectoral organisations, inevitably differs not only from state to state but from case to case, according to the local, social, economic and cultural context (see Curtin & Varley 1995). Nonetheless, from a policy perspective, there is an expectation that community organisations will play a role as equal partners in the development process and thus they have been afforded the power to influence development implementation and outcomes (LEADER European Observatory 1997).

Prior to LEADER, the structurally interventionist CAP had no communicative channels with rural civil society organisations. While the participatory development opportunities now fostered by the EU are a response to the shortcomings of the productivist CAP, the allocation of power to community organisations is also the result of an iterative policy discussion over many years, informed by arguments originating in liberal democratic EU member states. Prior to LEADER, there was an acknowledged capacity of rural civil society organisations (community organisations, farmers' organisations, tourism organisations, artisan and cultural organisations) in the EU15 to form a strong sectoral local agenda and be "competent actors in the development process" (Ibid.). Given this basis for the LEADER programme, its inception did not require the formation of rural interest organisations from scratch, but simply the will to utilise and develop them, considering their acknowledged capacity.

The conferral of power on local interest organisations has given rise to research on how local development, as influenced by local actors, takes form and how different cultures effect its operation (Curtin & Varley 1991, Osti 2000). The transposition of this governance-oriented system to the recently acceded post-socialist Central and Eastern European EU member states raises a number of interesting research questions concerning the influence of this new post-socialist rural context on the implementation of grass-root community development programmes. In the literature, there is considerable support for the 'bottom-up' approach in post-socialist EU Member States (See Nemes 1999, Bryden & Shucksmith 2000, Kovach 2000), on the basis of the democratic qualities of the approach and the acknowledged failures of structural policies in the case of the CAP in the EU15. Local conditions on the ground are nonetheless significantly different, and rural interest organisations and community organisations are not a given in their eastern counterparts.

The Ukmerge District[98] of Lithuania and the Rural Partnerships Programme

Since the fall of the socialist regime in 1991, the Ukmerge District of Lithuania has experienced a tumult of social, economic, cultural and political change. Typically for post-socialist transformation, the land and property of the former collective farms were restituted to farm workers as well as to previous owners (or their descendants), and, in Lithuania, rather uniquely in comparison to other post-socialist Central and Eastern European States, land-owners have tended to farm their mostly small plots of land themselves rather than leasing it out and in so doing giving rise to larger land owners (EC 2002). Therefore, while there is an average of two large farmers in each village of the Ukmerge District, almost all of the district's rural population is engaged in subsistence agriculture, as "post-socialist peasants" (Leonard & Kaneff 2004). There is little business activity in the villages of Ukmerge; most of the businesses are grocery shops, which take the form of either cooperatives or what are locally called "commercial" shops. Typical professions in the villages of Ukmerge today are teachers, post-office workers, and municipal employees such as librarians and cultural house workers[99], with all other professional (e.g. medical, legal) services located in the town of Ukmerge. The average salary in the district in 2002 was LTL (Lithuanian Litas) 708 (€ 205) per month while the national average was LTL 1,113 (€ 323), and the main source of employment is in the industrial (wood-processing) sector, and casual village maintenance work paid for by the municipal government. In January 2002, the number of those receiving unemployment benefits was 16.6% (Lieutvos Statistikos Departamentas 2002).

The Ukmerge district has 51,000 inhabitants, of which 22,000 live in rural areas. The district is divided into three administrative levels; the municipality, the *seniunija*[100] (below the municipal level) and the village. There are administrative offices both at the municipal level and at the level of the *seniunija*. There are eleven rural *seniunijas* in the Ukmerge district, in each of

---

98 The other implementation sites for the RPP were Salcininkai and Svencionys. Salcinikiai is a district where there is an ethnic mix of Lithuanian and Russian culture. Svencionys is a particularly poor district. The Ukmerge District is one which reflects more accurately the average Lithuanian rural environment and was chosen as a case study so as to avoid, in so far as possible, depicting an extreme or extraordinary case.

99 Cultural houses are the main venue for village social activity and have their origin in the socialist period, when every village had a full-time cultural-house worker to organise social events.

100 The English translation of *seniunija* is "ward". The person who is head of the *seniunija*, is called the *Seniunje*, and is translated into English as "warden".

which there are a number of villages. The population of the villages averages at 360, but ranges from 122 in Laumenai (in Zelva *seniunija*) to 842 in Sventupes (in Vidiskiai *seniunija*).

There were two registered rural interest organisations in the rural areas of Ukmerge in 2002; a Youth Club in the village of Zelva (Zelva *seniunija*) and a registered community organisation in the village of Jakutiskiai[101] (Deltuva *seniunija*). There were also 14 hunting clubs in the district, which were not formally registered. With respect to village social activity, there are 11 cultural houses, 20 libraries (usually located within schools), and 13 churches in the rural areas of Ukmerge. In many villages, cultural-house activities are still in operation, facilitated by a worker paid by the Department of Culture of the municipal government. In many cases, however, where the cultural house was located in a property that had been privately owned in the pre-socialist period, it was restituted to former owners and had either ceased to operate or had been transferred to the village school. As schools often house both cultural houses and libraries, the closure of rural schools poses a threat to village social activity (RPP 2000).

The UK Department for International Development (DfID) implemented a three year Rural Partnerships Programme (RPP), the aim of which was to reduce rural poverty and social exclusion in the three Baltic States, Lithuania, Latvia and Estonia. Three rural partnerships were established in each of the Baltic States, and Ukmerge was the site of one of the Lithuanian partnerships. The purpose of the programme in all the states was "to support the creation of a new rural development policy framework in which local rural people can work in partnership with national, regional and local authorities, to identify local needs, prioritise actions and manage strategies" (RPP 2003, 1). The RPP inception report refers to the EC First Thematic Evaluation Report on the Partnership Principle of EU Structural Funds (2001), conveying the policy context of the programme's emergence:

> It is clear that as the preparations for EU accession advance, governments in the candidate countries will be challenged to widen the debate on national, regional, and local development priorities. There is a need…to support decentralisation, which is related to the general effort to achieve three major objectives – the consolidation of democracy, the development of partnership and an increase in economic efficiency.

The programme recognised that in order to meet the policy challenges of EU integration such as the LEADER programme, there was a need for developing

[101] According to the villagers of Jakutiskiai, this community organisation existed "only on paper". The chairperson did not live in the village and was involved in a rural community discussion organisation in Vilnius.

ways to include local communities in the development process and to develop relationships between different sectoral organisations, by means of partnership. The stated RPP vision for Ukmerge was a "socially and economically developed district with active, influential, democratic and focused communities working towards better economic and educational opportunities for its members" (Ibid., p. 31). The partnership's mission statement was the following: "the partnership board is an active learning organisation striving to encourage community organisations and to develop the capacities of their members to take an active part in economic activities" (Ibid.).

The RPP acknowledged that the rural NGO/community sectors in rural areas of the Baltic States were not sufficiently developed and therefore a main strand of the programme involved the identification and training of potential community facilitators from the village population, with the view that they would establish community organisations in the villages. Villagers' involvement in local development was unprecedented in Ukmerge, and due to a lack of responses to RPP advertisements that sought potential community facilitators to volunteer, RPP personnel took active steps to identify villagers who were known to be somewhat active in village affairs. To do this, RPP personnel established contact with key actors in the Ukmerge district, such as the heads of rural *seniunija* (*Seniunje*), representatives of State agencies and municipal government employees, who were acquainted with active villagers. The heads of *seniunijas* in particular, were active at the village level in putting forward potential facilitators and helping to organise meetings at the village level, a reflection of their traditional prominence in village affairs.

The next phase was the holding of a meeting in the town of Ukmerge where 45 villagers signed up for training in order to become "community facilitators". This training focused on consultative processes in community formation and operation. The aim was that the community facilitators would use their skills to establish new community organisations in their villages, which in turn would lead to applications for community development projects being submitted to the RPP. In fact, it was a pre-requisite that funding applications would be considered by the RPP only from formally registered communities. Forty-five applications were received (that is, one application each from forty-five community organisations, and a total of nineteen community development projects (covering 14 villages in Ukmerge) were approved by the RPP.[102]

The establishment of each individual community organisation was a story in itself, and in many cases, they varied significantly. The comparative case-study presented in this paper focuses on the neighbouring villages of Petronys and Tulpiakiemis, both within the Siesikiai *seniunija,* and analyses the very different

[102] The approved projects were allocated a total of GB£15,000 (€ 22,810).

outcomes that emerged from each. There had been no community organisation in either village prior to the RPP. The two villages were comparable in terms of population, with 284 inhabitants in Petronys and 274 in Tulpiakiemis. One RPP-funded community development project was implemented in each village; in Tulpiakiemis, a project entitled "Encouraging the collective action of village youth by establishing a recreational centre" and, in Petronys, a project called "The Petronys village community craft house".

Taking each case in turn, the following sections describe in detail how the RPP-trained facilitators formed community organisations; how the organisations operated in practice and how their purpose was perceived by local villagers; the main actors; and issues of trust and mistrust that were generated from the organisations' operation. The empirical data are sourced from qualitative semi-structured interviews that were carried out with community facilitators, community chairpersons, community board members, and village inhabitants. In all, 33 interviews were carried out in Petronys and 24 in Tulpiakiemis.[103]

The formation and organisation of the Petronys Community

The RPP-trained community facilitator in Petronys was previously known to a number of municipal government employees as she was a key member of a small but well-known dairy producer organisation.[104] She was contacted by RPP

[103] The number of key actors in Petronys exceeded the number in Tulpiakiemis, as depicted in the following sections.

[104] This producer organisation was unique in the Ukmerge District and comprised a number of women in the village who were engaged in dairy farming. The organisation was the result of a key actor in the community, who had returned upon Lithuania's independence to the village, from the city of Panevezys where she had worked as a textile engineer. After the restitution of her family's land, she began a dairy farm and encouraged other women engaged in dairy farming not to sell their milk cheaply to the creamery but instead to produce and sell their dairy products (cheese, sour cream) privately at the market-place in the town of Ukmerge. There were 15 women in the village who agreed to this and the organisation joined the Lithuanian Women Farmers' Association and set up a local branch in 1994. Through the Lithuanian Women Farmers' association, a UK lottery-funded NGO called "Powerful Information" contacted the organisation, which was now seven strong, that same year and initiated a purposely-designed educational project on dairy production, with the aim of enabling the organisation to overcome problems they had encountered concerning the market's hygiene standards. As a result, the organisation initiated meetings with the Chairman of the Committee of Rural Affairs of the parliament and the Ministry of Agriculture and eventually succeeded in overcoming the obstacles to selling their produce at the market, by arranging a timescale for gradually meeting the health and safety, and bureaucratic requirements. As part of this project, the organisation also went on trips to areas where

personnel and attended RPP training. Once the training phase was completed, the task at hand was the formation of a community organisation, so the Siesikiai *Seniunije,* (in line with the traditional function of *seniunijas*) called a public meeting for village inhabitants to announce the setting up of the Petronys Community. At this meeting, the *Seniunje* appointed a community leader, an action protested by the trained community facilitator and the villagers who claimed that it was "our right to elect a community leader". It was agreed that an election should take place but those present thought that there was an insufficient number of people present to elect a community leader. After the meeting, the villagers discussed establishing their own community organisation independently from the *seniunija*, and the village cultural-house worker and RPP-trained community facilitator advertised a second public meeting. At this meeting, a community leader, a farmer from the area, was elected from among the seventy-eight people present, and volunteers were asked to sit on the community board. The board was made up of six of the women engaged in the Petronys dairy organisation (including the community facilitator) and eleven others. Following the election of the leader and the creation of the board, the community organisation was formally registered, with some administrative help from the community facilitator, as the "Petronys Community".

The second task at hand was to formulate an application for funding for a community development project, which would be submitted to the RPP. A public meeting, with forty-eight in attendance, was held where ideas for a potential community project were discussed. The idea of a craft house was proposed and endorsed by those present without the need for a vote. A project application was submitted to the RPP, which stated:

> After the registration of the Petronys Community, community meetings looked for ways to solve community problems and the idea of the craft house emerged. The craft house will help to some extent to solve the unemployment problem and to involve community members in collective action. We will have separate rooms for different crafts, such as bread and cheese making, wood-carving and wickerwork. All rooms will be adjoined to a common guest room. This project will unite community people in collective work and will encourage the learning of crafts.

The Petronys Community were successful in their application and received the maximum eligible grant from the RPP.[105] Regarding membership of the community organisation, the community chairperson explained in an interview

---

this kind of local dairy production was being practiced and brought their produce to agricultural fairs. The organisation also received funding from the UK NGO to purchase their own van for transporting their produce.

[105] LTL 10,000 (€ 2,896).

that the organisation was understood by the board to be representative of the territorial unit of Petronys, that is, all Petronys inhabitants. The Community as it was organised, however, had a system of membership whereby people would officially join.[106] In practice, however, villagers who did not officially register also used the craft house. The Community Board chairperson stated that in order to adhere to the articles of association relating to registered community organisations, records had to be kept of the number of community members, the number of people at community meetings and the number of votes on issues of community importance. In terms of the RPP project implementation, the project was managed (i.e. funds administered) through the Community Board.

The building that was going to be the craft house was owned by two villagers, who were jointly allocated the property during the period of land restitution. It was located in the centre of the village, near the cluster of Petronys dwelling units, (built by the collective farm under socialism)[107] and next to the local commercial shop. The owners leased it to the Petronys Community (without charging rent) as the development of private or state run property was prohibited under the funding regulations of the RPP. A list of tasks was drawn up for the completion of the craft house, and work commenced as soon as the project was approved.

Most of the RPP funding would go towards paying for building materials for the renovation of the building, which was in a state of disrepair, and there was a great reliance on volunteers to carry out the work. It was apparent from records of the work done and the names of those who had volunteered that a high proportion (31% of the total population[108]) of Petronys' villagers contributed. The result was a well-renovated building with a computer room and craft-making room, as well as a reception room. The craft house also served additional functions within the village, which are elaborated in the next section.

The purpose of the Petronys Community as understood by villagers

The nature of the RPP-funded project, which centred on the production of cheese, bread, and crafts, was, to a certain extent, economic. As a result of the

---

[106] People could join the community by filling out a form (name, address, age, what they would like to see the community accomplish) and by paying an annual membership fee (LTL 10).

[107] Cultural houses are the main venue for village social activity and have their origin in the socialist period, when every village had a full-time cultural-house worker to organise social events.

[108] Excluding the 14% of Petronys villagers that were over the age of 60 and the 15% under the age of nine at the time of the project's implementation, 44% of the remaining population became involved.

establishment of the craft house more grants have been obtained[109] and more people in the village have become involved in the dairy producer organisation which had dropped from 15 to 8 members after its initial establishment. After the establishment of the craft house, its membership increased back up to 12.

Apart from the establishment of the craft house, which was the economically-oriented focus of the initial RPP project, the house had also very obviously acquired the purpose of a territorially-oriented community centre. This was apparent from observing the actual activities of the new organisation, which ranged from social activities, to lobbying, to religious activities. The Petronys Community began to take up issues of village importance, such as the need for a bus-stop in the village and the need for local roads to be repaired. The organisation successfully lobbied the municipal government in order to resolve both of these issues. The organisation has also taken on board the issue of the village water reservoir, village ownership of which was the initiative of the collective farm leader at the time of the dismantling of the collective farm. In 2004, the craft house also set up a 'May altar', where people could say their prayers every evening throughout the month of May to celebrate a Roman Catholic tradition. This was widely used, particularly by elderly folk but also by children and families who did not have a means of transport to visit the church, which is located in Siesikiai, 12.5 km away.[110] Social events constituted a major role in the activities of the Petronys Community, demonstrating its close functional link with the socialist era's cultural houses.

Interviews with rural inhabitants revealed that the new community organisation in Petronys was seen as something very natural for the villagers to be involved in. Although it was admitted that such an organisation, in the formal sense, would never have been established without the impetus of the RPP, villagers made a conceptual link between the village social interaction, activity

---

[109] Additionally, in the aftermath of the RPP, the community applied for funding to the United Nations Office for Project Services (UNOPS) for a combined environmental and social project to disseminate information on ecological farming, and to further develop the craft house. As a result of this application, the community organisation received LTL 49,805 (€ 14,424) (May 2003 - September 2004). They also applied to the World Bank for funding to implement a business start-up training project in the craft house and received LTL 13,483 (€ 3,905) (April 2002 – May 2004). Smaller projects, such as a water-sports project (LTL 400 / € 117 in 2004); a basketball championship (LTL 500 / € 145, in June 2005); and a Whit Sunday celebration project (LTL 600 / € 174, in May 2005) were applied for, and granted by the municipality. The Lithuanian Youth Affairs Council granted LTL 1600 (€ 465) in June 2005 to the community to implement a project to encourage youth to care for the elderly.

[110] Apart from this, religion or religious actors did not play a role in community or village affairs in Siesikiai *seniunija*.

and events that were an existing part of the cultural house tradition, with the function of the community organisation. It was stated that:

> [V]illage events and celebrations are very important to us. We've had these events as long as I can remember, they continued in the cultural house after the collective farm broke up. Now most events are held in the craft house as it's cosier and it can accommodate far more people than the cultural house. There are also far more social events than before, as the community helps with the organisation and gets money from the municipality (Female, 38 yrs, Petronys).

Apart from the immediate tangible achievements and activities of the Petronys Community, how local villagers perceived both the newly-formed entity and its purpose, taking a long-term perspective, was also of crucial importance. Interesting opinions which were in many cases divided, emerged from the interviews. One common perception was that the institution of community necessary in fulfilling the diminished role of the cultural houses in the aftermath of socialism. Another was that the Community was inadequate in what it provided to the village, only fulfilling a proportion of villagers' needs. Those who were of the latter view expressed disappointment about the Community, stating that the Community had little or nothing to offer them. In such cases, villagers appeared to conflate the idea of the Community with the function of the collective farm. They explained that the collective farm had provided jobs, as well as health and childcare services and were doubtful about the purpose of the Community when it couldn't help in providing these life necessities. The Community Board chairperson claimed that:

> [P]eople don't understand that the Community is different than the collective farm board. We can apply for funding, but not to manage the village. People don't understand that the Community is theirs; that they must partake in the work and decision-making on a voluntary basis instead of expecting something from the Community all the time (Community Chairperson, Petronys).

Key Actors

The members of the farm board were of mixed educational and professional status, yet it was notable that all of the few professionals[111] in the village were on the board, and 14 out of 17 were women. Apart from the five full-time farmers, all the other Community Board members had small subsistence farms.

---

[111] The board included the Petronys post-mistress, teacher, librarian and cultural-house worker (who also owned the shop). There were also two teachers who worked outside Petronys, five farmers, two housewives, two pensioners, a handy-man and a postal worker.

When villagers were asked why they thought more women than men were involved, they replied that community work is women's work and that men mostly help out when there is physical work to be done, such as in manual work when it came to project implementation in the case of the RPP project. It was also argued that "more women than men work as cultural-house workers, teachers and librarians, and such people usually get involved in work like community work, it's their duty". On the question of whether villagers thought the Community Board was elitist, the same response was put forward, and that people who had such jobs "are expected to engage in projects like the RPP, it is natural for them to do so". In fact, it was apparent that villagers did not have an attitude of "us and them" towards the board but were of the opinion that they were working for the good of the village population, one villager saying "we are all in the same boat" (Quotations from an interview with a female resident, 42 yrs, Petronys).

Apart from the core organisation of female professionals, there was no other particular social organisation involved in the community organisation and its activities. The village population in general was significantly involved in decision-making processes at community meetings, and were also heavily involved in project implementation. The role of the *Seniunje* was notably weaker after the first community public meeting.

Trust and Mistrust

There was some scepticism about the nature of the Petronys Community Organisation, primarily due to the fact that the RPP-funded project was economic in nature. One villager expressed the view that "the community should have started out with a social issue, not an economic one" (Male, 58yrs, Petronys). A number of other villagers expressed the same opinion, saying that "the craft house is not for everyone, just for those who can profit from making cheese and bread". Nevertheless, all the villagers who expressed this opinion claimed that this did not stop them going to the craft house to attend meetings and events, or to use its computer. As one of them said, "I am free to go there if I wish to" (Male, 58yrs, Petronys), indicating a certain sense of public ownership.

The craft house producers and the Petronys Community Organisation have acquired some fame, featuring on two Lithuanian TV programmes, and the RPP-funded project is acknowledged as a successful rural economic project overall. The external interest generated by the project also gave rise to scepticism at the local level, concerning the relationship between the Petronys Community and international and government officials. One local claimed that a recent St. George's day celebration "had more officials present than locals"

(Female, 58 yrs, Petronys). Correspondingly, many villagers expressed the belief that the community is an institution that originates in the EU. A newspaper report on the Petronys St. George's Day[112] community event stated:

> Petronys people herded out a "eurocow" (a cow draped with the flag of the EU) for top officials from the Ministry of Agriculture to tend to it. In soviet times such rituals had a special word "*pokazucha*" (a Russian word for showing off). This is another example of how the EU is much the same as the USSR. A folk picnic was organised for representatives of the Ministry of Agriculture and a UN representative. National TV was also brought along to make an even greater spectacle. A fuss was even made of some ordinary fried eggs. When the TV camera focused in on a local, Mr. Algimantas, who was demonstrating how to fry eggs at the time, the spoon was taken away from him and all the agricultural clerks started to energetically beat the eggs in order to demonstrate their love of Lithuania and their understanding of agriculture. All the guests then took their seats and admired at the fried eggs as if this was the first time they had ever seen such a thing. All the while, the villagers were given the honour of entertaining the city lords, and village children sang and danced
>
> On 1st May, everyone who wants to celebrate will easily find an occasion. A number of holidays fall on the same day: Orthodox Easter, Catholic Mothers' Day, International Labour Day, the first anniversary of Lithuania's membership in the EU, the Pagan Cuckoo Festival, and the German Walpurgis Night. To your health! (Ukmerges Zinios, Balandzio 30, 2005).

In all, while it was clear that a degree of scepticism was present, the villagers' pride in and good-will towards the Community Organisation far outweighed it and disapproval never turned into public protest. Although the absence of public protest in this post-socialist society may in part be attributable to the socialist experience (as was the absence of rural interest organisations), all the villagers interviewed exhibited a certain degree of pride in the success of the craft house, particularly the computers (purchased under a UNOPS project) and how their children could use them. The Petronys Community was undoubtedly associated with progress in the minds of villagers, and the generally positive attitude towards it seemed to be reinforced by the fact that all the interviewees said that they were particularly proud of Petronys, both its history and to be living there today.

---

[112] St. George's Day is celebrated in rural parts of Lithuania by baking a loaf of bread for every farm animal, and allowing them to roam free in the fields. It is said that animals are not put to work and farmers are especially kind to them on St. George's Day.

The formation and organisation of the Tulpiakiemis Community

There was no established interest organisation in Tulpiakiemis before the inception of the RPP. The village became involved in the RPP when a villager saw an advertisement and contacted RPP representatives in Ukmerge. The villager attended the initial meetings and went on to attend the training course with a view to establishing a community in Tulpiakiemis and applying for a project grant from the RPP. The facilitator had recently renovated an old basket-ball court on a voluntary basis with five youths in the area, and he invited this organisation to form a community organisation with him, so that the Tulpiakiemis Community could be registered. The community organisation had the idea of making youth and sport the focus of the Tulpiakiemis village project and with the *Seniunje* (similar to the case of Petronys) held a village meeting to discuss the idea. The *Seniunje* appointed the RPP-trained community facilitator as the chairperson of the community and presented the idea of a Youth and Sports Club as the focus of the RPP application for community development funding. Thirty people from the village were present at the meeting, which was held in the local primary school, and upon hearing the community project proposal, many expressed the views that there were other more urgent needs in the community, such as a village wash-house with sanitary facilities. One organisation also expressed the view that they had the right to elect the community leader themselves and to decide the focus of the community development project by a vote.

Another meeting was held by those who wished to establish a community organisation independently (unattended by the *Seniunje* or the RPP-trained community facilitator) to exist alongside the organisation of which the RPP-trained facilitator was the chairperson. At this meeting, fifteen candidates put themselves forward for the position of community chairperson. Each of the 34 villagers present could vote for three candidates and the end result was a large farmer from the area being elected chairperson. The Tulpe (tulip) Community Organisation was then formally registered.

Each of the two community organisations competed for signatures of support from the village population, with the outcome that the Tulpe Community obtained a slight majority of signatures. Two applications for RPP funding were submitted by the Tulpe Community: one for a village wash-house, and one to develop a Youth and Sports Club. In selecting projects, the RPP was primarily concerned with the orientation of the project, and issues concerning popular participation. A crucial criterion was that the amount of funding sought in the application not exceed the maximum eligible grant[113] Due to the ongoing conflict caused by the communities' competition for RPP funding, RPP representatives visited Tulpiakiemis on numerous occasions to see if a solution or a compromise could be found in order to come up with a joint community project proposal. One application was ineligible due to the amount of funding sought, which exceeded the maximum eligible grant per project, and therefore could not be granted to the Tulpe Community. RPP representatives proposed that the youth project share its building with a smaller wash-house project. The leader of the Tulpiakiemis Community would not agree to this on the basis that a certain minimum amount of floor-space was required for most sports or games and that to reduce the space available would render the Youth and Sports Club only partially functional. Moreover, as demonstrated by the two community organisations' unwillingness to cooperate, relations between the organisations were extremely fraught, so much so that a deep divide was created in the village (Female, 36 yrs, Tulpiakiemis).

The result was that the Tulpiakiemis Community and the Tulpe Community went ahead with their individual applications. The Tulpiakiemis Community was allocated LTL 3,582 (€ 1,040) and the Tulpe Community's proposal was denied, due to the fact that the amount sought exceeded the maximum eligible grant. The Tulpiakiemis Community stated the following in its application:

> The aim of the project is to engage Tulpiakiemis youth in a voluntary collective work project, and to address how youth spend their free-time, by creating a recreational outlet which will prevent the development of anti-social behaviour.

The Youth and Sports Club was to be located in a dilapidated vacant building, which had been leased at no charge from Siesikiai *seniunija* to the Tulpiakiemis Community. As with Petronys, a work schedule was planned and although the costs of most of the materials required for carrying out the renovation were provided by the RPP, project implementation relied heavily on volunteering. The main implementers were the Community Board, which consisted of the community chairperson and five others interested in sport. A large farmer in the area was also involved at the outset, and loaned the organisation some machinery so that the work could be carried out more efficiently. The implementation organisation was small and there were no formally recorded community meetings or minutes of meetings during project implementation.

---

[113] LTL 10,000 (€ 2,900). The Tulpe Community wished to apply for LTL 50,000 (€ 14,510) arguing that this was the minimum amount required to achieve their goal, whilst the Tulpiakiemis Community applied for LTL 3,582 (€ 1,040).

The function of community as perceived by Tulpiakiemis villagers

The Tulpiakiemis Community achieved the goal of renovating a vacant building for the purposes of a Youth and Sports Club, which was well equipped with a snooker table, a table-tennis table and various board-games. Although the exact number of visitors has not been recorded, it can be assumed that most of the young people in the area began to use the facility, as groups of local schoolchildren interviewed claimed that "all young people here go to the club". Also, a significant number of adult villagers (who were formally against the idea of the Tulpiakiemis Community) stated that their children went to the club and enjoyed it. A refurbished room in the club, which could be used as a meeting room, was adorned with medals and trophies won by local sportspeople.

Unlike most other villages in the Ukmerge District, there is no cultural house in Tulpiakiemis, which, during the socialist period, was located on a large estate which has now been restituted as private property.[114] Therefore, collective activity such as village meetings and celebrations mostly ceased with the disappearance of the collective farm, with only a few events such as Easter, Christmas, and New Year celebrations taking place in the school. However, the Youth and Sports Club began to be used for funerals, and at a general meeting of the Tulpiakiemis Community (with 30 villagers in attendance), it was suggested that it also be used for fortnightly discos for the young people in the area and their friends. Despite initial protests about the Tulpiakiemis Community Organisation, from the holding of funerals and discos in the club it was evident that there was a sense of public ownership was nonetheless present with respect to the Youth and Sports Club.

The discos went ahead as planned and were organised and supervised by the community facilitator and the other five members of the community board. After two discos had taken place, however, a decision was taken by the Tulpiakiemis Community chairperson (reportedly unilaterally) not to allow further youth discos to take place in the centre due to damage that had occurred to the flooring. The chairperson also decided that funerals would not take place in the club either, because people who had used it in the past had not cleaned up afterwards. These decisions aroused considerable discontent among Tulpiakiemis villagers, yet the chairperson was the sole key-holder of the club and was supported by the *Seniunje*. The villagers had little power to intervene. Some vandalism occurred to the centre, and a bonfire was lit on the basket-ball

[114] Nor is there a post-office, which was also located on the estate. The library, which also was on the estate, is now located in a small room at the school. The majority of the communities established in the Ukmerge District as a result of the RPP used cultural houses as their base, and many RPP projects focused on the refurbishment of such houses.

court, which had been a prior project of the community chairperson and the organisation. In response, the community facilitator locked the youth and sport centre at all times, opening it only for a select few in the village. Parents were angry about this, reporting that "now children run home crying, saying that they have been turned away from the Youth Club" and their response was to contact local newspapers. In response, the *Seniunje* organised a village meeting in the youth and sports centre, which was attended by municipal government officials and was covered in a local newspaper which described the extent of the division between those in favour of the Tulpiakiemis Community and those against it – "Tulpiakiemis has clearly two communities – one inside the Youth Club and the other outside" (Ukmerges Zinios, Kovo 19, 2005).

The *Seniunje* suggested at this meeting that a community board for the Tulpiakiemis Community be elected there and then. Six people were elected onto the board, which would take over responsibility for all financial and managerial matters relating to the Tulpiakiemis Community, and the Youth and Sports Club, while the original chairperson remained in place without any major responsibilities. Today, the Youth and Sport Club is used for recreational purposes, for village meetings (organised by the *Seniunje)* for birthday parties, funerals and for youth discos (now supervised by parents)

It appeared that 'community' meetings of the Tulpiakiemis Community, as conventionally understood as representative of the village population, are very much identified with the Youth and Sport Club, and not the wider village population. One villager noted that "a general meeting is called in the village to discuss an internal problem in the youth centre, where's the point in that? It's only pretence" (Female, 55 yrs, Tulpiakiemis).

Soon after the opening of the Youth and Sports Club, its meeting room was used for village meetings when representatives from the unemployment agency or *seniunija* visited, and for meetings about EU membership and EU rural policy. The village meetings, however, were organised by the *seniunija* and while they addressed issues of general importance to the village, they could not be defined as an independent community (third sector) initiative. Upon observing one such meeting, although badly attended, issues of general importance to the village were indeed discussed. A representative from the police department was there to discuss a recent bout of crime in the village, and a representative from the labour exchange to discuss recent changes in unemployment benefits.

The Tulpe Community, on the other hand, has successfully lobbied the municipal government and the mayor of Ukmerge to finance the renovation of a vacant house into a wash-house and also to build a dam in the river that runs through Tulpiakiemis (Sventoje River), so that people can swim there in the summertime. When this work will take place, however, remains unclear. The chairperson and deputy chairperson of the Tulpe Community are also lobbying the municipal government to provide a proper road into the village; it is the only village among the 14 villages where the RPP was implemented that only has a dirt-road leading to and from the village.

More generally, when villagers were asked about their perception of the function of their community organisations – their answers related to both of the established communities – the most common answer was that "there are two communities, one for the youth and the other to address issues that concern the whole community. The youth community is active, and provides a place for children to go, but the other is inactive" (Male, 50 yrs, Tulpiakiemis).

The majority of the villagers interviewed said that they wished that the Tulpe community was more active, reasoning that they needed a unified organisation to act on their behalf if another funding opportunity came along. Villagers also said that they believed that the sports and youth centre was a useful meeting place, but the actual meetings themselves were identified more with the *seniunija* than the Tulpiakiemis Community Organisation. When asked what people would like from a community, a commonly perceived need was an active cultural house where people could socialise like they did in the days of the collective farm. As one villager put it: "We have no village building" (Postal worker, 48 yrs, Tulpiakiemis). Another villager said: "I imagine the community like a collective farm, with a leader and promise" (Female shop worker, 35 yrs, Tulpiakiemis).

Key actors

The chairperson of the Tulpiakiemis Community had moved to Tulpiakiemis five years prior to the commencement of the RPP and had become acquainted with a organisation of young men in the area who enjoyed playing basketball. In the absence of a court, they were playing in a disused gravelled area. The community facilitator had helped this organisation of young men to improve this site and make it more suitable for sports. This organisation of men initially formed the Tulpiakiemis community board and while they worked and resided in the capital city of Vilnius during the week, they returned to Tulpiakiemis at weekends to carry out the implementation work on the Youth and Sports Club. One of them owned a small business in Vilnius, three were semi-skilled workers, and one was a student at Vilnius University. An additional four volunteers from the village population helped out with implementing the project, but according to the chairperson and board members, not in a significant way.

There were three other main influential actors in the village of Tulpiakiemis: the *Seniunje*, the *Seniunje's* deputy located in Tulpiakiemis who is deputy chairperson of the Tulpe Community, and a large farmer who was elected chairperson of the Tulpe Community. The deputy worked with both the Tulpiakiemis and Tulpe Communities, while the chairperson of the Tulpe Community was not in favour of the Tulpiakiemis Community. The *Seniunje*, according to the traditional role of the position, was a key actor in organising meetings and village affairs in Tulpiakiemis. According to villagers, she was only in favour of the Tulpiakiemis Community, and it was reported that at the initial village meeting where the Tulpiakiemis Community was announced, she had said "there will be the Tulpiakiemis Community or no community", and had proceeded to appoint the RPP-trained community facilitator as chairperson. The *Seniunje* organises regular meetings at the Youth and Sports Club to discuss issues of village importance and thereby has extended the functional purpose of the Youth and Sports Club building.

The deputy of the Tulpe Community (who is also the deputy of the *seniunija*) and the chairperson of the Tulpe Community are described as "the basis for community activity in our village" (Former Cultural House worker, 70 yrs, Tulpiakiemis). Villagers respect the chairperson of the Tulpe Community, because he is "hard-working", "level-headed" and "honest". He is a native of Tulpiakiemis but left during socialism to join the army, only to return in 1998 and now owns one of two creameries in the village. The deputy chairperson and deputy to the *Seniunje* liaise between villagers and the *seniunija* on matters of importance such as: the organisation of village meetings, organising the attendance of guest-speakers at village meetings, and forwarding individual and organisation requests to the *seniunija*. The deputy also takes responsibility for the village-owned water tower and collects the maintenance fee required for its upkeep from the villagers.

In all, it is claimed that there are very few key actors in Tulpiakiemis who are willing to work voluntarily or engage in collective action. One resident argued that:

> Everyone cares just about themselves; people only communicate on a one-to-one basis. This is because the village is old. Young or very old people do not engage in village matters so we only have some 40-50 people who could potentially become involved. A number of these work in the town of Ukmerge, and have no interest in the village. Farming takes up most of the villagers' time, especially in winter when people have to cut wood and feed animals. There are some people who are willing to be leaders, but nobody especially talented (Male, 60 yrs, Tulpiakiemis).

Trust and mistrust

It was obvious from the interviews carried out, and from the dynamics of how Tulpiakiemis reacted to the establishment of new community organisations under the RPP, that there was a low level of trust among village inhabitants. This was evident in relation to the position of the leader of the Tulpiakiemis Community Organisation and to the very idea of the "community" itself. Mistrust was also evident between village inhabitants themselves and scepticism was manifest in the vast majority of interviews, as were predominantly negative views on the village's future. As one villager put it:

> People are secretive here. They drink too much and are angry and hungry. This is because they are unemployed and were left with nothing after the dissolution of the collective farm. In the collective farm, everyone had their own job and there was no need to argue (Female, 30 yrs, Tulpiakiemis).

This viewpoint which refers to the sense of loss experienced by village inhabitants upon the dissolution of the collective farm expanded into full-blown scepticism about the potential of community organisations to fill the void left behind by the disappearance of the farms. Alongside the testimonies that the Tulpikiemis Collective Farm workers experienced greater poverty in comparison to other farms in the district, it is clear that farm workers were left destitute after the dissolution of the collective farm. Self-protectionism, desperation and the unequal economic status of the villagers was identified by interviewees as the basis for their scepticism in relation to the cooperation of the villagers in the activities of the new community organisations:

> There was mistrust about all the nice words that were said about communities. We were told of success stories such as Petronys and Jakutiskiai. I thought it was unrealistic that people would do things for each other without reward (Female shop worker, 35 yrs, Tulpiakiemis).

Additionally, the leader of the Tulpiakiemis Community Organisation was regarded as a "profiteer" by a significant organisation of villagers (those in support of the Tulpe Community Organisation). Due to the RPP's association with the organisation, villages also regarded the RPP with mistrust:

> By the second meeting held about the community, everyone in the village was against the community leader, but officials from Ukmerge and the *seniunija* succeeded in keeping him in position by giving him money (Female shopkeeper, 35 yrs, Tulpiakiemis).

Implicit in the co-existence of two community organisations were issues concerning the representation of the Tulpiakiemis villagers, and whether the leader should be a native of the village or a non-native. The leader of the Tulpiakiemis Community Organisation was perceived as an outsider by many villagers:

> The head of the youth community is a man from a different place. He has an organisation of young people and they have a Youth Club. Not all young people are part of it. He hasn't managed to become a member of our village. People don't accept him. He's still an alien here. He doesn't fit in. His community is separate from the village. It's not for the village, only for a few. (Former cultural-house worker, 70 yrs, Tulpiakiemis).

The issue of trust was clearly prominent in the formation of the two community organisations in Tulpiakiemis and how their operation and roles were perceived by villagers. Experiences of poverty on the collective farm and the lingering effects of restitution clearly have an influence on how community organisations take form and operate in Tulpiakiemis today.

Community in Petronys and Tulpiakiemis: a different basis for operation

The establishment of community organisations in the villages of Petronys and Tulpiakiemis led to different local reactions and effects. The result in Petronys overall was a successful territorially-oriented community with wide membership, yet the result in Tulpiakiemis was conflictual and, with respect to the funded Tulpiakiemis Community, insular and inherently problematic. While every community organisation is unique depending on local economic, social and cultural conditions and the actors that become involved, it is also noteworthy that Petronys and Tulpiakiemis had different experiences under socialism. This section presents historical contextual information particular to the villages of Tulpiakiemis and Petronys that goes some way towards explaining the very different outcomes of their respective community organisations. Although the villages were located in the same rural *seniunija*, their experiences of the same socialist entity, the collective farm, were almost diametrically opposed: The *Ausra* (meaning dawn) collective farm in Petronys is remembered in a very positive way, while the Tulpiakiemis farm is recollected as strongly, but in negative terms.

The Petronys village inhabitants have demonstrably close social ties, with a heritage of largely positive collective experiences. Villagers spoke of their trust in the collective farm leader who was in place for 30 years. They claimed that he gave a voice to farm workers when they were concerned about a farm or welfare issue. The farm leader also conferred genuine power on the collective farm board, which was elected by the farm workers, to make the primary decisions about the allocation of goods, services, and how farm workers could efficiently parcel and farm their small plots of private land (an issue external to the management of the collective farm itself). This shed some light on Petronys villagers' ease in operating fair and consultative community procedures, where the board was formed by means of election, and decisions were taken collectively by consensus or by vote. The villagers' historical confidence in the collective farm board is also reflected in their generally positive attitude towards community organisation today. The overall management of the collective farm, which was evidently "by the people", also concerned itself with the welfare of its workers (e.g., the maximum profitability of private household plots).

The social environment of cooperation and solidarity continued on into the post-socialist period, as evidenced by an incident in 1999 when a family's barn and cowsheds burnt down and some livestock were killed. Neighbours of this family decided to organise a collective effort to help the family and approached the person who once had managed the savings bank in the collective farm to oversee it. The former savings bank manager, who is now a farmer, organised a collection and claimed that all but three families in Petronys had contributed to the fund, some very generously and others who were comparatively poor, donated hay or a day's work. Villagers claimed that:

> if such a thing happened in the collective farm, the collective farm board and leader would have arranged for the family to be compensated. We just did the same; except with this independent regime, we had to take it from our own pockets.

Petronys villagers explained that their leader worked hard to make the farm a successful one and that the farm workers, too, worked hard; pilfering and alcohol abuse were less common than in other farms. They claimed that the Petronys farm was one of the most successful in the district, and that they had better housing and living conditions than in most other areas. The community organisation, as well as its body of members today, has assumed a similar work ethic, demonstrated by the significant percentage of the population having engaged in the implementation work needed to renovate the craft house, and the monstrous efforts of the community to further its progress, proven by the additional grants that have been secured from the UNOPS, the World Bank, the Municipal government, and the Lithuanian Youth Affairs Council.

The farm leader, who still lives in Petronys,[115] explained that his main ambition as leader was to build as many houses as possible to accommodate

---

[115] The farm leaders of all the other 13 villages where the RPP was implemented had left the locality. Rural inhabitants explained that it was common for collective farm leaders to leave the village upon the dissolution of the collective farm, as they were generally disliked by the farm population. The Petronys collective farm leader claimed "if I was

young people, and to buy as much machinery as possible. Today, villagers claimed, every household inherited a piece of machinery from the collective farm and people feel fortunate, in comparison to other villages. One village inhabitant who had recently married into the area expressed her surprise at how well equipped the small farmers in Petronys were in comparison to other villages in the district. Due to the plentiful housing situation, people who were raised in Petronys tended to stay, and those who were transferred under socialism tended to come back on holidays and returned permanently upon Lithuania's independence. Even skilled workers and professionals were encouraged to stay in Petronys as farmers as they inherited machinery from the farm and were in a position to farm the land that was restituted to them, and because of family and social ties; it was claimed that "many families have four generations living here in Petronys" (Female, 42 yrs, Petronys).

This gave rise to a situation where, prior to the initiation of the RPP, a organisation of educated women set up a dairy producer organisation and after setting up a local branch of the Lithuanian Women Farmers' Organisation, went on to receive the support of a UK NGO. The stable population of the village also resulted in the continuation of the village school, library and cultural house, and the professionals employed in these institutions also contributed in a significant way to the establishment of the community and its progress.

In contrast, the term 'outsider' emerged frequently during interviews with Tulpiakiemis villagers, particularly in reference to the Tulpiakiemis Community chairperson. Tulpiakiemis is said to be unique as regards the high number of people that passed through it today and also throughout socialism.The Tulpiakiemis collective farm, according to villagers living there now, was a particularly unsuccessful one. It was explained that in the case of unsuccessful farms, their leadership was dictated by the central committee in Ukmerge which changed every number of years, and with each change, a new leader would be allocated to the failing farms. Once a new leader was instated, according to villagers, he would first equip himself with all the material needs he required, then came his family, and only then would the farm workers start to benefit. It was also claimed that "the farm leaders that came here more often than not were alcoholics and because they had no successful farm of their own, they were transferred to Tulpiakiemis" (Male, 48 yrs, Tulpiakiemis).

The authority and functioning of the collective farm board in Tulpiakiemis was also undermined by the farm leaders, the change of these leaders and the transient working population, and the overall failure of the collective farm. Some of the board members are living in Tulpiakiemis today and speak of their frustration at the way in which the farm was managed: "how could we be

---

corrupt or a bad leader, I would be in Vilnius or in another city now with all the other former leaders".

successful when our leader would be there for only a few years, and was disinterested because of the inefficiency of the farm?" (Male, 48 yrs, Tulpiakiemis). Farm workers also spoke of their poor treatment on the farm: "In the days of the collective farm, only people in the offices had good times. We worked like slaves" (Female, 70 yrs, Tulpiakiemis).

One of the main lasting effects of this was the transience of the farm workers who usually moved on from Tupiakiemis after only a short period of time. This was attributed to the lack of housing, especially individual houses, the building of which was the under the authority of the collective farm leaders, who usually built apartments more than houses.[116] Some of the Tulpiakiemis farm leaders built two or three houses and a block of apartments per year, whilst others did not build a single house over their entire five-year term with the result that there was a lack of housing. Therefore, young people who had grown up on the farm would leave to find work on another farm so that they could have their own house with its own plot of land, rather than an apartment. This, evidently, has given rise to the lack of trust and the unfriendly perception of 'outsiders' that is part of the social fabric of Tulpiakiemis today. Workers and specialists who came to Tulpiakiemis were often required to share flats and houses with others, and would leave the village at the earliest opportunity. Therefore, it was claimed, "it was difficult to have a sense of closeness in Tulpiakiemis, as even our children left and the people who did come here would stay for a few months and then move on" (Female, 55 yrs, Tulpiakiemis).

Also, in contrast to Petronys, the Tulpiakiemis farm was in debt when the collective farm was dissolved and, therefore, very little machinery was available to be allocated to the farm workers. Today, one resident claimed that "life in the village is very hard now. Most people don't even keep their land. There are those on benefits who don't even keep a cow." (Post-mistress, 48 yrs, Tulpiakiemis).

In 2001, twice as many people earned their living from farming in Petronys than in Tulpiakiemis, and double the number of people received unemployment benefit in Tulpiakiemis than in Petronys (16% and 8% respectively) (Statistikos Departamentas 2001).

Villagers who lived in the Tulpiakiemis collective farm explained that little effort was made by the collective farm leaders to keep workers at the farm. When the Tulpiakiemis collective farm was dissolved at the time of Lithuania's independence, workers, particularly specialists, were inclined to leave the area, if they had the means to do so, in search of better work elsewhere: "those who could, left Tulpiakiemis straight away to find a better place to live" (Female, 70yrs, Tulpiakiemis).

---

[116] Today, there is over double the number of apartments in Tulpiakiemis than in Petronys (Lithuanian Statistics Department 2001)

Now, in the post-socialist period, this has resulted in a situation where there is an absence of educated professionals, who have played a prominent role in community organisations elsewhere in Ukmerge. According to the 2001 census, only 1.8% of Tulpiakiemis residents have a higher education, whereas in Petronys the corresponding percentage is 5.6%. The usual presence of females of professional status on the community board (cultural-house workers, librarians, post-mistresses and teachers), as in the case of Petronys and in other documented cases (see Juska 2005a), was absent here due to the fact that "Tulpiakiemis doesn't even have its own teachers, they all come from outside" (Female, 70 yrs, Tulpiakiemis).

Neither is there a cultural-house worker in Tulpiakiemis[117] or a post-office, although a postal worker works from home, sorting the post in her living room, and delivering it to homes in the village. The elderly must also collect their pensions from her home. There is a small library in the village, located in the school, which was run by the same librarian that used to work in the collective farm. She, however, was replaced by the RPP community facilitator soon after the Youth and Sports Club was renovated,[118] a situation that gave rise to discontent among the village population. The absence of professionals in Tulpiakiemis, who have traditionally played a prominent role in the social activity that is associated with community in Lithuania today, has given rise, in part, to the perception amongst Tulpiakiemis villagers that the Tulpiakiemis Community Chairperson is somehow unqualified as he does not belong to any of these professions.

Today, it is claimed "the village will never be empty as people relocate from towns here because they can live so cheaply" (Male, 58 yrs, Tulpiakiemis). In 2001, 40 people (14% of the total population) of Tulpiakiemis inhabitants were originally from urban areas. Many local people are of the view that newcomers are "undesirables, often with criminal records and we don't want them here" (Female shop-worker, 35yrs, Tulpiakiemis). The former cultural-house worker spoke of her unfamiliarity with the ever-changing population and claimed "I

[117] There is no cultural house in Tulpiakiemis, but a limited number of social events are held in the school.

[118] Although she said that she resigned voluntarily, she also said that she felt under pressure to resign as the RPP community facilitator was more skilled than she was. She had been involved in organising annual Easter, Christmas and New-Year celebrations in the school since independence, and recently the library had celebrated its 50th anniversary. She said that, when the community facilitator came to live in the community, five years earlier, "he became head of the community, with links to the authorities. I saw that I wasn't as good an organiser as he. I don't have the skills, therefore I left". (Former librarian, 45 yrs, Tulpiakiemis).

don't know anybody around here, I don't have the kind of experience needed to organise events among strangers. People won't go".

The different outcomes of the newly established community organisations in Petronys and Tulpiakiemis show that there can be different bases for collective action in villages that have had different experiences of the collective farm. This comparative case study shows that there is a stronger base for community formation and action in Petronys as the community is an extension of collective farm structures in which there was popular trust in the Soviet period, and the idea of community action is not therefore so new and unfamiliar today. The undermining of the institution in which trust had been invested, the collective farm board, as well as the historic absence of trust in the farm leader has given rise to a problematic basis for community action in the case of Tulpiakiemis, where the leader failed to consolidate unified action. While in Petronys, there was scepticism among villagers regarding the funded community project, which was primarily economic in nature and therefore estranged from the common conception of what community projects should entail, the project and the community succeeded nonetheless. In the case of Tulpiakiemis, the project was entirely social in nature with no potential for economic gain, yet the lack of trust resulted in the lack of an established community.

Conclusion

This paper has sought to depict some of the crucial determinants of community action in a post-socialist context, so as to shed light on variations of the path-dependent operational reality of third sector participation in future EU rural development. The paper has described and analysed in context the formation and operation of community organisations in the neighbouring villages of Petronys and Tulpiakiemis. In Petronys, the outcome was generally successful, indicated by popular support for the community organisation and by the fact that it evolved to address issues of concern for the whole village. In Tulpiakiemis, on the other hand, the establishment of a community organisation gave rise to conflict among village inhabitants, resulting in the formation of a second community organisation.

In attempting to explain the different results in community formation and operation in neighbouring villages, this paper suggests that the main explanatory factors lie in the villages' different experiences of the collective farm; the crucial determinants in this comparative case arising from the farm leader(s). The basis for the success of the Petronys community was that villagers, historically, had a trustful relationship with the farm leader who had been in place for 30 years prior to the dissolution of the collective farm. The leader bestowed power on the collective farm board, which was elected by the farm workers and had a mandate that extended beyond farm management issues to matters relating to workers' welfare. The farm leader prioritised the provision of housing and the purchasing of machinery, which encouraged workers, as well as professionals, to remain on the farm. Even after the dissolution of the collective farm, they benefited from these policies.

In Tulpiakiemis, on the other hand, the collective farm was particularly unsuccessful, and the change of the collective farm leader every five years, as well as the neglect of the provision of housing, resulted in a situation where workers usually moved away from the area after only a short period. This gave rise to a situation where there was little or no trust and weak social ties, a prominent issue today being the presence of 'outsiders' in the village.

A second effect of the success of the collective farm in Petronys, and the lack of success in its counterpart in Tulpiakiemis, relates to the presence of professional women in the villages. In Petronys, the role of the cultural-house worker, teacher, librarian and post-mistress (professions that are generally dominated by women) was significant in establishing a successful community due to their traditional involvement in village social activity dating back to the socialist period. In Tulpiakiemis, on the other hand, there is a lack of such professionals, which is attributed to the fact that after the dissolution of the collective farm, everyone who could do so left the area in search of a better living environment. The departure of professionals from the area was also caused by the privatisation of the cultural house, library and school, due to the farm not having built its own buildings for these facilities. Given the lack of professionals who traditionally undertook socially-oriented tasks and the lack of experience of consultative processes on the collective farm, the basis for community formation and leadership was unclear. The community chairperson was perceived as an outsider and his position was seen as illegitimate.

The confidence of the Petronys villagers in comparison with their Tulpiakiemis counterparts is further illustrated by the former's unified stance against the attempt of the *Seniunje* to put in place a community chairperson. They responded by independently electing a chairperson and establishing a community on their own terms. Despite some degree of protest, the *Seniunje's* attempt to do this in Tulpiakiemis was more succesful, as demonstrated by the formation of two separate and conflicting communities. It is notable that now, the *Seniunje* organises all public meetings in the Tulpiakiemis Community building, yet in Petronys, it is the *Seniunje* who is invited to meetings organised by the community.

Apart from deductions reached on the basis of historical social and economic experiences, conclusions can also be made on community formation in a project-based framework. In Petronys, a dairy producer organisation had formed endogenously within a relatively confident village society, and only then profited from external funding agencies and projects. This dairy organisation was a pioneering post-socialist development in the village, and the RPP project constituted a further development of an already existing process, whereas the project in Tulpiakiemis represented a new phenomenon as there was no tradition of association prior to the RPP. In Tulpiakiemis, the villagers did not exhibit cohesion, nor were there any natural leaders. The emergence of a community facilitator from this kind of environment and the effect of this on the impetus of a funded project was somewhat random, the popular reaction unknown. The result of the RPP community development project in Tulpiakiemis was that the trained community facilitator, who was perceived as an 'outsider', was, nevertheless, placed in the position of community chairperson due to the fact that the funding application of the Tulpiakiemis Community was granted. The application of the Tulpe Community, on the other hand, although the organisation had a chairperson of some popular legitimacy within the village, was for practical reasons denied.

From the research findings of this paper, it can be seen that although there was a virtual absence of rural community organisations in the post-socialist rural district of Ukmerge prior to the RPP, there was a heritage of collective action, albeit in different forms to those that exist in the EU15. It is also apparent, that despite the uniformity of socialist rural policy, there were significant differences in how collective farms operated in practice and these variations have given rise to different post-socialist rural environments for the operation of new community organisations. It is clear that small-scale programmes, such as the "Information is Powerful" initiative implemented in Petronys, and the RPP, are crucial in preparing post-socialist villages for the increasing autonomy afforded to community organisations through programmes such as LEADER.

References

Beksta, A., & A. Petkevicius (2000) *Local Governments in Lithuania in Decentralization: Experiments and Reforms, Local Government and Public Service Reform Initiative*. Open Society Institute, Budapest.

Bryden, J,. & M. Shucksmith (2000) *EU Enlargement in the context of Late-Modernity*. Conference paper given at Arkleton Centre for Rural Development Research, July 2000.

CEC (1988) *The Future of Rural Society*. Directorate General for Agriculture, CEC.

Curtin, C., & T. Varley (1994) Shellfish Co-operatives in North West Connemara: A Successful Case of 'Collective' Endogenous Development? in *Beyond Modernisation: The Impact of Endogenous Rural Development* ed. by J. Van Der Ploeg & G. Van Dijh. Assen, Van Gorcum, 386-99.

Curtin, C., & T. Varley (1995) Take Your Partners and Face the Music: The State, Community Organisations and Area-Based Partnerships in Rural Ireland, in *Secularisation and the State in Ireland*, ed. by P. Brennan. Caen University Press, Caen, 119-46.

Curtin, C., & T. Varley (2002) Changing patterns of leadership and local power in rural Ireland, in *Leadership and Local Power in European Rural Development*, ed. by K. Halfacree et al. Aldershot, Ashgate, 12-32.

Curtin, C., T. Varley & K. O'Donoghue (1991) The Theory and Practice of Community Development in Two West of Ireland Community Councils, in *Rural Development: Problems and Prospects,* ed. by H. Buller & S. Wright. Aldershot, Avebury,

European Commission (2002) *The Agricultural Situation in the Candidate Countries, Country Report on Lithuania.* Directorate General for Agriculture, July 2002.

Gazaryan, A. (1995) Local Government in Lithuania in the Transition period, in *Local Government in Eastern Europe*, ed. by A. Coulson. Aldershot, Hants, p. 291.

Intitut für Agrarentwicklung in Mittel- und Ost-Europa (IAMO) (2004) *The Future of Rural Areas in the CEE new Member States*. IAMO, Germany.

Kazlauskas, D. (2005) *Talka. Jurgines, O gal Valpurgijos naktis?* (translation: Spring Cleaning, St. George's Day, or maybe Walpurgis Night?) Ukmerges Zinios, Balandzio 30.

Kovach, I. (2000) LEADER, a New Social Order, and the Central and East European Countries. *Sociologia Ruralis*, 40 (2), 181-89.

Labanauskas, S. (2005) *'Karas' isvarino Tulpiakiemis dvaro giventojus.* (translation: "War" has worn down the inhabitants of the Tulpiakiemis Estate). Ukmerges Zinios, Kovo 19.

LEADER European Observatory (1997) *Organising Local Partnerships; Innovation in Rural Areas.* Notebook no.2.

Leonard, P. & D. Kaneff (2002) *Post-Socialist Peasant?* Macmillan, New York.

Nemes, G. (2003) *Rural Development and Pre-Accession Preparation in Hungary – is there an alternative way?* OSI International Policy Fellowship Final Policy Paper, UK

Juska, A., A. Poviliunas & R. Pozzuto (2005a) *Resisting Marginalisation: The Rise of the Rural Community Movement in Lithuania,* Sociologia Ruralis 40 (1/2), 3-21.

Juska, A., A. Poviliunas & R. Pozzuto (2006) Rural Grass-roots Organizing in Eastern Europe: the Experience from Lithuania. *Community Development Journal* 41 (2), 174-188.

Taylor, L. (1990) The River Would Run Red with Blood: Community and Common Property in an Irish Fishing Settlement, in *The Question of the*

Commons: The Culture and Ecology of Communal Resources, ed. by B. McCay & J. M. Acheson. (2nd printing of 1987 edition.) Arizona Studies in Human Ecology, University of Arizona Press, Tucson, AZ, 1-36.

Slee, B. (2000) *W(h)ither the Small Farm? Rural Development and Agricultural Restructuring in Transition Economies with Particular reference to the Baltic States*. Conference paper presented at Arkleton Centre for Rural Development Research, July 2000.

Statistikos Departamentas (2002) *Statistikos Departamentas prie Lietuvos Respublikos Vyriausybe*s. (translation: Lithuanian Statistiks Department) Vilnius, Lithuania.

Macken Walsh, A. (2005) *Community Action in the Post-Socialist Countryside: the case of Lithuania.* Conference paper presented at XXII Congress of the European Society for Rural Sociology, Keszthely, Hungary.

CHAPTER TEN

"INDUSTRIALIZED VILLAGES" IN POST-SOCIALIST COUNTRIES – STEPS TOWARDS AN INTEGRATIVE RESEARCH CONCEPT

INGRID OSWALD

Introduction

The term "industrialized village" arose in the course of our research project on societal change in rural regions throughout post-socialist Eastern Europe.[119] Using the instruments of qualitative research (narrative and biographic interviews, field studies and participant observation), the team compared living and working conditions in six villages in several transition countries, one each

[119] The project "Beyond the big cities. Rural living and working conditions in post-socialist Eastern Europe" focused on the life worlds in transition countries, and was financed from the year 2002 to 2005 by the German Research Community ("Deutsche Forschungsgemeinschaft" DFG). Applicants were Eckhard Dittrich (University Magdeburg) and Ingrid Oswald (then University Magdeburg, now Humboldt University Berlin); the main co-ordination lay in the hands of Viktor Voronkov ("Centre for Independent Social Research" CISR/ St. Petersburg). Originally the study was comprised of four villages: two Russian villages, one in the region of Novgorod and one in the region of Krasnodar; one village in Estonia, near Tartu; and one in Bulgaria between the towns Plovdiv and Burgas. After some months, researchers from the Irkutsk "Centre for Independent Social Research and Education" (CISRE) voluntarily joined the project under the guidance of Michail Rozhanskij. They brought in the cases of two Siberian villages in the Irkutsk region and could, after a while, get a fee from the "Stifterverband fuer Wissenschaft" (Scientific Founders Association). The village in East Germany was added to the comparison via contact with the Thuenen Institute for Regional Development in Mecklenburg-Vorpommern. Main contributors to the project, besides those already mentioned, were: Elena Bogdanova, Olga Brednikova, Natalja Cheremnykh, Elena Chikadze, Frank Ernst, Rumiana Jeleva, Sergej Karnaukhov, Aleksandra Kasjanova, Aleksandr Manujlov, Elena Nikiforova, Tatjana Timofeeva, Olga Tkach and Tuuli Toomere.

in Bulgaria, Estonia and East Germany, and three in Russia, specifically in the South (Krasnodar region), the North (Novgorod region) and in Siberia.

Although the following suggestions do not contradict the main results provided by agronomy and business studies, the methodology is very different and opened another perspective on the specific "path dependencies" of societal change in rural areas of Eastern Europe – areas which are processing not only decades of socialist transition but also now a variety of legal reforms and a dramatic price decline for agricultural produce (see Stark & Bruszt, 1998).

At an early stage of our empirical work it became clear that there was a need for a specific interpretation scheme because the societal change taking place in the post-socialist countries in question does not obviously support traditional rural ways of life but is developing a broad spectrum of living patterns and working conditions depending on the previous socialist transition. The methods mentioned above are those of cultural anthropology and point primarily to a description (of a situation, a social or cultural phenomenon); that is, they illuminate particularities. However, following Ember and Ember (2001, 2), explanation requires comparison. Comparative studies aim at general statements that seek to answer why variations exist and to enable differences to be identified.

Cross-cultural comparison is possible only on the assumption that the phenomena in question are connected by certain similarities although they exhibit different qualities. The differences are not variables as in quantitative research since there is a continuity of variations with, of course, extreme poles. In order to find the "kinds of phenomena that occur repeatedly" (Ember & Ember 2001, 3), research designs have to formulate a qualitative standard on an abstract level, a "*tertium comparationis*" (Matthes 1992), which is, in our case, the model of the "industrialized village". It consists of the basic elements of ruralness in the course, and as a consequence, of socialist and post-socialist socio-economic reforms in order to compare the villages studied on their different developmental paths.

The concept of the "industrialized village" works as a sort of Weberian "ideal type" (Weber 1988). As a theoretical approach it contrasts with the concept and social practices of the "old European village of family farms" which was brought to an end by the socialization of property. Initially, post-socialist reform programs defined the revitalization of family farming as one goal, among others, that could not be realized at all. In this paper I will show why. Therefore, I will, on an abstract level, formulate some of the basic elements of socialist and post-socialist rural ways of life in order to compare the different paths of post-socialist transition in Eastern Europe. In opposition to the assumptions of the classic theory of "ongoing modernization" (Zapf 1996), societal transformation is not seen here as a short-term process of institutional system change, in which, according to the model of Western Europe, functioning institutions were introduced. The research design refers to the cultural embeddedness of transformation by referring to actors and actor constellations and by focusing on daily life rather than on the processes of institution-building alone. "Social structure sets certain limitations on actors, and actor dynamics cause a change of structure with, however, a certain time lag in between" (Schrader 2004, 8). Thus, the destruction of socialist agriculture did not automatically lead to a reformation of rural society. The re-establishment of private property in land and agrarian markets should produce capitalist and democratic structures, but, as S. Eisenstadt (1978) points out, the elimination of habitual milieus and infrastructure can just as well lead to "disorganization, delinquency and chaos" (see also Rosa 2003).

The concept of the "industrialized village" can help to describe the tensions within the post-socialist rebuilding of rural settlements. Thus, it clarifies the main thesis that the peasant village in Eastern Europe no longer exists, and that it won't be revived. Socialism changed rural daily life so deeply that there are only very rare starting points for the "re-invention of traditions". At present, something new is emerging. In other words, new rural ways of life and new habits are developing that are different from those in "the West" and different from pre-Soviet ones.

In introducing my arguments, I will, firstly, give a short survey of the concept, followed by a presentation of the categories employed. A comparison of the villages examined in this project will close the paper, illustrated by the example of a failed state-run project in one of the examined villages.

The concept of the "industrialized village" and the main research questions

At first sight, the term "industrialized village" might conjure up images of the industrialization of agriculture that was such an important element of Soviet modernization from the 1920s onward. But, more significantly, Soviet agrarian reforms aimed at the "equalization of town and country" and carried with them the "industrialization" of villagers' lives. It is often said that a socialist plant's operation represented the world in miniature. In the countryside the plants were *sovkhozes* or other agrarian co-operatives, ruling not only production but also the social reproduction of its members (recreation, child care and so on). Thus, the socialist plant was especially decisive for its members' lives. The workers and their families were integrated into its social institutions and infrastructure, which included kindergartens, canteens and shops with special prices, apartments and cultural institutions, even holiday camps and sometimes schools, training courses and stipends for the workers' children. Although these aspects are known (Narojek 1980/81), the "totality" of public care and supply in the country should be emphasized. In the course of farm collectivization and the industrialization of agriculture many competences were transferred from the community and the family to the plant and thus came under state control. Whereas in the late socialist period, townspeople were provided with a broad spectrum of cultural and educational institutions, the villagers were dependent upon their plant's operation and their families.

The industrialization of agriculture and the strict tying of daily life to the plant's operation were elements of a modernization strategy specific to all societies of the Soviet type. There were, of course, differences in time and extent, but, on the whole, rural subsistence and rural ways of life were brought to an end.[120] For centuries, rurality was bound to property and a concept of the family as an economic unit which as such (and not as members of a certain collective) acquired its status within the village's social hierarchy. Post-revolutionary socialist transition brought an end to the traditional peasantry, and rural families and households were integrated into collective farms, separating working individuals from their property. The introduction of "urban" principles meant a waged labour and – via a collective plant – integration into a central social system that organized every aspect of life according to a uniform principle.

Several elements, having constituted rural life for centuries, were fundamentally re-organized within only a few decades. The first element was rural self-subsistence which was replaced by industrialized agriculture. Then, property (of land and/or holdings) was socialized, and only little pieces of land (household plots) for personal needs were left in the hands of agricultural workers. The third element refers to forced but dependent individualization: Whereas the traditional household unit was the family with its own life, the collective farmer was a wageworker in huge agro-industrial complexes in a centrally planned economy.

The decisive factor is not the industrialization of agriculture – this happened everywhere, including the West and is even present in so-called eco-farming. The crucial point is the industrialization of people's lives which resulted from the complete entanglement and integration of everyday life with, and into, the cycles of the collective farms.

---

120 The collectivization of farms and the establishment of an agro-industrial complex did not dominate all socialist countries. In Poland, for example, there was always a high percentage of small family farms, and aside from the Soviet core regions where collectivization had already begun in the 1920s, rural ways of life were not totally forgotten when the Soviet system collapsed. The concept of the industrialized village should be able to accommodate these differences systematically.

Thus, the rural population became “de-ruralized”. However, they could not become townspeople because socialist modernization never really bridged the “antagonism between town and country”. Modern infrastructure did not reach the villages (or at best it reached them in fragments, as our example will illustrate), but the all-embracing care offered by the agro-industrial complexes nourished certain expectations, even if the state did not entirely fulfil its promises, because the supply was on a low level.

This disastrous connection between a solicitous but overambitious state and its dependent but demanding citizens is well-known and shall not be discussed here (see e.g. Ledeneva 1998; Schrader 2004), except to emphasize that paternalism ruled the countryside even more than the cities. Because rural areas – lacking of urban infrastructure and the institutional setting of a city - could not offer regular alternatives to official operational supplies, country-people had to help themselves. This was the reason for the formation of huge informal sectors and tight social networks which – sometimes in fragments or having been reconstituted – continue to exist today. Villagers could not escape the industrialization of their lives but they could create parallel supply structures via informal arrangements, one of the most important being the extension and care of household plots.

Some post-socialist paths of agricultural re-organization

The paternal organization of production and reproduction showed signs of dysfunctionality at a very early stage, but, over a rather long period, tremendous subsidies and efforts at providing rural infrastructure could compensate for these failings to some extent. Nevertheless, in the 1980s the relatively low productivity of large collective farms compared to that of household plots, and the misuse of collective property and infrastructure for private purposes led to massive problems. Most of the agro-industrialized complexes had to be re-organized since the planned economy and state subsidies had come to an end, and the collective units were dissolved and liquidated. Sometimes collective farms were privatised and restructured, but most of them were simply closed by dismissing the whole staff.

Of course, the restructuring of the great agro-industrial complexes and the re-organization of agriculture followed different paths of transition in each post-socialist society and created different starting points for new forms of rural life and economy. In Estonia, Bulgaria and East Germany reforms started with the restitution of property in order to stimulate agricultural production, whereas in Russia re-organization, de-collectivization and even privatization took a slow and sometimes contradictory course. But privatization as such does not seem to be the best solution for the problems of post-socialist rural areas. Although the former country people were by now mostly agro-industrial workers, the idea, or rather dream, of traditional life in a village, and its revival after the breakdown of state socialism, had survived, even at the highest official level and, thus, it arose in the first versions of several reform programmes. This is why the first post-socialist agrarian reforms aimed at a broad re-establishment of family farms, subsistence economy and market production.

The instruments of these reforms were the privatization of land (arable land) via sale or property transfer, and sometimes – in Bulgaria, Estonia and Eastern Germany – the restitution of land to its original owners or their descendants. Ten or fifteen years later, one has to state that this aspect of reform more or less failed in the countries that were the focus of our research. The new economic units in these countries are large holding companies or miserable "dwarf economies" (very tiny units) rather than family farms (Conte & Giordano 1999, Laschewski & Siebert 2001).

Why didn't it work? Why couldn't a traditional peasantry be revived with self-sufficient families making a living? Although at the beginning of the 1990s a majority of the collective farms were closed, largely due to the ending of state subsidies, villagers could not simply return to a farmer's life. There are many reasons for this.

The first is that agro-industrial workers might have been specialists, with perhaps a diploma, but were not necessarily competent across the whole spectrum of agricultural knowledge. Another reason is that the descendants of former farmers (that is, in pre-socialist times) are nowadays mostly townspeople with corresponding professions and habits. Even if they receive some arable land they are not able or are not willing to cultivate it; sometimes, for example in Bulgaria, they can sell or lease it and try to live on the proceeds. An important point is that, as a rule, the amount of land returned to any single owner/descendant is too small and, thus, uneconomic; big agro-companies in the European Union can always produce more cheaply than new small farms in Eastern Europe. And finally, it has to be stressed that very few aspiring new farmers have enough initial capital to start farming in a competitive market on a tiny piece of land. Credit is rare, so there is no money for seed, technical equipment, or seasonal workers.

Given this background, one had better forget myths of a return of post-socialist Eastern Europe to its original rurality. Perhaps there are regions in Siberia or in Central Asia where the lack of opportunities and competition have given pre-industrialized ways of life a chance; but if this is so, it should not be idealized. But in the peripheries of the joint European market there is no place for traditional peasantry if it is not linked with business ideas such as tourism or eco-farming.

Since a return to pre-socialist rurality no longer seemed to be an option, the post-socialist re-organization of agriculture followed specific paths largely determined by existing legal and political preconditions.

For example, in East-Germany, namely, in the federal county of Mecklenburg-Vorpommern, some collective plants were transformed into capitalist stock companies and are now among the most productive high-tech agro enterprises within the European Union, but, at the same time, they only employ a small number of their former staff. They are like islands of high performance amidst socio-economically devastated regions since there are only a few (non-agrarian) industrial enterprises to provide ex-collective farm workers with jobs. Even in villages where a new agrarian enterprise has opened, the locals do not profit from it because the shareholders usually live elsewhere, and the local people have lost both their jobs and the other social benefits they used to receive from the old plant. The once socially embedded villagers now live on welfare or on other aid money (Laschewski 1998, Laschewski & Siebert 2001).

In contrast to all the other post-socialist countries, in East-Germany only a few ex-workers of the former LPGs (*Landwirtschaftliche Produktionsgenossenschaft*, Agricultural Production Co-operatives) run a household plot. There is no need for a subsistence or dwarf economy because home-produced food is much more expensive than the food found in any supermarket. The people who have not left their villages are alienated from their professional skills and cannot expect to find any other job. Whereas villagers now rely on the supply line of the state (welfare aid, pensions or other social benefits) that affects every aspect of their lives, the communal administration has neither the financial nor the other resources required in order to fulfil its tasks. Thus, the village as an administrative unit is as marginalized as its inhabitants, with no hope of escaping from its extremely low social status.

In Estonia and Bulgaria, state-run agro-plants became either private enterprises or co-operatives producing for the (capitalist) market. Estonia, after joining the EU, is in a better position to develop successfully. Above all, the connection between restructured agro-complexes and the rest of the food industry seems to be working well, and the first steps to promote the countryside for tourism and recreation have been made (Nikiforova & Toomere 2003).

A social movement called "*Kodukant*" ("neighbourhood"), which was formed in order to re-establish rural self-government, has played a leading role within this "success story", although financial shortcomings often weaken the ability of rural communities to act. *Kodukant* is an NGO, whose stated primary goal is to develop rural life in Estonian villages. Thus, it is a totally new actor in the countryside bringing together various social groups, big and small entrepreneurs and local administrations. *Kodukant* is one of Estonia's new civic society institutions and faces a lot of problems and difficulties that sometimes tend to overshadow the creative and more enjoyable aspects of its activities. Nevertheless, the *Kodukant*-NGO could bring jobs to the village and encourage the communal administration to be more active, and many villagers could restructure their lives so that they would not be totally dependent on the state.

In Bulgaria, the reformers faced the severe problem caused by the restitution that there would be not enough interested and capable farmers to restructure rural production. So the referred to the long, even pre-war, story of co-operative movement in the country. Land or rural property was – as in other transition countries – returned to its former owners or their descendants who, for the most part, neither work or live in the countryside and do not see a return to the land as a realistic option (Ernst 1999, Dittrich & Jeleva 2005). Bulgaria is an interesting case as the country experienced rapid urbanization especially after World War II, so although most Bulgarians today live in cities or towns, they still have close family or mental ties with the country. The unification of many small land owners in co-operatives made sense in terms of establishing competitive businesses. There are now many new co-operatives giving "farmers" the chance to earn a living whilst providing their urban family members with a certain dividend. In addition, several private large-scale agro-companies have been established. Since these demand a considerable amount of starting capital they are not wide-spread.

A common way of life in Bulgaria involves a sort of "town-country-symbiosis": some family members, above all the elderly, live and work on restituted or newly acquired small or middle-sized plots, whereas the rest of the family lives in town. This is not simply a return to traditional agriculture but the formation of a new special type of household economy, a life based mainly on urban households. The latter "delegate" some family members for a season or a weekend to the countryside where they run the garden plot, thus combining rural and urban resources. In these cases, a household's income consists of home-grown agrarian produce, wages, pensions and other transfer payments (for children, disabled persons, war veterans and so on). Since the provision of public utilities is poor, life is family-centred leaving little room for individual decision making.

As in Bulgaria, the keeping of household plots was wide-spread in the Soviet Union. The collective farmers could cultivate their own small piece of land with the use of the collective's equipment. This provided them with a reasonable income as the produce could partly be sold in town markets nearby. This once typical practice continues to this day, but post-socialist reforms have also enabled villagers to keep middle-sized garden plots consisting of land separated off from the former collective farm. Although this garden economy is also run on a modest level, with manual labour predominating and the keeping of animal hardly possible, it is decisive for most rural households. But, these households are severely pauperized since a dwarf and garden economy can only cover some immediate material needs and are completely unable to provide villagers with the services and social security once provided by the former collective farms.

Given this background, it becomes clear that replacing these social and other services is a family task. The Bulgarian picture of big co-operatives alongside private farms and small household plots is quite similar in South Russia. Because the former system of state-run social security has decayed to an even larger degree than in Bulgaria, households have to take many functions upon themselves. Thus, life is centred on households rather than individuals and aims, as in Bulgaria, at a combination of urban and rural resources. The "town-country-symbiosis" is less tight because distances in Russia are considerably greater than in Bulgaria, and because the rural population has been "de-ruralized" for several generations, that is, it has become accustomed to an industrialized way of life.

Agriculture in South Russia has been partly restructured as private investors have reorganized many of the former state-run agro-plants. Mainly through the use of informal arrangements, they have gained a certain degree of influence over the local authorities and have rebuilt some elements of the former social and technical infrastructure like schools, kinder gardens, hospitals and highways. The most prestigious positions in the community seem to be occupied by a few successful entrepreneurs and their families in something resembling a "clan" structure.

Villages in Northern Russia and Siberia are extreme examples of the drastic consequences that followed the suspension of subsidies were. After a transitional period, most of the state-run collective farms were closed which caused severe problems for the local food industry. The villagers have been left to fend for themselves and try either to emigrate or to survive without the collective plant's infrastructure and with only a miserable level of protection in the form of central transfer payments. If such northern regions are not subsidized, if there is no-one, either native or foreign, with a reasonable amount of capital to invest and if the infrastructure does not receive a considerable amount of investment, then only in exceptional cases will it be possible to establish or maintain large-scale or even middle-scale agricultural enterprises. As a rule, the small plants that remain operate with the help of the stock (equipment, buildings, feed etc.) of closed collective farms, that is, on a very low and uncompetitive level. Households also keep tiny pieces of land near the house, but it is quite unusual to keep more than one cow or cultivate a middle-sized garden plot.

Only a few villagers have – low paid – jobs in the villages; most of these are women who have jobs in administration, schools or kindergartens. The other villagers commute to nearby small towns, and increase their income by picking berries and mushrooms and illegally cutting trees and selling the wood (Bogdanova et al. 2004). Once all these resources have been used up, these villages will be abandoned or "closed". Some of them, located not far from big cities (like St. Petersburg or Novgorod), may have a future as *dacha* colonies, i.e. as summer resorts for city dwellers.

Table 10-1 Transitional paths of "industrialized villages" in post-socialist societies

	East Germany	**Estonia**	**Bulgaria**	**North Russia**	**South Russia**	**Siberia**
Political context	Market reforms/ High transfer payments	Market reforms/ Access to EU	Delayed market reforms	Agrarian + legal reforms Instable Institutional vacuum		
Legal context	Restitution	Restitution	Restitution	Ambivalent Privatization slowed down		
Dominating types of farms	Large-scale agro-enterprises	Large-+ small scale agro-enterprises	New co-operatives + private farms	Subsistence Dwarf economy	Large-scale agro-enterprises	Subsistence Dwarf economy
Self-government	Formally existing, but weak	Restructured	Under construction	Top-down principle Dominance of informal arrangements		
Household plots	Rare	Sometimes	Yes	Yes	Yes	Yes
Life arrangements	Supported by transfer payments	Restructured	"Town-country-symbiosis"	Archaic	"Town-country-symbiosis"	Archaic
Social security	State-run	State-run & communal	By plant's operation/ state/ family	By family	By family	By family
Social status	Marginalized	Restructured	Via family/ "clan"	Marginalized	Via family/ "clan"	Marginalized

Such examples clearly demonstrate that the collapse of the industrialized life of rural areas and the failure, in most cases, of new institutions to replace former institutions has not enabled villagers to return to a traditional rural way of life.[121] The necessary preconditions for this are lacking: the villagers' economic basis is largely insufficient for running a private and competitive farm; there is no social actor willing to transfer administrative functions from the former collective plants to the communities, although a legal basis for this exists; and finally, the people concerned are accustomed to having dependable jobs whereas management and economic decision-making is strange to them. Because climatic conditions in Northern Russia and Siberia are less favourable to agriculture than in Bulgaria or Southern Russia the situation has become far more problematic, resulting in partly "archaic", and in any case anachronistic, ways of life. For a better orientation see Table 9-1.

Comparative aspects within the concept

The concept of the "industrialized village" does not coincide with classic modernization theories because it does not define backwardness in the course of uniform modernization but wants to analyse how particular paths of modernization based on the industrialization of agriculture, the collectivization of resources and ways of life, are tightly connected with a collective plant's operation in rural regions. This special form of modernization proceeds today along a set of different transitional paths partly revoking or correcting socialist structural elements.

In the following, I would like to comment on three aspects of post-socialist development that are fundamental for a comparison of transitional paths: the informalization of social relations (the circumventing of formal arrangements, of contracts) that is typical for rural regions in societies experiencing transformation and which displace villagers into an "institutional vacuum"; the transformation of socialist rural populations into rural industrial workers; and finally, the different migration patterns resulting from de-ruralization, de-collectivization and privatization.

---

[121] Political speech sometimes appeals to a post-socialist "rebirth" of the village, but this ideal is based neither on a serious political agenda nor on science. Up to the middle of the 1990s, there were great hopes of a revival of family farming, but these were to be disappointed.

Institutional transfer and informalization

For a long time, Eastern European societies of the Soviet type experienced a "permanent crisis of management", a steady struggle against targets of the planned economy, with the informalization of social relations being one element of this crisis. Since the state promised, but could not deliver, total socio-economic security (in return for political obedience), citizens were forced to help themselves using informal arrangements on the edge of legality, which were politically illegitimate though largely tolerated. This self-help was carried out in professional circles, in age groups or among friends and relatives, that is, in social networks. On the one hand, they stabilized the system. On the other hand, they undermined official, formal ways of integration (Srubar 1991). Whether this ought to be called "pre-modern" is a matter of discussion, but without a doubt it was the basis for social phenomena like the shadow economy, the second economy, a self-help mentality, insider deals and corruption (Ledeneva 1997). The transformation of these informal arrangements into formal ones is gradually being realized in urban areas, but beyond the cities informality continues to be the most common social practice.

Above all, this is evident in Russia, where a village is considered an independent administrative unit, which, however, cannot solve problems because for financial, technical and other reasons. It is difficult to speak about "self-government" since villagers obviously do not know and do not care about the principles and functions of a top-down installed administration. A woman who was appointed an "honorary" assistant of the administration could not explain the nature of her job:

> I do nothing. I didn't decide for anything. They put me on the list. Look, we had a meeting in the district administration. Sometimes some people come in and decide some questions, they invite us. We have many such authorized persons but we cannot do anything. We have authority only on the street level. There is much. But I do not have anything. What shall I do when the people brawl or something like that?

It is not that villagers are deviating from formal rules since the corresponding institutions do not work; rather, they act informally in an "institutional vacuum". Their behaviour patterns are based on self-help in an elementary sense: they use their reciprocal relations and try to adapt to top-down installed rules, the meanings of which are hidden from the people they affect.

Bulgaria and, above all, Estonia, unlike Russia, succeeded in their administrative reforms. The villages are managed by different authorities, secular and religious, who discuss the prospects for future development strategies. A handful of candidates apply for the mayor's post, and establish the community as a forum for democratic discussion and social organization. An important role in this process is played by the social movement *Kodukant* as already described above. Therefore, communal self-government in Estonia has a less ornamental character than in East Germany where villages, with their high unemployment rates, are so dependent on transfer payments that they are not able to make their own decisions.

Rural population without rural skills

I have already suggested that the rural population of Eastern Europe, in spite of de-collectivization, cannot return to a traditional rural way of life. The collective "farmers" were wageworkers, agricultural producers with special skills as milker, stockbreeder, cultivator, tractor driver. So, although regular work schedules and social security are lacking in the villages today, most of the former agricultural workers want to participate in the benefits of modernity including material goods like TVs and cars, and methods and procedures of modern administration and contemporary education. These demands concern local planning as well as personal lives.

And, last but not least, they adapted their lives to the organizational structures of large-scale plants. These plants affected not only work but also leisure, weekends and holidays, as well as childcare and housekeeping. Life could not simply be re-traditionalized. Since women as well as men were included in the management structure of the collective farms, the former clearly outlined gender roles for a peasant and his wife no longer exist, nor does the old division of labour.

There was an "urbanized" life, which was inculcated over generations and which developed certain expectations and pretensions. But now many professional spheres have disappeared from the countryside and from agriculture because privatization has meant rationalization and/or the abolition of all other employment options in the villages. Women, who seldom became rural entrepreneurs or farmers, and who avoid commuting to distant towns seem to face a premature end to their aspirations. For a certain transitional period, villagers have only two options: if they are among the younger and better educated ones they can decide to migrate, temporarily or permanently, to urban areas. Otherwise, they are forced to radically reduce their needs and concentrate on surviving with the help of their household and garden plots.

One could interpret this way of life as a "return" to pre-modernity or as a problematic mixture of modern and traditional elements, but it is more a question of modernization of already modernized living conditions, even if it is poor: a question of people who, to begin with, lost their property and traditions, then lost the organized shelter of the collective plants and now, facing totally new forms of social relations and economic necessities, have had to "invent" new forms of survival and, moreover, new, significant structures of meaning, of life-sense. At present, they do not live in "traditional" conditions since they have lost their social embeddedness. Reciprocity and activities within social networks are elements of an "emergency economy", referring to functional deficits, since the industrialized life has lost its basis and has not been replaced with an equally satisfactory alternative.

Migration patterns in rural regions

The classic social theory conceptualizes the "village" – in contrast to societal associations – as a community with a high level of social control which defines its members by a close sense of belonging built up over generations and by an equally sensitive reaction against outsiders (Sorokin & Zimmerman 1929, Struff 1999). But collectivization, resettlement and urbanization all destroyed "authentic" village cultures that could bestow identity and protect resources. The longer these processes continued, the clearer the effects of a forced industrialization requiring high mobility became, as it was the case in most Soviet regions.

The Bulgarian pattern of migration concerning the "town-country-symbiosis" was already mentioned above. Here, I will briefly outline migration in rural Southern Russia. This specific migration pattern can be found with more or less sharp contours throughout all rural regions in the post-socialist countries of Eastern Europe, but it does not exist in a non-socialist rural context. A segment of an interview with a young woman who was born in a Southern Russian village will illustrate this complex migration pattern. As a little girl she migrated with her parents to rural (Soviet) Turkmenistan, but after the death of her mother she returned to her native village and has been living there with her grandmother.

> No, she [the grandmother – I.O.] came from Belorussia, but she has been living here for a long time. Actually they were nomads – all over the former Soviet Union. She and my grandfather met in Lithuania... They had two children in Lithuania. I guess my elder uncle and my mother, and then they moved to the Kustanaj region [in Kazakhstan – I.O.] and lived there for around ten years. They had another child, my younger uncle, and after that they moved here. For a certain period, they even lived in Tikhoreck [near Krasnodar – I.O.], where I was born. They migrated in this way. My grandmother worked all her life in a *kolkhoz*, but my grandfather commuted to Shevchenko [Ukraine – I.O.] as a miner.

These few sentences display a panorama of Soviet daily life. We notice that villagers did not live in some pre-modern enclave amidst an ultra-modern society, but in settlement types (around collective farms) specific to socialist industrialized societies. In these villages were people who had always lived in the country and worked in agriculture but, at the same time, were socialized in modern institutions and preserved certain individual and moral expectations.

The migration pattern of a Southern Russian village consists of many layers beginning with migrations during World War I and the revolution, and then the first collectivization waves, followed by resettlement and deportation, and then flight and evacuation in the course of World War II. After that came several phases of collectivization accompanied by rural exodus on the one hand and rural development with migration into the country, on the other. These migrations did not slow down until the 1970s. In the 1980s, there were the first remigration waves, when labour migrants to Soviet Central Asia and the Caucasus returned to Russia. This process accelerated when the Soviet Union collapsed and continues to this day. A similar remigration process involves the return of people from industrial areas in the North and in Siberia. Earlier, millions of people from poor rural or provincial regions had migrated to these vast areas in search of work. The present de-industrialization process has forced them to remigrate, and many of them have no other option than to return to their original villages.

Each of these migration waves reached rural regions and reorganized them. But it is important to emphasize that the liquidation of villages, the foundation of new rural settlements, and the temporary employment of specialists and skilled or unskilled labour were only possible in so far as villagers were gradually transformed into rural wageworkers. Everywhere they settled, these people found the same living and working conditions. Thus, an industrialized life includes the standardizing of infrastructure and the material base, the gradual disappearance of regional qualities, the breakdown of local power, the dependence on central structures and organizations, all of which leads, ultimately, to a permanent alienation from traditional ways of life. As the interviewee mentioned, Soviet people became nomads in a socialist modernity and – to remain within the picture – migrated between state-run industrial oases.

Today's life in industrialized villages

In conclusion, I would like to illustrate some actual living and working conditions in post-socialist villages with an example from Northern Russia. This is, perhaps, a harsh, but by no means extreme or isolated, case capable of demonstrating the logic of this article

The village has around 250 inhabitants; there is a school, a kindergarten and two shops. In the 1970s, the village was regarded as one "with a future", and people from smaller villages around it were resettled there. It is the seat of the district administration and has a library and a medical practitioner. An old church was reopened three years ago.

At first glance we see an idyllic village – little wooden houses and garden plots. But this first impression is illusory as next to this pastoral scene lie the ruins of the former *sovkhoz* for pig and cattle breeding. The village had been the appendage of an agro-industrial complex which had not been built for the sake of the village.

Fig. 10-1 The stone house

© Elena Bogdanova

On the contrary, this village grew up around the collective farm, and with the breakdown of the latter the village also began to decay. Today there are around ten jobs whereas before there had been more than two hundred. Villagers try to use the few resources available to survive. As we will see, villagers who live in stone houses with two stories are especially unable to cope with the new living conditions.

The stone house is an allegory for the attempts of socialist states to dissolve the antagonism between urban and rural areas. Village life was held to be backward, and the state wanted villagers to become urban dwellers partly by living in a certain "urban" type of housing. They were built in the 1970s in order house urban specialists who were sent to the village or people from so-called "villages without prospects". Because "our" village was considered a unit full of prospects, it experienced massive enlargement at the expense of the surrounding smaller villages. But the vision of the state often does not coincide with that of its citizens who do not want the state to impose its schemes on them (Scott 1988). Results may be open to protest, passive agreement or refusal; in this case it resulted in cultural decay.

This special house on the photo was built in the end of the 1970s, and is made of stone not wood, the traditional construction material. Despite this urban façade, there was very little comfort. The residents, even those on the second floor, have to fetch water from a well. The house does not have running water, or gas. Although there are balconies, giving the ensemble a certain absurdity, there are no asphalted roads, and no cellars or attics for storing food or the harvest, as was the case in traditional wooden houses. And there are no garden plots. Like all the other villagers, the residents of the stone house are now forced to do household farming. They received land, but because there was no land near the house, it is located on the edge of the village. So, not only do the residents have to travel a long way to get to their land, they also have to bring water and everything else they need a long way as well. Furthermore, they cannot effectively protect their property against thieves. Since everything is very complicated, in particular keeping animals, the residents have stopped doing it.

The house was built 25 years ago and has never been renovated. The material used in its construction was poor, water is dripping everywhere, and the toilets – because there is no canalization – have constant problems, and so on. The residents suffer from these problems, but they are not prepared to do anything to solve them. One reason for their indifference is that they do not have sufficient means – neither money, nor tools. But the more profound reason is the fact that the house no longer has an owner. Once it belonged to the *sovkhoz*, but now it is an orphan, and the residents do not even know to whom they should pay the rent.

There is bitter misery. It is a matter of survival. To find adequate survival strategies is difficult enough for the residents of frame houses, but it becomes more and more impossible for those in these stone houses. Nonetheless, all the villagers are caught between two cultures. They live, so to speak, between the relics of traditional village culture on the one hand, and the unfulfilled promises of an urban culture and an effective central administration on the other. For the time being, they are forced to live their anachronistic lives in settlements fit neither for modern times, nor for a return to a traditional rural way of life.

Conclusion

This article has discussed the concept of the "industrialized village", which helps to compare the specific "path dependencies" of the post-socialist transition of rural areas throughout Eastern Europe. Whereas the dramatic fall in agricultural production in the early 1990s and the restructuring of the large socialist agro-industrial complexes during the following decade are quite well documented and researched, the enormous changes in the living and working conditions of the former collective-farm workers are still underestimated.

The "industrialized village" was a special type of rural settlement which only existed in socialist countries and was built around great collective farms (*kolkhozes* and *sovkhozes*), firmly integrating the workers and their families into the operational logic of the collective farm. In this respect, the crucial feature of socialist agriculture was not the industrialization of agriculture but the industrialization of the lives of the villagers, the organizing of all aspects of their lives according to a uniform principle.

This happened more or less in all societies of the Soviet type, with the exception of those regions where agriculture was only partly collectivized, as was the case in Poland. Therefore, the model provides researchers with an instrument to compare post-socialist developments in rural regions, and highlights the processes of societal change.

Since the concept is shaped on a highly abstract level, concrete cases are required in order to bring to light the manifold differences of contemporary rural life in Eastern Europe. Comparative research has shown the value of the concept. For example, the problems of informal arrangements in all aspects of daily life, or of specific migration patterns in rural regions are, of course, topics of research on transition societies. From the perspective of the industrialization of life, these issues have to be reformulated and, therefore, show an exigent desideratum for research.

References

Bogdanova, E., O. Brednikova & E. Chikadze (2004) *Die Agrarreform in Nordrussland* [The agrarian reform in North Russia]. St. Petersburg Unpublished project report.

Conte, É. & C. Giordano (1999) Pathways of Lost Rurality. Reflections on Post-socialism, in *Es war einmal die Wende... Sozialer Umbruch der ländlichen Gesellschaften Mittel- und Südosteuropas* [Once, there was the change...

Societal radical change in rural societies in Central and Southeast Europe] ed. by É. Conte & C. Giordano. Centre Marc Bloch, Berlin, 5-33.

Dittrich, E. & R. Jeleva (2005) Wirtschaftliche Restrukturierung auf dem Lande: Ein Beispiel aus Bulgarien [Economic restructuration in the country], in *Transformation als Typ sozialen Wandels. Postsozialistische Lektionen, historische und interkulturelle Vergleiche* [Transformation as a type of societal change. Post-socialist lessons, historical and intercultural comparisons], ed. by R. Kollmorgen. Lit, Muenster, 259-274.

Ember, C. & M. Ember (2001) *Cross-Cultural Research Methods*. AltaMira Press, Lanham, Walnut Creek, New York, Oxford.

Eisenstadt, S. N. (1979) *Tradition, Wandel und Modernitaet* [Tradition, Change and Modernity]. Suhrkamp, Frankfurt, Main.

Ernst, F. (1999) *Von Bauern und Anderen. Handlungsstrategien unter sich veraendernden oekonomischen und politischen Bedingungen am Beispiel der mecklenburgischen Gemeinde Tranlin* [About farmers and others. Strategies of action on changing economic and political conditions, the case of a community in Mecklenburg]. Birkhaeuser, Bern.

Frolkova, A. & A. Manujlov (2004) *Zur Agrarreform im Gebiet Krasnodar* [On the agrarian reform in the Krasnodar region]. Krasnodar. Unpublished project report.

Hann, C. M. (ed.) (2002) *Postsocialism. Ideals, Ideologies and Practices in Eurasia*. Routledge, London.

Kotkin, S. (1995) *Magnetic Mountain. Stalinism as a Civilization*. CUP, Berkley.

Labrianidis, L. (ed.) (2004) *The Future of Europe's rural Peripheries*. Ashgate, Aldershot.

Laschewski, L. (1998) Continuity and Changes – Agricultural Restructuring in East Germany. *Eastern European Countryside* 8 (4), 37-48.

Laschewski, L. & R. Siebert (2001) Effiziente Agrarwirtschaft und arme ländliche Ökonomie? Über gesellschaftliche und wirtschaftliche Folgen des Agrarstrukturwandels in Ostdeutschland [Efficient agriculture and poor rural economy? On the societal and economic consequences of the structural change agriculture in East Germany]. *Berliner Debatte – Initial* 12 (6), 31-42.

Ledeneva, A.V. (1997) Practices of Exchange and Networking in Russia. *Soziale Welt* 48 (2), 151-70.

—. (1998) *Russia's Economy of Favours*. CUP, Cambridge.

Matthes, J. (1992), The Operation Called "Vergleichen"[The operation called "to compare"], in *Zwischen den Kulturen? Die Sozialwissenschaften vor dem Problem des Kulturvergleichs [Between cultures? Social sciences facing the problem of cross-cultural comparison]* ed. by J. Matthes. *Soziale Welt* Special Number (8), 75-99.

Mormont, M. (1990) Who is Rural? Or, How to be Rural? Towards a Sociology of the Rural, in *Rural Restructuring – Global Processes and Their Responses*, ed. by T. Marsden et al. David Fulton, London.

Narojek, W. (1980/81) The Sociology of a Socialist Economy. *International Journal of Sociology* 10 (4), 32-46.

Nikiforova, E. & T. Toomere (2003) *Estonia: Legislative Changes and Its Consequences for Konguta Vald.* Tallinn, St. Petersburg. Unpublished project report.

Oswald, I., E. Frank & E. Dittrich (2005) Das industrialisierte Dorf. Zur Transformation laendlicher Lebensweise in postsozialistischen Gesellschaften [The industrialized village. On the transformation of rural way of life in post-socialist societies], in *Transformation als Typ sozialen Wandels. Postsozialistische Lektionen, historische und interkulturelle Vergleiche* [Transformation as a type of societal change. Post-socialist lessons, historical and intercultural comparisons], ed. by R. Kollmorgen. Lit, Muenster, 241-257.

Rosa, H. (2003) Social Acceleration. Ethical and Political Consequences of a De-Synchronized High-Speed Society. *Constellations. An International Journal of Critical and Democratic Theory* 10 (1), 3-52.

Schrader, H. (2004) Introduction, in *Trust and Social Transformation. Theoretical Approaches and Empirical Findings from Russia*, ed by H. Schrader. Lit, Muenster, 7-14.

Scott, J. (1988) *Seeing Like a State: How Certain Schemes to Improve the Human Condition Have Failed.* Yale University Press, New Haven.

Sorokin, P. & C. C. Zimmerman (1929) *Principles of Rural-Urban Sociology.* Holt, New York.

Srubar, I. (1991) War der reale Sozialismus modern? Versuch einer strukturellen Bestimmung [Was the real socialism modern? Essay on a structural definition]. *Koelner Zeitschrift für Soziologie und Sozialpsychologie* 43 (3), 415-32.

Stark, D. & L. Bruszt (1998) *Postsocialist Pathways: Transforming Politics and Property in East Central Europe.* CUP, Cambridge.

Struff, R. (1999), *Regionale Lebensverhältnisse: Sozialwissenschaftliche Dorf- und Gemeindestudien in Deutschland, Teil 2 [Regional living conditions: Sociological studies on villages and communities, Part 2]*, Forschungsgesellschaft für Agrarpolitik und Agrarsoziologie e.V., Bonn.

Swain, N. (1999) *From* Kolkhoz *to Holding Company: Social Capital in the History of a Hungarian Agricultural Producer Co-operative.* Frankfurt Institute for Transformation Studies, Discussion Paper 2. *Frankfurt, Oder.*

Weber, M. (1988 [1922]) Die “Objektivität” sozialwissenschaftlicher und sozialpolitischer Erkenntnis [The “objectivity“of knowledge in social sciences and social policy] in *Gesammelte Aufsaetze zur Wissenschaftslehre* [Collected essays on methodology], ed. by M. Weber, Mohr, Tuebingen, 146-214.

Zapf, W. (1996) Modernisierungstheorie in der Transformationsforschung [Modernization theory in research on transformation], in *Politische Theorien in der Ära der Transformation [Political theory in the era of transformation]*, ed. by K. v. Beyme & C. Offe. Westdeutscher Verlag, Opladen, 169-81.

CHAPTER ELEVEN

NENETS AND RUSSIAN DISCOURSES ON NORTHERN LANDSCAPES

KARINA LUKIN

Introduction

One of the most frequently mentioned themes one comes across when reading about the Nenets is their mobility. Whether it is some early or late ethnographic description or a Nenets folklore text, movement across the landscape is *the* striking feature. Outsiders are usually amazed or tired by the constant activity of packing, travelling, unpacking and once again packing. The British biologist Aubyn Trevor-Battye was amazed and enamoured when he visited Kolguev Island at the end of the nineteenth century, and left the following description:

> The packing of the sleighs was done with that exactness which one would expect from a nomad people, constantly on the move, because of their reindeer. Can you imagine what this means – the discomfort, the unrest of it? They can stay in one spot only just so long as the deer find plenty to eat. But a large herd of deer soon clear a district and every day they feed farther and farther from home, and it becomes more difficult to bring them in. So after a day or two there is nothing for it, but to pack up all your belongings, and move away to new pastures. (Trevor-Battye 1894, 163)

But it is not just outsiders who tend to emphasize the pros and cons of this nomadic way of life, the Nenets themselves also do this. Characterizing the world of Nenets epic songs, the *syudbabts*, *yarabts*, and *hynabts*, Andrei Golovnev (1995, 198) observes that:

> In the folklore the distance of the travels of the heroes are not measured in remoteness, but in years. In the real life, the status of a reindeer herder is measured in the plenty of the tundras he uses, but the strength of a mythical figure is highlighted with the time frame of his travels. The big heroes, godly men in their Odysseys conquer the whole space of the life without fail and after

> piecing together the Earth, they conquer the world beyond, traverse the oceans and conquer the heights of the mountains. Both in everyday and the mythical life the harmony between man and the world is expressed with the combination of the two endless: the space and the migration.

This quotation reminds me of the Russian expression *širokaja natura,* vast nature with its evocation of spiritual vastness and unending space. Indeed, on a certain level we may find many common features between the Nenets and Russian understanding of space. Consider the famous fragment from Gogol's *Dead Souls* glorifying the speed of the *troika* rushing across the endless plains. Elena Hellberg-Hirn (1998, 231) has described Russian sentiments toward space as essentially ambiguous:

> The endless, open landscape with the *troika*, and the protectively sealed space of the decorated Easter egg – the two contrasting symbols of Russia – convey the paradox of Russia's vast territory. While the *troika* denotes the centrifugal movement of escape and freedom, but also insecurity, the egg symbolizes the centripetal contraction of space into a seamlessly closed and safe refuge, perhaps a prison, surrounded by protective walls that separate Self from Other.

It probably comes as no surprise that this resemblance turns out to be rather false, or even superficial. With a closer examination of the ways the Nenets live in their landscape with their reindeer herding and nomadic way of life, on the one hand, and the settled agricultural life of the Russians, on the other, we can find many differences (see Siikala & Ulyashev 2003, 15).[122] These differences, in turn, contribute to the way the Russians and the Nenets think about their environment today. Although inhabiting the same physical space, the Russians no longer engage in agriculture, and the Nenets have given up their nomadic existence. Thus, it is not the physical space, or environment, that matters, but how both groups perceive it.

In this article I will show that there are, in rural areas of post-Soviet Russia, multiple ways of seeing and knowing the landscape. These ways do not derive only from common Soviet practices, but also from complex local patterns which have a long history of encounters and interplay with other practices. This multiplicity of practices is illustrated by considering the differences between Russian images and Nenets images of the North and by examining the two central living environments found in the North, namely, the tundra and the village.

---

[122] Siikala and Ulyashev deal with Khanty place conceptions. Although Khanty culture was traditionally based on hunting, fishing and small-scale reindeer herding, one can notice certain resemblances with Nenets place conceptions. This is probably due to their mobility, although in many ways it is a different kind of mobility.

Kolguev and Kolguev islanders

The basic material for this article consists of data collected in the village of Bugrino, which is located at the southern end of the island of Kolguev in the Barents Sea. I began conducting ethnographic fieldwork on the island in 2000, and the last field trip I made was in the beginning of 2005. On my most recent trips I concentrated on collecting historical narratives and place names, but the material naturally includes many kinds of information. My field trips have been between two weeks and three months in length – and the idea has been not so much to live for a long period in the community but rather to visit it on short-term trips. Besides the diverse field data, my analysis also rests on archival material.

The island is a big flat round swampy area in the Barents Sea. Sitting on the shore, I have sometimes felt agoraphobic with endless sea ahead and flat tundra behind me. Having grown up in a village in Southern Finland with forest coming right up to the back garden, I have often found myself crying about the 'nothingness' of the entire landscape in Kolguev. Especially in the wintertime, the tundra seems to be confusingly empty of features. At such times, it is easy to turn towards the village of Bugrino, in the hope of finding, amongst its houses, some sign of life, and the life of the community. For an outsider, it is also easy not to realize, or if one does to forget, that for many Nenets the tundra is still a rich and meaningful landscape quite apart from, or despite, the village.

Hence, although my field trips have concentrated on Bugrino — I have also stayed in the Kolguev tundra and in the city of Nar'yan-Mar — it is very important to note that my material is not limited to the village. It is clear that although most of the Kolguev Nenets live in Bugrino, it does not represent the community as a whole. In the course of my fieldtrips, I have learned that, on the one hand, the village with its name misleads you into thinking that it is the community, and, on the other, that the flatness of the swamp isn't a meaningless space.

The community lives all over the island and in the city of Nar'yan-Mar. The place is not a community; its actions create it (Cf. Glassie 1982, 19). There is life all over the island, and beyond. The community then extends further than just Kolguev. I have been going to Bugrino to study village life and the village community, but it has become clear to me that the little spot on the map signifying Bugrino, or the four rows of houses that make up the village, is not enough to understand the village community and its life. In everyday conversation, Bugrino is not only set against the tundra, but also against the city of Nar'yan-Mar. Being part of the Nenets autonomous district[123] is also an

[123] Nenets autonomous *okrug*, district is administratively part of Arhangel′sk *oblast'*, region. The district is one of the objects of the Russian Federation.

important part in people's sense of place here and is particularly evident when talking about Nar'yan-Mar. The tundra, the reindeer, and movement are all part of everyday conversation here as is life in Nar'yan-Mar, *v gorode*, in the city, as the Kolguev Islanders say. In this article, I will concentrate on Kolguev Island and thus the opposition between tundra and village.

Before the Nenets settled to the island, Kolguev was probably used seasonally for hunting various sea mammals by Russian *Pomors*[124], the now extinct *Sirtja*[125] and by the Nenets who were probably settled on the island by Russian merchants later. Nowadays, the Nenets are considered the indigenous population of Kolguev. Although the island is found on the first maps of the Northern seas, it has not been studied as much as the Novaya Zemlya or Vaigač. This is why there is less information about the history of Kolguev than about Novaya Zemlya, although it was probably populated later.

Bugrino arose as place where Nenets and Russian merchants and priests used to meet during the short summer season. Written sources about these contacts go back to the nineteenth century, but the locals say that these contracts go back at least to the eighteenth century. Bugrino developed from being a small meeting point with a little chapel and a few warehouses into an administrative and educational centre and then into an economic collective's centre and village in the Soviet and Russian North, where all the Nenets, Russians, and Ukrainians on the island today live.

The similar development is found in many Northern villages (Cf. E.g. Grant 1995; Bychkova Jordan& Jordan-Bychkov 2001). Villages usually sprung up in places where locals used to meet in pre-Soviet times. Many of the villages were abandoned when bigger collectives or *sovkhozes* were created, but Bugrino never had to go through that. Still, some Russians and Ukrainians moved to Bugrino, mainly in the 1950s and 1960s, to build a new life in the North. In these same years many Nenets families from Novaya Zemlya were forcibly moved to Kolguev.

Of the Nenets, children and women were the first ones to move seasonally to Bugrino – the men came later. The men continued herding and hunting in the tundra, but women were considered to be unproductive labour force and thus obliged to leave their home. After they started the ship herding system in the 1970s, everyone was settled to Bugrino. Nevertheless, some pensioners continued to live in the tundra; now, they have also moved to village. The change from tundra to village life has been very fast.

---

[124] Pomors is a group of Russian who have settled to the Northern shores of European Russia around from the eleventh century on. See Berštam 1978 for details.

[125] Sirtja lived in the Northern tundras before Nenets and Russian moved there. They are known mainly by archaeological evidence only. See Golovnev 1991.

The problems of Northern villages or villages on Russia's peripheries in general are widely known: the many social and economic problems are accompanied with growing uncertainty about the future. From the point of view of the villagers, the most severe problems concern housing and schooling. The residential houses and the schools are old, and new ones are needed. Still, the parents would also like their older children to have the opportunity to study in Bugrino – rather than the boarding school in Nar'yan-Mar where the children are sent after four grades, when they are about eleven years old.

Unemployment in Bugrino is about 25%, which is quite high when compared to other parts of the Nenets autonomous district. Most of the people work in the village administration or in the "Kolguev" co-operative, which owns most of the enterprises in Bugrino. Despite, or mainly because of, unemployment, people are very busy trying to make some sort of living: fishing, hunting and collecting, "making ice" (which they then melt for drinking water) or "preparing coal" (the houses are heated with coal). Lately, this has been described as a set of multiple strategies for making a living. It has also been stressed that these multiple strategies are not characteristic only of the Soviet or post-Soviet Russian North, but have "always" been available.[126]

Northern post-socialist villages are usually described with reference to negative things and in negative ways. I agree with Petra Rethmann (2001, xiv) who, in describing Koriak life, argues that:

> […] an emphasis on social suffering places indigenous peoples in a discourse of endangerment that leaves only little room for recognizing their imaginative and creative efforts to forge new futures. […] Koriak women and men seek social possibilities and opportunities to create forms of dignity and respect.

Thus, it is very important to remember that beyond these easily illustrated images of social and economic hardship are everyday lives, which do not come together only around difficulties, but extend over many spheres of life.

From the very beginning, studying the life and community of the village was not that easy. First of all, an ethnographer studying something modern is considered rather odd in the post-Soviet north, because ethnography there is still understood as a historical science. Secondly, not only were people constantly working and employing their multiple strategies, but they were also frequently on the move between village, tundra and city. Ethnographers have come to realize that their fields aren't just physically bounded places and that it is not proper to represent them as such, consequently, multi-sited research has been

[126] This point was illustrated and discussed in an excellent way in papers by Tuula Tuisku and Florian Stammler in a working group at the Alexander Institute's Conference in 2005. See also Humphrey 1998, 444-67.

suggested as one solution to this problem. In his article, George E. Marcus (2001, 231) suggests that ethnographers should try to constitute the social through strategic movement among different sites and hesitate to use non-ethnographical constructions as the basis of ethnography.

The idea is tempting, but, nonetheless, makes me doubtful: don't we come to emphasize the meaning of place and the stagnation of the natives, if *we*, the ethnographers, are the ones who move. (Cf. Appadurai 1988, 37) I prefer Jukka Siikala's (2001, 42) view about the relationship between the physical and conceptual world and fieldwork when he says that: "an interpretation of that conceptual world is possible only by analyzing practical activities in a specific location. The unseen becomes understandable through its relation to those activities." In Bugrino, the tundra is as unseen as the community as a whole. In the same way, the community seemed to open up as I looked beyond the imagined (by me) village borders.

Dwelling, telling and perceiving spaces

I am not the only one who hasn't appreciated the tundra. The common image we tend to have of the tundra is that of an empty and uniform space. It would appear that people who live in more wooded or hilly areas do not understand or appreciate such flat and empty terrain. James Fernandez (1988, 21) noted that his Spanish interviewees from the mountainous region of Asturia "have difficulty in placing themselves or even recognizing that flat and disappearing landscape as a place at all", when they came to the central plateaus of Spain. Realizing that the Sámi[127] perceive some things in the Northern landscape that an outsider not acquainted with Sami thinking does not, has led the Swedish ethnographer Håkan Rydving (2002) to distinguish between visible and invisible landscapes.

Rather than dividing space into something objective (visible) or subjective (invisible), I would suggest that we think of it as something embedded in social constructions. Thus, space is always seen from an angle, with some basic assumptions and cultural notions already in the gaze no matter how physical the gaze itself. Edward Casey (1996, 19) has put it clearly like this: cultural practices and social institutions "pervade every level of perception [...] the perception remains as *constitutive* as it is constituted."

On these phenomenological points I would like to add Peter Gow's concept of lived space. A lived space is "known by means of movements through it, seeing the traces of other people's movement and agency, and through the

[127] Sámi speaking peoples live in the Northern Scandinavia and Kola Peninsula. In his article, Rydving is interested in the so called Southern Sámi living in Sweden.

narratives of yet other people's agency" (Gow 1995, 59). It is important to note, that we usually move in places with others, in the company of other people. Although places or senses of places are constructed of local topography, personal associations and socially given systems of thought, it is these last ones, which organize the experience itself and are thus more interesting from an ethnographical point of view (Basso 1996, 57, 84).

We should not think that senses of places are something totally separate from the natural surroundings. I'm keen on Keith Basso's idea of the *interanimation* between places and the ideas and feelings about places. "This process of interanimation relates directly to the fact that familiar places are experienced as inherently meaningful, their significance and value being found to reside in (and, it may seem, to emanate from) the form and arrangement of their observable characteristics." This, it seems to me, means that our experience of a place always arises from the cultural practices and physical characteristics of that place, or, more precisely, that they are interconnected (Ibid. 55–56).

A simple example of this interanimation would be place names, the meaning of which is often revealed by some observable feature in the landscape. However, place names do not always refer to physical features. The Nenets name *habyi nye sedye*, that is, "the hill of the foreign woman", refers not only to a hill but also to a well-known narrative about an ugly Komi girl sitting on the hill waiting for suitors to come to her. Knowing the story, one already knows a lot more than the geographical place itself or its place name. To cite Basso: "the toponym [...] acquires the stamp of human events, of consequential happenings, of memorable times in the life of a people" (Ibid. 66).

One important point about places is the theme of movement which is connected to the body and the bodily implications when sensing, or more accurately, perceiving a place. Casey argues that the role of the body is most evident when we are moving from one place to another and that it is precisely through the body and synesthetical perceptions that we emplace our world. Casey (1996, 39) introduces a term *interplace* to describe briefly visited or merely traversed places which "are never uneventful, never not full of spatiotemporal specificities that reflect particular modes and moods of emplacement. Even on the hoof, we remain in place. We are never anywhere, anywhen, but in place."

We could then ask, what happens when a domestic space is an interplace, a camp site between journeys on the tundra, as for nomadic Nenets? And what happens when this kind of portable, moving domestic space is transformed into a non-nomadic, constant village, as has happened to many Northern peoples? To set the living body on tundra of the past against the one now in the village, is to see, on the one hand, a living body constantly on the move in a big area with a home on the move and, on the other hand, a body walking on duckboards in a relatively small area with a fixed house. The difference is huge. The Nenets in their constant state of migration were not dislocated, but, sadly enough, in their national villages, they are.

Russian space and images of the North

It would be oversimplifying and wrong to say that the village is a Russian space and the tundra a Nenets one. Nevertheless, in the following section, I will consider some Russian views on space and the North in order to contrast and compare them with Nenets views, past and present. Remembering that much of what we perceive is constructed through culturally given systems of thought; I argue that the village is a different kind of space for the Nenets, as they give it a different set of interpretations and meanings compared to Russians.

Already mentioned at the beginning of this article, ambivalence seems to characterize the Russian concept of space, from many points of view. The Russian Federation covers a huge territory with population centres scattered across it. This ambivalence is also present in central images that reveal both a love for spaciousness and a tendency to demarcate.

Looking at a map of the Russian North or Siberia, one can easily notice that whereas small or average size cities are absent, big cities have emerged and are still growing in size. This is due, on the one hand, to unsuccessful planning and, on the other hand, the attractiveness of cities during the Soviet period (Helanterä & Tynkkynen 2002). According to Mikhail Epstein (2003, 277),[128] there is a certain spatial orientation in Russian history, which means that "historical periods are not marked by purely temporal changes but rather by dislocations and expansions in space." Russian history is a history of a constantly expanding state the outcome being a state too vast to experience. But the paradox lies not in the vastness itself, but in the concentration of population in cities already too densely populated, in communal apartments and so on. To quote Epstein (Ibid. 280): "Russian closeness is born of desperate, heroic resistance to an equally Russian spaciousness."

This concentration of population has its administrative aspects, which have led to the current administrative-territorial units with their symbolically maintained differences, and resulted in the scattering of the Nenets over three different administrative areas. Today, most of the Nenets live in either the Nenets, the Yamalo-Nenets or the Dolgano-Nenets autonomous districts, and it is already customary to distinguish between the *evro-nency* (that is, Nenets who

[128] See also the seminal article Medvedev 1999 [1997] dealing with Russian space concepts.

live in the Nenets district), and the *yamal'skie nency* (Nenets who live in the Yamalo-Nenets district). These differences are not considered to be only administrative in nature, but to have deeper cultural connotations.

But Russia, as a whole, is not a very coherent administrative unit, anyway. Thus, instead of noting the "artificiality" of Russia as a nation-state (Cf. Medevedev 1999, 25–27, 32–36; Anderson 2000, 17) – and wondering if there is, in fact, any such nation-state – I would prefer to consider, on the one hand, how the unity of Russia was built and, on the other, how the boundaries between the *evro-nency* and the more Eastern Yamal Nenets have been created. How have these once so artificial borders, created only for the purpose of settling people and controlling their movements, become genuine borders in organizing everyday practices and experiences.

Of course, the general tendency to control by making borders and reshaping them is part of the ambivalence of Russia's space. Elena Hellberg-Hirn (1999, 51) mentions *zabor*, a fence, as one of the indicators of this concern with boundaries. What is interesting is that the demarcating of one's own is so strong, that Russians tend to see fences even in places where they do not exist. Hence, a Russian journalist describing Bugrino notes: "From far off, this all seemed like a malformed encampment of pipes, antennas, *fences*, clothes lines, doghouses, stacks of wood and even smaller warehouses." (Golovanov 2002, 97. Emphasis added.) There is not a single fence in Bugrino, which Golovanov must know very well. In the mind of a Russian, fences are just part of a village and they inevitably come to mind when thinking of a village.

There are two Russian notions referring to the North, that don't quite fit Kolguev. The first one is *Sibir'*, Siberia, where Russia's spatial ambivalence seems to come to rest. Unlimited freedom, a treasure trove of all kinds of riches is combined with captivity and terror (Hellberg-Hirn 1999, 54). In these images, it is often forgotten that there is another image of Siberia, or of its localities, that is, the image of home. "[T]he mythologizing of Siberia's endless landscapes and never-ending resources has led to reckless exploitation and desecration of the territory" (Fryer 1999, 106). To be accurate, Kolguev is not part of Siberia as it is situated on the European side of the Ural Mountains, but many of the spatial notions referring to Siberia come close to those referring to the European tundra. As for Kolguev, it is, even inside the Nenets district thought to be a harsh and peripheral land where the oil and gas are of better quality than anywhere else. Thus, it is a microcosm of Siberian images, a place where ideas of Siberia seem to exist in concentrated form.

Another concept, namely, that of *Russkij Sever*, the Russian North, does not really apply to Kolguev either. *Russkij Sever* usually refers to North-Western Russia and its arctic areas: the Kola Peninsula, Karelia, Arhangel'sk region and sometimes the Komi Republic. The present Nenets district is hardly part of the

Russian North, let alone Siberia. Nikolai Terebihin (2004, 5) has described the sacred landscape of the Russian North:

> The ethnocentric, [i.e. Russian] model of the world is founded on the opposition between the sacred, Russian and orthodox, and the profane and ktonic. This is also reflected in concepts about Northern lands inhabited by foreigns (*inorodcy*), as another world beyond, where everything was the other way around, according to those who travelled there. Therefore, the whole Russian North is characterized as antiworld, where people with the power to bewitch live.

Terebihin describes the world of the *Pomors*, a group of Russians living in the Russian North. For them the crosses, chapels and churches in the landscape are the most sacred of all places, but the whole of the *Russkij Sever* as such is also a sacred landscape. The forests and areas even further north than the *Russkij Sever* are as awe-inspiring as the strange people living in them. Even today, the Nenets are described as savage and crude although the land has been tamed. Working in the State archive of Arhkangel'sk region, I heard several times the Nenets referred to as *dikie,* savages.

The opposition between village and forest or tundra can be compared to similar ideas of the European suburban middle class in the nineteenth and twentieth centuries, for whom towns and their surrounding countryside were regarded as opposites, yet at the same time also as complementary to each other (Hirsch 1995, 2–3). This distinction between the social and economic environment and the natural and ideal is not intrinsic to the minds of the nomadic Nenets for whom the tundra is a place, a landscape where they live. Even today, the distinction between the tundra and the village exists, but the pattern is, in many ways, a different one. I will return to this distinction later.

The strong emphasis given to the Russian North during the Soviet period was driven by the idea, among other things, of conquering this Northern wilderness and "demonstrating that climate, a lack of relevant technology and remoteness could not stand in the way of the socialist economy." (Round 2005, 707) Working in the North had a strong propaganda value both at the centre and on the periphery so that some have described the Soviet discourse concerning the North in terms of an Arctic myth (McCannon 2003). The Arctic was a land of heroes who lived the idealized life of socialist propaganda. The propaganda value of conquering the North is easy to appreciate when set against descriptions like Terebihin's.

It was also rather easy to encourage people to move to the North; some of these pioneers still live in Kolguev. Now, many people in the North want to leave and return to central Russia, but this has not been very easy to organize due to a shortage of accommodation in the Russian heartlands. So Russia is now faced with the problem of supporting huge populations in remote and climatically harsh areas. Running down the infrastructure of the North does not affect only the life of those Soviet settlers who are not willing to move away from their adopted homelands. The indigenous population also requires infrastructure. Hence, paradoxically the achievements of the Soviet Union have become major problems for post-Soviet Russia (Round 2005; Helanterä & Tynkkynen 2002).

What was not so easy was to encourage or persuade the tundra's inhabitants to settle in villages – in a sense to resist heroically Russia's spaciousness – and ultimately force had to be used to make them do so.

The village, the tundra

Now, turning to the Nenets concepts of space, we have to put the mythical notions of the North and Siberia aside. I would like to begin with a place narrative told to me by a Nenets elder[129] who was born and lived in the Kolguev tundra, but who has also lived in the village of Bugrino a long time. Most place narratives somehow animate the place or explain the physical characteristics or names of places. But we can also approach these narratives from a different angle. Not animating, and being animated by, geographical places, which is inevitable, but telling about past and possibly also contemporary ways of structuring experience and perception – what Basso (1996, 84) calls "the notional particulars of socially given systems of thought". The narrative goes as follows:

> [...] And about thirty kilometers - twenty or thirty - to the east from here is a place where they buried a person who attracts people to himself. All the time, no matter what kind of weather. If a man roams not knowing the land very well or is lost in thought, he immediately starts [to be pulled] towards the cemetery. I already know. Once, on a clear day, there was only a slight mist on the ground. Only on the ground was there mist and the sun was clearly visible and it was quiet, quiet weather. I started to follow the spoor of fox but there wasn't any spoor to be seen after this cemetery. I was with the *buran*[130], hunting with the buran. And the entire spoor [disappeared], I looked around and there were no spoor at all on the surrounding ground. And the mist went away. I thought: fine, I'll go back to the village, home. I lit a cigarette, smoked, and followed my tracks back. There was no wind. I went back along my tracks again. I went on and on and at some point I couldn't see my tracks anymore; I lost my own tracks. Oh, it appeared that I had got back to the same cemetery again, but from

---

129 As I cannot discuss differences between generations, or between different social groupings, of Kolguev Islanders in a short article, I will concentrate on the images of people who have lived in the tundra.

130 A snowmobile.

> the other side. But I thought I would leave anyway and I intended to follow back along the tracks I had made when I came to the cemetery. I went and looked carefully for the tracks on this clear day. I looked and looked and I went on and on and again I was driven to the same cemetery along the tracks that I had followed. And I did this again, a third time [and I came to the same place] and I sat down and thought: alright, I don't believe those fairy tales. In the old days, they said that you had to have cigarettes – if you cannot get out – you have to leave cigarettes to be able to get out. You will only be able to leave if you leave cigarettes there. I smoked, but I don't believe in this [I thought] and I left. Alright, the visibility was even better now and I was wondering, how had I got lost like that. I never get lost. And I went on and on and again, from another side, I came back to the same place. Alright, I smoked and left, threw cigarettes there to him and went away. Alright, I said, fine, I served him that way. And I went and didn't even notice how fast I was going, you see, so I didn't even notice that I was home again.

The man who told me this story is said to be one of the best experts on the places of the island. Not only because he has lived in the tundra most of his life, but also because he was seriously ill in his childhood and his grandfather told him "everything about Kolguev". Obviously, his knowledge doesn't include the village, which wasn't a very important institution when the man was suffering from his illness or when his grandfather was still alive. The context of this knowledge is the tundra as home and the village as a Russian place which does not order the ways of thought. Obviously this knowledge was not about the geographical characteristics of the island either: it has something to do with cultural particularities.

These kinds of narrative can be designated – depending on the point of view – as, for example, place narratives or memorates.[131] They are told in various everyday situations; the most usual being around a cup of tea. What is interesting is that only male interviewees have told me these narratives with the tape recorder on. Women hesitate to tell memorates "to the recorder", but are eager to recollect them in more conventional communicative situations.

It is also worth mentioning that I have noticed that when telling narratives, which have some religious implications, the Nenets lower their voice if some Russians or Ukrainians are around. This can of course be due to many things. As some Ukrainians in Kolguev have laughed in my presence at the Nenets way of still speaking about dead shamans and other supernatural phenomena, I have interpreted this lowering of the voice in this context. Hence, I think it is a way of avoiding the uncomprehending and probably derogatory views and comments of outsiders. This manner also implies that there is a difference between Nenets, Russian and Ukrainian perceptions and experiences of Kolguev Island. Nenets

[131] A narrative describing a supernatural experience.

tend to interpret getting lost as being due to some characteristics of a place. In the narrative above, it is a dead shaman who pulls people to the cemetery, no matter how well they know the island. By contrast, Russians and Ukrainians living in Kolguev interpret getting lost as being due to their poor knowledge of the landscape.

Lived space: narratives in motion

For most adult Nenets in Kolguev, the tundra is a lived space, at least, for those adults who have lived in the tundra. It could be said, as Anna Kerttula has noted in relation to Sireniki's Chukchi, that the Nenets also associate strongly with the tundra, which is their point of physical, cultural and symbolic reference (Kerttula 2000, 124). The Nenets association with the tundra is based on past practices of reindeer herding and hunting and on the nomadic way of life, and it is impossible to understand this association without appreciating these past practices. They relied on a network of places and routes that were known and used in everyday life.

Andrei Golovnev and Gail Osherenko (2001, 39-42) have described the rhythm of tundra life and the long-sightedness of the Nenets in their approach to the tundra. According to them, hurrying in the tundra is not considered wise:

> The 'slowness' has its own rhythm, predetermined by external reality, a reality that cannot be made 'faster', that might in fact suffer damage or even turn hostile if dealt with too hastily [...] People 'find' a rhythm in nature, instead of imposing one on the environment.

I wouldn't go as far as to reduce the rhythm totally to nature, but there is something in this slowness and its relation to the tundra.

On the one hand, I would associate Golovnev and Osherensko's views with the bodily implications of perceiving place. I have heard more than once from my Nenets interviewees that one senses the environment more thoroughly when travelling by sledge or walking. When, on the other hand, you are driving a snowmobile, you don't sense the tundra and can easily get lost. As you move on a snowmobile or on a *vezdekhod*, troop carrier, your body does not have the same kind of relationship with the place that it has when walking or on a sledge. The pace is faster, the sound-world is different and the sense of the ground is different. The narrative can be interpreted as referring to the bodily implications of perceiving place. The man is moving on a *buran*, which leads his thoughts out of the landscape to something else.

The tundra is not only a point of reference because of the past nomadic way of life. It is still used and referred to by most Kolguev Islanders. The places and the landscape have not become irrelevant, although the people are now settled in the village. Many have little huts in the tundra, which are used for hunting, fishing and gathering – and also just for relaxing. And when people visit the tundra, the elders are often questioned for their knowledge (Cf. Kharyuchi 2004, 161).

On the other hand, I would see this rhythm as referring to a "flexible manner of 'knowing' the place", even if nowadays this knowledge is not based on a constant presence in the tundra. This means that the tundra is dwelled according to the characteristics in the moment of moving there, not according to what there should be, according to "externally imposed measures of time and space." (Anderson 2000, 15)

Besides of moving, everyday conversation, talking also provides insights into, and knowledge about, the tundra. The narrative above is one example of this kind of conversation, which constantly shapes the views people have on the tundra – and on the village. The elders questioned do not base their knowledge only on the physical conditions of the environment but advise people to move in the tundra according to knowledge gained by their previous travels there and from talking about the tundra. Thus, this flexible manner of knowing the place consists of multiple forms of knowledge.

Being in the tundra nowadays differs from how it used to be even for people who spend more time than most there, that is, for the herders. They live in the tundra with only an occasional interval in Kolguev. In the tundra they live in small huts for a month or so and then return for a rest in Bugrino and are replaced by other herders who have rested a month and who now go back to the herd. This shift herding system was developed during Soviet times, but was only introduced to Kolguev recently, at the end of the 1970s.

As previous studies on Nenets reindeer herding have observed, the shift herding system was not readily accepted by everyone. The older herders in particular question the system's benefits, although the younger herders have already adapted to the shift system (Tuisku 1999, 143–149). Moreover, in the Yamal peninsula, the herders and the authorities were convinced, even in the Soviet period, that the shift herding system would not be efficient or advisable (Stammler 2005, 13). Thus, there are huge differences between and within Nenets communities, over the relationship between the tundra and the village.

I argue that the narrative above reflects both nomadic and settled ways of perceiving place. First, it can be interpreted as talking about places in terms of a network and in terms of belonging to a system of moving around the tundra. This is clearly seen in the religious connotations of the narrative. The traditional belief system is naturally an inherent part of the nomadic way of life. Its foundation lies in the network of holy places scattered around the tundra and in round forms such as the conical tent, *mya''*, and the camp site where the tents are always arranged in a semi-circle (Golovnev 1995, 199-206).[132] At some point in my fieldwork, I believed that the old beliefs were dead, because, as every one said, Nenets beliefs cannot live in the square-shaped houses of villages. The point is that the beliefs don't live in these houses. They live in the minds and are accessible to outsiders through the narratives.

I would argue that most of my interviewees considered themselves to be non-religious people and yet they still believed that you would get lost near the old graveyard of shamans unless you threw some cigarettes as an offering. The official[133] atheism of the Soviet period explains some aspects of this attitude: it used to be considered shameful to believe in this sort of thing, as it was considered backward. Only the elderly or non-modern or non-Soviet people believed in such things. Official atheism left a strange legacy in Russia. There are people now claiming to be atheist and orthodox Christians at the same time. Some people don't, for example, associate Christianity with Easter very strongly. Orthodoxy is more connected to Russian nationalism than to religiosity, and Easter is a lovely holiday with eggs rather than a feast of the Resurrection. On the other hand, Alexander Agadjanian has noted that, after the collapse of the Soviet Union, religion has been thought of mostly as something instrumental. Religion can be used to promote cultural arguments or collective memories and as a source of symbolic power which is needed just as much by the smaller constituent entities of the Russian Federation as by the Federation itself (Agadjanian 2000, 251–252).

Arno Survo has described the ways this atheism created a conflict of dialogue between Soviet and local religio-ethnic characteristics (Survo 2001). This conflict has been resolved in many ways in different places and times in the area that used to be the Soviet Union. Locating religion outside the Soviet or Russian village, has been one of the resolutions. This is why it seems that religion had died when the "last" shamans were buried, but as long as the whole island is a space for the Nenets, the shamans will be part of the experience of these places.

Secondly, the narrative highlights the fact that the network of places has remained meaningful even for the settled Nenets who still use the tundra. It shows how important it is for a man leaving the village to hunt, to be able to know where he is going on the basis of the whole repertoire of knowledge he has about the landscape. Through the place narratives the tundra remains a

---

132 It was intriguing to note that these same bases and forms are also part of the Sami landscape (Rydving 2002).

133 I use the term *official* atheism here wilfully, following Arno Survo (2001, 183): "the sweeping generalizations engendered by terms such as 'Soviet', 'totalitarian', and the like, merely help to build hollow explanatory models. At least the attribute 'official' questions, if only obliquely, the relevance of 'atheism' in everyday life."

meaningful space. Though not currently living on the tundra, my elderly interviewees have lived there most of their lives. They have a sense of place that is connected to their experiences on the tundra. They have grown up on the tundra hearing narratives about its places. But the village also represents a lived space for them.

Dichotomy upside-down

In the narrative the tundra is the opposite of the village. It is from the village that a man departs to go hunting and he goes back to the village when he wants to go home. The current opposition between the village and the tundra seems to be common amongst Northern minorities in Russia.[134] The concept of the tundra should still be made clearer, which can be done by still another opposition. Tuula Tuisku (2001, 43) has written that:

> For the Nenets, 'tundra' is a culturally and socially constructed term having two different meanings. First of all, it is the opposite of the camp area, which is itself located on the tundra. Secondly, the tundra is the opposite of villages, which are stable spots also located on the tundra as a vegetation zone.

I interpret the quotation as saying that the village–tundra opposition is only of secondary importance, with the camp-tundra opposition having primary importance. In addition to this tundra-camp opposition we must add, that the nomadic Nenets consider the tundra as their home – and not just the conical tent that is built again and again in the camp sites. The whole tundra being a home means that it is a meaningful space as a whole. Being a meaningful space, on the other hand, means that the landscape is lived space with individual, communal and cultural meanings in it. If a man or a woman and their society moves in the tundra from year to year and bases their living on this movement and space, it cannot be meaningless.

One of my informants, now 60 years old, said that he had thought many times of moving back to the tundra where he would be free and could go where he wanted when he wanted without worrying at all about his livelihood. The nomadic way of life is considered to be a guarantee for the preservation and continuation of the Nenets way of life in general as the village inevitably means the death of Nenets culture. The Nenets mentality lives in the tundra.

There is something romantic about these ideas, a sense of nostalgia for the past. Considering the present, it is important to note that the village and the tundra are not only oppositions, but also complement each other. What is

---

[134] See e.g. King 2002; Kerttula's (2000) study on the Yup'ik and Chukchi adds the opposition of sea and village, or sea and tundra.

important is the gaze which comes from the tundra. The village is seen from this tundra perspective, not the other way round.

The village, on the other hand, has very different kinds of meanings as the agency of people is different, and the people who first moved and lived in the village were of a different kind. And the dichotomy has been turned upside-down. As their way of living has been transformed from a nomadic to a settled one, the younger generation has a very different kind of sense of Kolguev. They haven't lived the space and moved around the tundra with reindeer and they cannot understand all the narratives connected to places. We should, nevertheless, remember that these narratives are not just told to outside ethnographers like myself. The younger generation has also heard them many times. Thus, these narratives are also part of their sense of place although many of them haven't physically visited the places.

The narrative above does refer to a village, a place to which the narrator hurriedly returned. Regarding the tundra as the only "true" place of association for the Nenets would be to forget and underestimate a large part of their life. Today, Bugrino is a centre of activity where most of the Kolguev Islanders live. During the Soviet period, the village was also a centre for the economic collective, whose meanings reached far beyond the economic. Thus, it is important to remember that according to local imageries the best reindeer herders, the most qualified meat, and quantum leaps of the Nenets *okrug* were made in the *kolkhoz* "Kolguev". People have not only lived in the village, they have built it, worked for it, improved its conditions and built its reputation. There was "a lifelong interest in building a community which approached the standards of comfort and refinement in the Russian centers of high culture" (Anderson 2000, 43).

The above narrative includes both the village and the tundra. It brings out very clearly, that the Nenets have not stagnated in their traditional way of living, in their traditional culture, in the tundra. But it also reminds us, that the traditional is still part of their everyday thinking, speaking and in their perception of the landscape. The village does not denote the death of the Nenets culture, but is part of their network of places – part of the tundra.

Conclusion

Bugrino is a strange place. It is a Soviet invention, an attempt to create a different way of life in the North; an attempt to settle nomads in a small space in a typically Russian way. The rapid and violent manner in which the reforms and renewals were enforced between the 1930s and 1970s left little room for free adaptation and created a strong sense of rupture which worked for and against Soviet ways (Cf. Ssorin-Chaikov 2003). Nevertheless, I want to emphasize that adaptation did take place, or to be precise, something more than just adaptation. People have moved to villages with their thinking systems and cultures, shaped the life of the villages and actively participated in the life of such villages.[135]

The village has grown up and become part of the Nenets structure of places. In the Soviet period, the village meant the *kolkhoz*, with which the people identified themselves very strongly. The communities were known in terms of the results and the conditions of their *kolkhoz*. Just as the construction of the *kolkhozes* was one of the most violent epochs in the history of the Nenets and the Soviet Union, so too has the abolition of the *kolkhozes* been an attack against "imagined communities" that had become very real. The villages were left without the prime symbol of their action, the *kolkhoz*. Fortunately, activity previously conducted and centered around the *kolkhoz* "Kolguev", now continues around new and inchoate institutions.

Patterns related to the nomadic way of life are still the basis of the Nenets community in Kolguev – patterns related to a settled way of living are constantly created within the older patterns.

In this article, I have tried to describe some differences between Russian and Nenets ways of seeing the landscape, the North and the village. The Russian point of departure has often been one of conquest. Looking from the Nenets, and nomadic, point of view, the whole idea and reality of conquering the North, looks absurd. The ambivalence of spaciousness and resistance to it are not part of Nenets landscape thinking. There is nothing heroic about living in the North – it is not a land of horrible creatures, but a home. The Soviet Union has ignored these differences in spatial thinking. Today, with the abandonment of the Russian North and the problem of maintaining its infrastructure, is the time to consider local views. In the meantime, the culture and landscape of Kolguev will continue to be restructured.

References

Agadjanian, A. (2000) Russian Religion in Media Discourse – Entropy Interlude in Ideocratic Tradition, in *Religious Transition in Russia,* ed. by M. Kotiranta. Aleksanteri Institute, Helsinki, 251–88.

Anderson, D. (2001) *Identity and Ecology in Arctic Siberia. The Number One Reindeer Brigade.* Oxford University Press, Oxford.

Appadurai, A. (1988) Putting Hierarchy in Its Place. *Cultural Anthropology* 3 (1), 36–49.

---

[135] For an excellent discussion on the mental construction of places totally anew after migration in the Soviet Union, see Hakamies 2005.

Basso, K. (1996) Wisdom Sits in Places: Notes on a Western Apache Landscape, in *Sense of Place*, ed. by S. Feld & K. Basso. School of American Research, Santa Fe, New Mexico, 53–90.

Bernštam, T.A. (1978) *Pomory. Formirovanie gruppy i sistema hoziaistva.* [The Pomors. Formation of the group and the system of household.] Nauka, Leningrad.

Bychkova Jordan, B. & T. Jordan-Bychkov (2001) *Siberian Village. Land and Life in the Sakha Republic.* University of Minnesota Press, Minneapolis, London.

Casey, E. (1996) How to get from Space to Place in a Fairly Short Stretch of Time: Phenomenological Prolegomena, in *Sense of Place,* ed. by S. Feld & K. Basso. School of American Research Advanced Seminar Series.Santa Fe, New Mexico, 13-52.

Epstein, M. (2003) Russo-Soviet Topoi, in *The Landscape of Stalisnism. The Art and Ideology of Soviet Space,* ed. by E. Dodrenko & E. Naiman. University of Washington Press, Seattle & London, 277-306.

Fernandez, J. (1988) Andalusia on Our Minds: Two Contrasting Places in Spain As Seen in a Vrenacular Poetic Dual of the Late 19th Century. *Cultural Anthropology* 3 (1), 21-35.

Fryer, P. (1999) Heaven, Hell, or ...Something in Between? Cobtrasting Russian Images of Siberia, in *Beyond the Limits. The Concept of Space in Russian History and Culture,* ed. by J. Smith. Finnish Historical Society, Helsinki, 95-106.

Glassie, H. (1982) *Passing the Time in Ballymenone. Culture and History through an Ulster Community.* University of Pennsylvania Press, Philadelphia.

Golovanov, V. (2002) *Ostrov, ili opravdanie bessmiyslennyh putešestvij.* [Island, ora defense of senseless journeys.] Vagrius, Moskva.

Golovnev, A.V. (1992) Sihitja in Mythology and Archaelogy. *Specimina Sibirica* tomus V, 79-93.

—. 1995 *Govorjaščie kul'tury. Tradicii samodijcev i ugrov.* [Talkingcultures. Traditions of the Samoyedes and Ugrians] Rossijskaja akademija nauk, Ekaterinburg.

Golovnev, A. V. & G. Osherenko (1999) *Siberian Survival. The Nenets and Their Story.* Cornell University Press, Ithaca & London.

Gow, P. (1995) Land, People, and Paper in Western Amazonia, in *The Anthropology of Landscape. Perspectives on Place and Space,* ed. by E. Hirsch & M. O'Hanlon. Oxford University Press, Oxford, 43–62.

Grant, B. (1995) *In the Soviet House of Culture. A Century of Perestroikas.* Princeton University Press, Princeton.

Hakamies, P. (2005) New Culture on New Territories. The Karelian Isthmus and Ladoga Karelia in Post-war Years, in *Moving in the USSR. Western Anomalies and Northern Wilderness*, ed. by P. Hakamies. Finnish Literature Society, Helsinki, 91-109.

Hellberg-Hirn E. (1999) Ambivalent Space: Russian Expressions of Russian Identity, in *Beyond the Limits. The Concept of Space in Russian History and Culture,* ed. by J. Smith. Finnish Historical Society, Helsinki, 49-69.

—. 1998, *Soil and Soul. The Symbolic World of Russianness*. Ashgate, Aldershot, Brookfield, Singapore & Sydney.

Helanterä, A. & V. Tynkkynen (2002) *Maantieteelle Venäjä ei voi mitään.* [Russia cannot help its geography] Ajatus Kirjat, Helsinki.

Hirsch, E. (1995) Introduction: Landcape. Between Place and Space, in *The Anthropology of Landscape. Perspectives on Place and Space,* ed. by E. Hirsch & M. O'Hanlon. Oxford University Press, Oxford, 1-30.

Humphrey, C. (1998) *Marx Went Away – but Karl Stayed Behind.* Rev. ed. of Karl Marx Collective. University of Michigan Press, Ann Arbor.

Kerttula, A. (2000) *Antler on the Sea. The Yup'ik and Chukchi of the Russian Far East.* Cornell University Press, Ithaca & London.

Kharyuchi, G.P. (2004) The Nenets Sacred Sites as Ethnographic Landscape, in *Northern Ethnographic Landscapes: Perspectives from Circumpolar Nations*, ed. by I. Krupnik, R. Mason &T. Horton. Smithsonian Institution, Washington D.C., 155-76.

King, A.D. (2002) Reindeer Herders' Culturescapes in the Koryak Autonomous Okrug, in *People and the Land. Pathways to Reform in Post-Soviet Siberia*, ed. by E. Kasten. Dietrich Reimer Verlag, Berlin, 63-80.

Marcus, G.E. (2001) Multi-Sited Research as a Departure from Regulative Ideals of Classic Fieldwork, in Anthropology in *Departures. How Societies Distribute Their People,* ed. by J. Siikala. Finnish Anthropological Society, Helsinki, 217-34.

McCannon, J. (2003) Tabula Rasa in the North: the Soviet Arctic and Mythic Landscapes in Stalinist Popular Culture, in *The Landscape of Stalisnism. The Art and Ideology of Soviet Space*, ed. by E. Dobrenko & E. Naiman. University of Washington Press, Seattle & London, 241-60.

Medevedev, S. (1999) A General Theory of Russian Space: A Gay Science and a Rigorous Science, in *Beyond the Limits. The Concept of Space in Russian History and Culture*, ed. by J. Smith. Finnish Historical Society, Helsinki, 15-47.

Rethmann, P. (2001) *Tundra Passages. History and Gender in the Russian Far East.* Pennsylvania State University Press, Pennsylvania.

Round, J. (2005) Rescaling Russia's Geography: the Challenges of Depopulating the Northern Periphery. *Europe-Asia Studies* 57 (5), 705-27.

Rydving, H. (2002) Synliga og osynliga landskap. Några samiska exempel, [The seen and unseen landscape. Some Saami examples.] in *Ting og tekst*, ed. by E. Mundal & A. Ågotnes. Bryggens Museum, Bergen, 65-77.

Siikala, A-L. & O. Ulyashev (2003) Landscape of Spirits: Holy Places and Challenging Rituals of the Northern Khanty. *Shaman* 11 (1&2), 149-76.

Siikala, J. (2001) Tilling the Soil and Sailing the Seas: Cadastral Maps and Anthropological Interpretations, in *Departures. How Societies Distribute Their People*, ed. by J. Siikala, Finnish Anthropological Society, Helsinki, 22-45.

Stammler, F. (2005) *Reindeer Nomads Meet the Market. Culture, Property and Globalisation at the 'End of the Land'*. Lit verlag, Berlin.

Survo, A. (2001) Words about the Wor(l)d: Ingrian Lutheranism in the (post) Soviet Cultural Space, in *Departures. How Societies Distribute Their People,* ed. by J. Siikala. Finnish Anthropological Society, Helsinki, 179-216.

Ssorin-Chaikov, N. (2003) *The Social Life of the State in Subarctic Siberia.* Stanford University Press, Palo Alto.

Terebihin, N.M. (2004) *Metafizika Severa.* [The metaphysics of the North] Pomoskij Universitet, Arkhangel'sk.

Trevor-Batye, A. (1895) *Ice-Bound in Kolguev,* Archibald Constable, Westminster & Co.

Tuisku, T. (2001) The Displacement of Nenets Women from Reindeer Herding and the Tundra in the Nenets Autonomous Okrug, Northwestern Russia. *Acta Borealia* 2, 41–60.

—. (1999) Nenetsien ankarat elämisen ehdot tundralla ja kylässä. Poronhoidon sopeutumisstrategiat ja delokalisoitumisprosessi Nenetsiassa. [The severe living conditions of Nenets in tundra and village. The adaptations strategies and the process of delocalization in Nenetsia.] Lapin yliopisto, Rovaniemi.

CHAPTER TWELVE

VILLAGERS AND *DACHNIKI*[136] IN POST-SOVIET RUSSIA: A COMPLEX RELATION

NATHALIE ORTAR

Introduction

One of the consequences of decollectivisation in Russia has been an increase in the number of *dacha*s. Several forms coexist in the villages: inherited old peasant houses (*isba*), old houses bought by workers or employees, new houses built by wealthy people, but they are all *dacha*s since they are used as second homes. The owners of those houses are working in towns and come only for their vacations and/or, when they do not live too far, during the week-ends. They are either native to the village or its surroundings (either themselves or their parents), or came by way of relationships with other *dachniki* or villagers. Although this is changing with the development of new housing markets, a newcomer to a village usually has some connection with someone who is already a member of the community – another *dachnik* or a villager, a kin, a colleague or a friend. Moreover, those second home owners represents a wide range of professions and positions in society, which reflects the fact that some people have inherited or bought an old *isba* whilst others have built new wood or brick houses, the size depending on their wealth. These people maintain or develop new relationships with the locals on the basis of family networks and the exchange of services (helps) amongst the *dachniki* and/or between the *dachniki* and the villagers.

*Dacha*s influence the organisation of time of the *dachniki* and their conception of life and family. If gardening and the upkeep of the *dacha* consume most of the *dachniki's* time, they also interact a lot with other *dachniki* and villagers. The nature of the exchanges can be economic or cultural. *Dachniki* interact with the rural world and change it. The needs of the *dachniki*

[136] Name given to *dacha*s owners in Russia. *Dacha*s are Russian second homes.

create new job opportunities for the villagers, but they also influence the way villagers look at their cultural heritage. However, such change cannot happen without generating a degree of tension between the two populations.

The fieldwork was undertaken around Yaroslavl' and Rybinsk among a population of *dachniki* owning houses in allotments[137] (Ortar 2005) and villages, using a social anthropological approach. The fieldwork was conducted in two villages and three collective gardens[138] (*kolektivnye sady*) in the summers of 1999-2003. Altogether, I stayed with five different families in two villages and two collective gardens. I returned every year in order to be able to follow the lives of the people I had met and observe any changes. Over this period, I conducted thirty-five interviews, mostly with *dachniki,* but also with villagers. Most of them were made while staying in villages and collective gardens, but I also made ten interviews while visiting other *dacha*s and allotments around Yaroslavl'. I also interviewed ten families both at their *dacha*s and at their flats or offices in the city in order to observe different aspects of their life. To complete the picture, I conducted five interviews with town or transport planners and architects.

Rybinsk (234,000 inhabitants) is located in Yaroslavl' *oblast*[139], around 350 kilometres north east of Moscow, on the river Volga. Rybinsk was renowned for its airplane-engine factories and has been strongly affected by unemployment over the last fifteen years. Yaroslavl' (600,000 inhabitants) is the main city of Yaroslavl' *oblast*, and has been less affected by unemployment. Knowledge of the urban context furnishes some keys to understanding the role of the *dac*ha. Indeed, the development of these two cities has followed rigid urbanisation patterns. In Rybinsk, plans for the region were conceived at the beginning of the 1930s when the city had only 100,000 inhabitants. At that time, the plans envisaged a city of 700,000 inhabitants, a size never reached. The agglomeration stretches over twenty kilometres along the Volga-river. Land was allotted to companies which built residential buildings for their employees

---

[137] The wealthiest people during the soviet period and furthermore since the end of it, can own a *dacha* in allotments: on the contrary to the collective gardens (see bellow for a more precise definition) *dachniki* were not required to grow up vegetables and the plots were the house was settle were bigger (between 800 to 1,000 m^2) than that of the collective gardens.

[138] Collective gardens are allocated land managed by a cooperative. Inside the cooperative plots of 600 m^2 are given to families. Gardeners are required to grow up vegetables and can build a 25m^2 house. The plot, called dacha, can be passed on to parents, children or spouses, and they could without qualification be inherited Lovell (2003) or Traven (2005). This aspect of the research will not be under discussion in this paper.

[139] An administrative region in Russian.

according to pre-established plans, repeated *ad infinitum*.[140] Whole districts composed exclusively of buildings of seven to twelve stores, divided into flats looking all alike, were built around the factories without any overall coherence. Consequently, residential areas can be located several kilometres away from the town centre. *Isba* belonging to old villages, forested areas, fields, and waste land remain between these districts. In some of these areas, individual houses and new buildings dedicated to Russia's new upper class are beginning to be built. Yaroslavl' has been developed according to a town-plan similar to that of Rybinsk. Therefore, much time and energy is devoted to commuting to and from work every day. In this urban, work-related context, *dacha*s are places of rest, relative freedom and somewhere for people to work in their gardens.

The collective gardens and villages where I stayed were located around these two cities. In the villages, *dachniki* from a wide social spectrum live together. This is a feature of the countryside. The *dachniki* I interviewed ranged from unemployed people to employed workers in unskilled jobs with poor living standards to well-off business men and women, doctors, and teachers working in international schools. The poorer *dachniki* live in towns close by except when the *dacha* is inherited, the more well-to-do *dachniki* live either in Yaroslavl', Moscow or Saint Petersburg.

Dacha time organisation

In spite of the fact that recent development of dachas in rural areas is closely linked to food shortages that Russia underwent since the fall of the Soviet Union till the very beginning of the twenty first century and the emergence of a desire for space, second home ownership and a country life, the phenomenon of occasional commuting between rural and urban spaces (*maâtnikovaâ migratsiâ*) has been known and studied by sociologists such as Basil Kerblay (1973, 1985) for quite a long time. However, most of the research on dachas has been conducted since 1990. Ronan Hervouet (2003) has studied *kolektivnye sady* in Belarus and Jane Zavisca (2003) has studied *dacha*s in Kaluga, a medium-sized central Russian city. Both, as well as Nathalie Ortar (2005), were influenced by Simon Clarke's (2000) research on the *dacha*s' economic role. Apart from Simon Clarke, this economic role has also been analysed by Richard Rose and Evgeny Tikhomirov (1993), Ronan Hervouet (2003), Jane Zavisca (2003) and Nathalie Ortar (2005) in their attempt to understand the broader meaning of the *dacha*. This aspect will not be specifically analysed in this article. Two research works conducted with a historical approach must also be mentioned: those of Stephen Lovell (2003) and Vlada Traven (2005). Both contribute to the

[140] Architects could choose between two types of buildings.

understanding of the origins of the different forms of *dacha*s that can be observed today.

Residential migrations between the city and the country can be of two types. If the *dacha* is located nearby, trips to the *dacha* do not have a seasonal character: city-dwellers favour short but frequent trips or weekends, as long as the weather is good enough. Some even visit their dachas in the winter. In contrast, when the second home is far from the main residence, the commuting journey is made over a long distance. In this case, trips to the *dacha* preserve both their holiday character, and their long duration (several weeks or months at a time). Trips to the *dacha* also depend on the fact that the house may be shared by more than two generations.

Several factors lay behind the evolution of people's trips to their *dacha*, this back and forth movement between urban and rural spaces. The most important factor is simply the economic means at people's disposal. Then the various means of transport available and the quality of the road network determine distance thresholds. The distance to the *dacha* also determines the various uses to which it is put. The distances people travel to their *dacha*s varies enormously from some dozens of kilometres for the inhabitants of small- and medium-sized cities, to hundreds of kilometres for residents of regional and national capitals such as Moscow or Yaroslavl'. It should be noted, however, that substantial increases in the price of petrol recently and, therefore, in travel costs has served to encourage people to spend more time at their *dacha*s. M. and Mrs Smekalov[141], a working-class couple, live in Saint Petersburg and have a house near Rybinsk, which was bought from family members. During the 1980s, they used to come by car not only for the summer holidays but also for shorter visits of between three days and one week. The economic recession obliged them to sell their car and travel by train: now as a result they come only during the summer but they stay longer. They save up all their annual leave for this one summer holiday, except for a visit with their son in his car, at the beginning of spring to plant seeds in the garden.

As mentioned above, the question of the garden and its use is central to understanding the *dacha* and its evolution. For example, in 1999 it was unthinkable not to cultivate the garden oneself or give it to a poorer family member. A rich Muscovite owner of *dacha* around Rybinsk left the garden, rather condescendingly, to her sister to grow potatoes. On the same allotment owned by the elite of Rybinsk, flowers were rare. However, three years later, beds of flowers had appeared replacing the seedlings of potatoes and gherkins, and the gardens known as Alpine or Japanese gardens are a veritable success. Other vegetables and berries persist but are relegated in more hidden places of

[141] All the names of the people met are changed.

the garden. If such changes can be noticed among wealthy people, for others, especially those on low salaries and pensioners (Rimachevskaïa 1997), growing vegetables are still an indispensable part of their lives (Ortar 2005). So, depending on the wealth of the person who owns them, *dacha*s may be interpreted as sites of consumption or of production, economic necessities or status symbols (Zavisca 2003).

The rural residence: a reference point for lifestyles

The phenomenon of the *dacha* in rural areas says a lot about the potential of rural space to appear as a central point of reference for lifestyles. A sense of belonging to the rural world is then claimed. If it is true that both one's professional life and part of one's social life are located in the city, we can only grasp the essence of both when the rural dimension is taken into account. This link with the rural environment and the effect it is seen to have on one's identity holds true whether the dacha was inherited, or was purchased in a village in which one had no kin (Ortar 2004). Nevertheless, the presence of kin seems, in a *de facto* fashion, to justify a claim on identity as can be noticed in other countries, in France for example (Ortar 1999, Perrot 1998). Therefore, the conceptual dimension of roots appears very rapidly in speech. When considering the importance of an identity revealing itself through speech, one also has to take into account the ways in which family memory is built. Anne Muxel (1996) points to the importance and productivity of the presence of holiday recollections, which take up the greater part of the space available to one's memory, even when holidays represent only a short period compared to the time taken up by one's daily routine. However, these periods correspond to time spent together. In this rural "unity" of the family, which can be contrasted with the "dispersion" of the city (Gotman & Léger 1999), the beginning of an explanation for the incapacity of the city to confer legitimate territorial identities can be found.

The importance given to the rural world gives way to new strategies developed for maintaining contacts. First of all they take the form of a purchase or additional rental for children, relatives or friends. Within a territory where the family has no ties of origins, this can bring family members together, including sometimes a couple's first cousins. In order to avoid discord, relatives can also invest either in building land, or in restorable houses, so that every sibling can possess his own home in the future, while at the same time giving the family the chance to protect its integrity. For example the Manilov bought a piece of land to build a *dacha* in 1996. In 2002, they started looking for two other parcels of land in the same village in order to be able to build two houses for their sons one day.

Acquisition can also be a strategy to increase a family's wealth as in the case of the the Netsvetaïev, a working-class family. The parents had a *dacha* in a *kolektivnye sad*, and had two sons, both married and both fathers of three children. One of the sons obtained another *dacha*, which was a long way from his home. The two *dacha*s were sold to buy a peace of land twice as big as those on which staid the dachas, in a village within reach by bus. The Netsvetaïev built two houses there — which would have been impossible in the old allotments — where wives and children spend the summer growing vegetables. These kitchen gardens are vital for those families. Nevertheless, thanks to the deployed strategies and the work of each family member, this family, whose income has remained constant and therefore modest, has an environment offering a real quality of life and has considerably increased its capital. This is only one example among many of the real estate strategies implemented around second homes, which are of both a financial and symbolic nature, revealing the complexity of the connections elaborated by the *dachniki*.

Exchanges in the environment of the second home

The presence of the *dachniki* and the frequency and length of their visits are the source of a variety of exchanges between them and other *dachniki* and villagers which contribute to the revitalization of the countryside.

Economic exchanges

The contacts that emerge between the *dachniki* and local villagers often take the form of an exchange of services (e.g. looking after the house during the winter, taking care of the garden, repairing the house, etc.). Some of these services are paid and this injection of capital stimulates the local economy. *Dacha*s — which are for the most part left uninhabited during Russia's long winter — benefit from minor repair work or from improvements thanks to the year-round residents of the village. These local year-round residents thus help maintain the houses and also guard them in the winter in order to reduce the risk of burgling. Flowers and vegetables are planted in the spring. When the *dachniki* visit on holiday, the locals provide them with various foodstuffs: Mrs Baklouchine, a widowed teacher, sells milk from her cow to several families during their visit; the Fomitch also provides the Manilov with milk and sells what the Fomitch's grand-mother and children gather (e.g. mushrooms and berries) and also help out in other ways. Not all these services and goods are paid for with money. Instead, they can be paid for in the form of gifts of vodka, second-hand clothes, courses given to children, or help in finding somewhere to live when one of the villagers' children goes away to study.

However, in many cases the *dachniki* do pay for these services and goods with money, which provides an important source of income for many unemployed or underemployed locals. It is interesting to note that after the fall of communism, some Russians left the cities to live in the countryside, sometimes in an *isba* belonging to their parents, hoping to find a better standard of living. Mr Souchilov is one such person. Unemployed for several years, he has started a new life by planting potatoes and onions in his parents' field, which had been left unexploited for several years. He and his family moved back to town during the winter when he tried to find work as a private policeman. To improve his income he also started to work as a mason for people who wanted to build a *dacha*. This activity has become so profitable that it now occupies all his time, providing him with an income for his family.

The use of workers has a very marked seasonal character in Russia. Nevertheless, it is characterized by the consolidation of existing commercial networks and by the creation and development of the various sectors involved in building and restoration. For example, several of the *dachniki* observed hired the services of a mason skilled in building old fashion stoves, and/or a wood-carver and a joiner. This trend can also be seen in the remarkable development of retail outlets for building materials.

Among the multiple ties that bind secondary residents to their *dacha*, as well as binding the *dachniki* to each other, like between the *dachniki* and the villagers, a certain number are expressed in the form of an informal economy, within a system of debt always renewed. The exchange of services is not always paid for, and it can assume extremely different forms. For instance, it can correspond to the transport of the family to and from the *dacha*: Mrs Ivanova is regularly driven by friends to her *dacha*, which she bought with their help. She had given free courses to their son in order to help him enter to medical school a few years earlier. Car-pooling, arranged among friends or relatives, is rarely done on the basis of a money payment. An obligation incurred can very well correspond to the repayment of another debt. Local acquaintances go well beyond the framework of the second home, to exercise their influence in helping to enrol children in a school, find work placement. The strength and the number of these ties are as old as the *dacha*s themselves. They bear witness to the importance of the second home as a place of exchange and contact between groups which would not meet outside this context.

Cultural exchanges

Social relationships between *dachniki* and local people do indeed contribute to the development of territorial (regional or local), social and occupational identity. Social players are consolidated and fixed in roles which are established initially in informal exchanges and daily contacts and then given concrete expression by a network of interpersonal relations, notably through sponsorships and referrals. These same social identities are reaffirmed through the organization of social events or activities having a symbolic and unifying character.

Certain forms of social relation are new. For example, in the hamlet of Velikovo, in a rural district of the region of Yaroslavl, city residents who have bought old *isbas* in order to restore them as second homes, share an area adjoining an established rural population which is not very mobile, because few own a car and most of them are elderly. These city residents (without any experience of working the land) benefit from the advice and know-how offered by their older neighbours, who can advise them on the choice of plant strains, and how to grow them. In return, the *dachniki* bring seeds and grain, which are still difficult to find in small rural markets, to the village.

The practice of exchange is also encouraged through the practice of buying supplies together. The absence of a local grocer's shop, or if there is one, its inability to meet all the local needs, promotes practices of mutual aid which include both car-pooling for travel to larger urban centres, and shopping done for nearby neighbours and/or friends. The totality of these relationships added to the various types of exchanged services actually forms a tight network of mutual aid and mutual debt that binds temporary and permanent residents together.

Those exchanges are also accomplished through the exchange of symbolic possessions. Permanent residents transfer not only some of their historical and cultural knowledge of the area to the *dachniki*, but also the legitimacy to be a member of the village. In return, permanent residents receive the added value conferred on them through the interest developed by urban residents in the rural way of life, which was formerly abandoned or belittled. These symbolic exchanges occur within a general context of a search for stable reference points of identity in modern ever-changing European societies (Ortar 2004). An example of those exchanges was the rebuilding of a village church financed by wealthy *dachniki*. By rebuilding a wooden church in the old style, the aim was to revive the church in order to give back what was perceived as the village's unity.

Conflicts and tensions

The rural character of this social exchange expresses itself through making acquaintances, which is useful for cementing social ties. A tacit obligation is imposed upon the newcomer to adhere to the network of the village, at the risk of being stigmatised as a person who refuses to play according to the rules of the game. *Dachniki*'s integration is measured by their involvement in local rural life. To remain an outsider, to refuse to get involved in an activity, not to be available for a festival or for a service, is to be met at once with disapproval, while subscribing to village social exchange — through creating social ties or through benefiting from an established network of family or friends — allows the *dachnik* to be closer to the group of villagers.

The relationships that the two communities maintain allow them to express their vital economic, social and political interests, as well as those pertaining to their identity. These interests can generate tensions, as well as the permanent search for balance.. Tensions are revealed by the ambivalent way in which each community perceives the others. Indeed, permanent and secondary residents constantly criticize each other while at the same time maintaining daily, and varied, cordial personal relationships with members of the incriminated community. So, the forms of social exchange actually experienced reveal that social practices can widely deviate from ideal models.

One of the limits of mutual social relationships lies in the competitiveness that can crop up among different groups. If competitiveness appears between locals and *dachniki* during fights over political interests, it also occurs among *dachniki* for access to the territory of the village and to its use.

In the region of Rybinsk, the *dachniki* who have already become established members of the village community are trying to slow or to oppose the influx of new residents by using their influence in the rural land council which has the power, among other thing, to decide who is going to be able to buy the land and which peace of land are going to be sold. By mobilising their network of acquaintances within it, they intervene so that plots of land that are still available are allocated to individuals of their choosing or "even reserved" for their own personal projects, whether these are practical in the medium- or long-term future. Mr. Manilov bought a plot through a friend who wanted to thank him for having put up his son in Moscow. A few years later, Mr. Manilov was informed that new land will be put on sale. The family of his friend is interested as is he himself, for his children. However, as he cannot pay at the time, the authorities agreed to freeze the sale until such time as he could afford the first instalment.

Conflicts of interest may also arise over different uses of the land and to whom it is sold. Existing tensions over access to the land have taken on more of an economic than a political character. To have the power to sell the land favours the development of corruption; this accompanies the mobilization of support and sponsoring. The beneficiaries of this corruption, local and regional civil servants, are also responsible for land surveying, and take advantage of the rivalry which develops among secondary residents, while ensuring their own power.

Conclusion

The relationships between *dachniki* and villagers are very intricate and are not devoid of tensions. If a renewal of rural social exchange can be observed, it is also because the actors, whether rural or urban, permanent or secondary, share the same source of common cultural representations, which find their basis in the rural past of the Russian population. Those relations ensure continuity in the relations between cities and villages and feed all kinds of exchanges. Moreover, part of the population of *dachniki* is starting to live permanently in villages around the towns, first signs of a suburbanisation.

Actually, if the State, through the companies still offers lodging access, this supply is often in a bad shape and concerns only flats. Since the beginning of the twenty first century, a private market is developing, and while in the city dwellings remain rather rare and expensive, it is easier to find houses and apartments available for rent or for purchase around the towns (Prokofieva, Grichanov & Kortchagina 2003).

This movement of population is not the first one to be observed, since at the beginning of the 1990s, an initial migratory movement from city dwellers to the countryside, was regarded as the first sign of re-urbanization. These first migrants were often unemployed and were hoping to find better living conditions and job opportunities in the countryside (Lezean 1997). Nevertheless, since living conditions in the cities have improved, large parts of this new rural population have returned there. During the late 1990s, only those who were not able to find another solution continued to commute daily between the city and the countryside (Lezean 1997). However, since the beginning of 2000, along with the continuing improvement of living conditions, city dwellers are once again attracted to the countryside. These people are wealthier than those of the first wave, and tend to keep their jobs in the city. The starting point for this new suburbanisation is either a *dacha* or a village first used by the *dachniki* and still used as a summer residence for some and full-time residence for others: a situation which also depends greatly on the state of the road network. *Dacha* and suburbanisation are becoming more and more intricate and a more urban way of using rural land is appearing in Russia.

References

Clarke, S., L. Varshavskaya, S. Alasheev & M. Karelina (2000) The myth of the urban peasant. *Work, employment and society* 14 (3), 481-99.

Gessat, E. & N. Ortar (2006) Circuler entre ville et campagne. Evolution de l'usage des résidences secondaires en France et en Russie [To move between town and countryside. Changes in the use of second homes in

France and Russia], in *Nouvelles urbanités, nouvelles ruralités en Europe* [New towns, new countryside in Europe], ed. by Y. Luginbühl. Peter Lang. Bruxelles (to be published).

Gotman, A., Léger, J.M. (1999), Variations saisonnières de la famille : enquête sur les secondes résidences [Seasonal changes of the family: a survey on second homes], in *D'une maison l'autre* [From one house to the other], ed. by P. Bonnin & R. de Villanova. Créaphis, Paris, 177-212.

Hervouet, R. (2003) Dachas and Vegetable Gardens in Belarus. Economic and Subjective Stakes of an Ordinary Passion. *The Anthropology of East Europe Review: Central Europe, Eastern Europe and Eurasia* XXI (1), 159-68.

Kerblay, B. (1973) *L'isba d'hier et d'aujourd'hui* [*Isba* from yesterday and today]. L'Age d'Homme, Lausanne.

—. (1985) *Du mir aux agrovilles* [From *mir* to agrotowns]. Editions de l'Institut d'études slaves, Paris.

Lezean, E. (1997) *Bilan et perspectives de la réforme agraire dans les terres non noires: oblast de Iaroslav* [Results and forecasts of the agrarian reform in the Yaroslavl' *oblast*]. Mémoire de maîtrise de russe, Institut national des langues et civilisations orientales, Paris.

Lovell, S. (2003) *Summerfolk. A History of the Dacha 1710-2000.* Cornell University press, Ithaca & London.

Muxel, A. (1996), *Individu et mémoire familiale* [Individual and family memory]. Nathan, Paris.

Ortar, N. (1999) Les multiples réalités de la résidence secondaire [The different symbolic aspects of the second home], in *D'une maison l'autre* [From one house to the other], ed. by P. Bonnin & R. de Villanova. Créaphis, Paris, 139-55.

—. (2004) Territoire d'origine et migration : la construction identitaire des résidents secondaires en France et en Russie [Homeland and migration: construction of identity of second homes owners in France and in Russia], in *Actes du colloque Identité(s)* [Annals of the Congress "Identities"]. Presses universitaires de Rennes, Rennes, 195-206.

—. (2005) Les multiples usages de la datcha des jardins collectifs [The multiple uses of the allotments dacha in Russia]. *Anthropologie et sociétés* 29 (2), 169-85.

Perrot, M. (1998) La maison de famille [Family houses] in *L'autre maison [The other house]*, ed. F. Dubost. Autrement, Collections Mutations, No. 178, Paris, 38-67.

Prokofieva, L., V. Grichanov & I. Kortchagina (2003) Pauvreté commune et marché à la marge. Les conditions de logement dans la Russie urbaine des

années 1990 [Urban Russia in the 1990s]. *Annales de la recherche urbaine* (93), 77-85.
Rose, R., & E. Tkhomirov (1993) Who Grows Food in Russia and Eastern Europe? *Post Soviet Geography* 34 (2), 79-110.
Rimachevskaïa, N. (1997) Le troisième âge et la transition en Russie [Old age and transition in Russia]. *Le courrier des pays de l'Est* 420, 34-46.
Traven, V. (2005) *La datcha en Russie de 1917 à nos jours* [Dacha in Russia since 1917]. Editions du Sextant, Paris.
Zavisca, J. (2003) Contesting Capitalism at the Post-soviet Dacha: the Meaning of Food Cultivation for Urban Russian. *Slavic review* 62 (4), 786-810.

CHAPTER THIRTEEN

THE STATUS OF THE YOUTH ON KARELIA'S RURAL LABOUR MARKET

MARIA DYAKONOVA

Introduction

The recent radical socio-economic reforms in Russia have affected all aspects of life. They have had a direct influence on the labour market. There are two contradictory tendencies in the Russian labour market. On the one hand, the appearance of new forms of ownership, the creation of new types of enterprises, and the development of entrepreneurial activity have led to a diversity of forms and places of employment, and increased the opportunities for people to realize their economic potential. On the other hand, economic crises have led to the impoverishment of the population, the appearance of unemployment, and an increase in discrimination against various groups of the population (e.g. by gender, age, place of residence). Overcoming the negative situation in the labour market is one of the priorities of Russian social policy (Sergienko et. al. 2001). Problems in the labour market are particularly acute in rural areas. Life in rural settlements is beset with difficulties related to the remoteness of villages and weaknesses in the economy in general.

Nowadays, the study of rural communities is of crucial importance. The last decade's economic performance and social exclusion regarding the Russian labour market have been studied by V. Gimpelson and A. Nikonov (1995); Z. Kalugina (2001, 2004, agrarian reforms, agriculture labour market); T. Zaslavskaya and T. Maleva (1999, unemployment, labour market, social reforms); V.Radaev and N.Rimashevskaya (2003, human potential); and R. Ryvkina, and V. Patsiorkovsky (2003, rural settlements, the family and household capital). Researchers have focused attention on analysing processes in the sphere of employment, and have created models of economic activity for different groups of the population. Furhermore, V.Artyomov, P.Elchaninov and A.Nikulin (2002) and O.Fadeeva (1999, 2004) have studied the problem of creating a rural labour market and the specific nature of that market, more generally, economic activity and unemployment in rural areas.

In this article I will concentrate on the problems of youth employment. Youth is the most mobile, adaptive and innovative strata of society. It quickly and sharply reacts to change in social, economic and political situations. I. Kon (1988) gives the following definition of the youth: "it is a social-demographic group allocated on the basis of a set of age characteristics and features of social status". The periodisation of life and notions about the properties and opportunities of individuals in each age group are closely connected with the age structure accepted by, and existing in, a society. In modern Russia (as well as earlier in the USSR) the youth is defined as a group of people between 15 and 30 years old.

In contemporary Russia, the youth suffer a special pressure of public problems; this especially concerns rural youth. The first part of this article highlights the main factors which influence changes in the labour market. In the second part, this paper looks at the youth's position within the Karelian rural labour market. The purpose of this section is to identify features of youth employment and unemployment on the base of sociological data. Some proposals of inadmissibility of social exclusion on a rural labour market are given in the conclusion. Approaches for solving youth employment problems are also developed.

With the purpose of studying of rural communities, their problems, and economic and social status, several surveys of Karelian villages were carried out by the research group of the Institute of Economics, the Karelian Research Centre, and the Russian Academy of Sciences under the supervision of T. Morozova. Interviews with the heads and experts of local administrations and enterprises have been carried out during trips since 1998. The problems of rural areas and ways to solve them were considered during our work. The status of the youth in the Karelian labour market was one of our research questions.

The target region is the Republic of Karelia which is located in the North-West of Russia. It is part of the Northern economic region of the Russian Federation. Karelia extends over an area of 180.5 thousand square km (1.06% of the total territory of Russia). Karelia borders on Finland in the West, on Leningrad oblast in the South, and on Murmansk and Archangelsk oblasts in the East. In the North-West the Republic lies on the White Sea. The northern border line of Karelia coincides with the state border of the Russian Federation. According to the All-Russian population census of 2002, the population of the Republic of Karelia was 716,000. The urban population represents 75% (537,000 inhabitants), and the rural population 25% (179,000 inhabitants) of the total population of the Republic. 37% of the population lives in the capital of the Republic – the city of Petrozavodsk. The population density of the Republic is four persons per square kilometre. The Republic consists of 19 municipal districts and 808 settlements.

Factors influencing changes in the labour market

The rural labour market, as well as the Russian labour market in general, is characterised by a decline in the economic activity of the population, the occurrence of new kinds and forms of employment, and a low registered unemployment level in comparison with a significant amount of latent unemployment. The main features of the rural labour market are the low level of economic activity, the high level of unemployment, and significant seasonal fluctuations. The qualitative characteristics of the labour force are poor and wages are low; payments in kind and unpaid labour are widespread. Another feature is the extremely limited range of alternative workplaces (Sergienko et al. 2001, 166).

There are several factors which influence changes in the labour market. Among the most important are problems with rural schools, changes in legislation, the imbalance between supply and demand in the labour force, and general transitional processes, which have led to the transformation of the ownership structure and a structural reorganisation of agricultural enterprises.

The problems of rural schools. Graduates of rural schools are in a much worse position in comparison with graduates of urban schools because the general level of training was traditionally lower in rural areas. The opportunity to receive a higher education is four times lower for rural youth than for urban graduates. Furthermore, there is an inequality of opportunities for the youth not only between village and city, but also between large cities and small remote towns. In order to create equal opportunities, it is necessary to carry out a modernisation of rural schools.

Small schools in rural areas are in the process of being reorganized. Small rural schools are being closed, some classes are being abolished and being merged. All these changes have significant social consequences for rural society and encounter resistance on the part of the population. In the opinion of the rural population, this is not merely a reorganisation but a wholesale closure of rural schools. They consider that the closing of schools will not yield economic savings or benefits because pupils will have to be transported to other schools, which in turn will entail additional expense. Apart from this, there is the other problem of the low quality of the roads.

Changes in legislation. There are two aspects to this question. The first is connected to the official registration of the unemployed after the adoption of the Law on Employment, and the re-organisation of the public employment services in 1991 (Mezentseva 2000). The second aspect directly affects the youth. In the

Soviet Union, the terms under which the youth (university graduates) entered the labour market were regulated by legislation. There was a centralised system of graduate job placement for the first three years after graduation, the most unstable period. In 1990 the centralised distribution of graduates was cancelled by the Council of Ministers of the USSR[142]. On the one hand, this allowed the youth to choose for themselves the type of job they were interested in. On the other hand, the general reduction of workplaces during the transition to a market economy has led to the growth of youth unemployment.

The imbalance between supply and demand in the labour force. This is a very real problem for Russia as a whole and for rural areas in particular. One of the main reasons for this ambivalence is that professional training is not taking into account the needs of the economy. Another one is the abolition of the centralised distribution of graduates. The result has been a divergence between what the educational system is producing and what employers are demanding. Our sociological data confirm that the majority of the problems which arise when a young person enters the labour market are the result of the imbalance between professional training on the one hand and the demands of the labour market on the other. According to our data, 70.3% of the youth have reported the need to acquire new skills. The need for retraining was higher for the respondents who had a general secondary education. Among the main causes for this, we can note the desire to receive a higher salary (49% of respondents) and the aspiration to realise one's own potential (27%).

General transitional processes. Since the beginning of the market reforms and the transformation of ownership structures, life in rural areas has become worse. The volume of social services, the level of electrification and gas supply as well as road and transport services have all experienced a decline. Transferring social services from agricultural enterprises (which were taking care about services during Soviet time) to local administrations has led to the reduction or closure of a number of institutions in the field of rural cultural, educational and public health services. The market reorganisation of collective and state farms has led to the majority of them going bankrupt.[143] As a result there was a drop in production; a rise in unemployment; the emergence of latent unemployment; the expansion of the informal sector which attracts labour that has been excluded from the formal labour market; the emergence of new modes of labour behaviour (such as entrepreneurship, self-employment, various types of job-combination); changes in the forms of hiring of workers (such as the emergence of temporary contracts) (Mezentseva 2000); and a decline in living

---

[142] 19.12.1990 № 1311

[143] According to interviews conducted during socio-economic surveys in Karelian villages (Velikaya Guba, Tolvuya, Pyalma and others) carried out under the guidance of T.V. Morozova during 1998-2004.

standards. The reduction of workplaces has coincided with a period that has witnessed a significant contingent of young workers entering the labour market.

The education and occupation of rural youth

The educational/training system has been slow to adapt to the new economic conditions, and the quality of the system suffered during an extended period of economic stagnation. Now, many new enterprises require a highly trained labour force.

In the Soviet period, working-class occupations were appreciated and well paid. Workers typically received higher wages than specialists. The youth with higher education and vocational education was employed in working-class occupations. Now there is an increasing mismatch between the supply of workplaces and the requirements of the youth on the labour market. The value of working-class occupations in the opinion of the youth has fallen considerably. At present, young people with vocational training are not interested in the kind of work that corresponds to their education.

Fig. 13-1 Occupational structure of youth by education in Karelia, 2004*

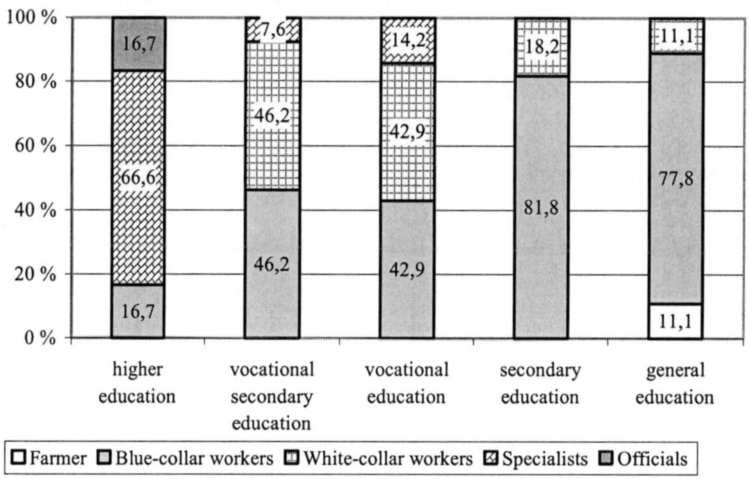

Source: Surveys data

Our sociological data provides information about young people's education and their subsequent occupation. Fig. 13-1 reveals the occupational structure of the youth, by education. In 2004 the majority of young people worked as blue-collar workers and had vocational secondary education (46.2%) and secondary education (81.8%). Among those who had received a higher education, 66.6% were specialists and 16.7% worked as officials. Only 16.7% worked as blue-collar workers. Young people with a higher education do not want to work as blue-collar workers because they regard blue-collar salaries as inadequate. The youth today want work which pays well and, at the same time, requires a minimal amount of effort. Given these aspirations, any future revival of industrial production requiring skilled workers might face difficulties in finding them on the labour market.

The changing structure of rural youth employment

The structural transformations that have taken place in the Russian economy have caused changes in the live of young people in the Republic of Karelia. Our data show that in 2004 the number of students has increased in comparison with 1998 by 26.8 %. The value of education, which in many respects declined in the eyes of young people in the early 1990s, is now once again assuming new importance. This growth in the importance attached to education began slowly but subsequently increasing. The share of employed youth also increased from 38.9% in 1998 to 44.9% in 2004. The growth in the number of students and of employed youth can be explained by rising entry figures higher schools and by the appearance on the labour market of children born. Over the period studied between 1998 and 2004, the share of unemployed youth fell by 15.3 % and was 11.5 % in 2004. (Fig. 13-2) It is possible to use 1998 as the indicator, because in that year it a significant rise in unemployment was observed not only among the youth but also among the whole population. In rural areas, this was more apparent because of the closure of important enterprises which had been the main or sole employer in the area.

The transformation of the economy has led to the appearance of different forms of property, such as cooperative, collective and private ownership. This transformation has also created new spheres of labour use, accompanied by new forms of employment (Table 13-1).

Fig. 13-2 Distribution of rural youth by economic activity in Karelia[144]

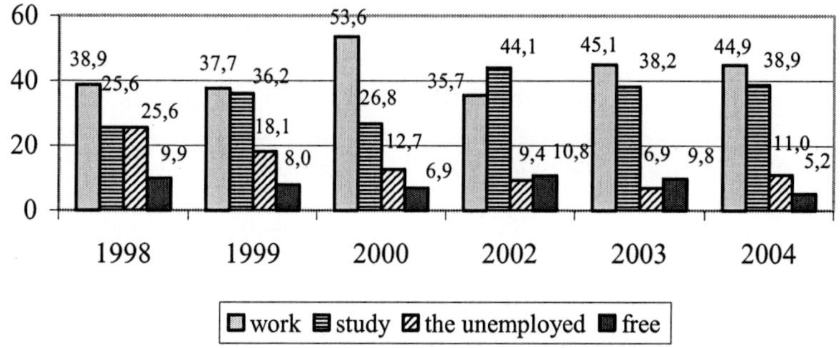

Source: Surveys data

Table 13-1 Distribution of rural youth by form of ownership of enterprise in Karelia, in percent

Year	Public enterprises	Joint-stock companies	Private and family farms	Joint and foreign enterprises	Entrepre-neurship
1998	79	21	-	-	-
1999	62,8	34,6	1,3	-	1,3
2000	41,3	45,5	3,3	4,1	5,8
2002	65,6	22,4	6,9	1,7	3,4
2003	50,4	37,6	3,8	1,4	6,8
2004	47,1	49,1	1,9	-	1,9

Source: Surveys data

Nowadays the main employers in rural areas are agricultural enterprises (former collective and state farms) and enterprises in the timber industry. In 2004 about 47% young labour force were employed in the public sector. In comparison with 1998 the number of youth working in the public sector has halved. Besides agriculture and the timber industry, there are jobs in transport and construction, in trade, in sewing workshops, and in services concerning the social sphere of the village. The largest number of jobs is in the social sphere: schools, infant schools, and cultural and public-service institutions. However,

[144] People in the category of the unoccupied (outside the labour market) are either on maternity leave or are housewives.

the number of such workplaces has fallen recently. Jobs in this sphere of employment belong to a scarce category which provides regular incomes. In 1998 about 20% of employed youth worked in new collectively-owned enterprises (joint-stock companies). The data from 2004 suggests that there was a transfer of some youth from public to private enterprises: joint-stock companies employed 49% of the youth, which is more than double the figure for 1998. For the entire population, the number employed in the public sector fell by 19.2% in comparison with 1998 and stood at 55.9% in 2004. At the same time, the number employed in joint-stock companies increased by 7.2% reaching 21.9% in 2004.

The new realities (market reorganizations and transformations in the economy) have pushed people into secondary employment and into a more intensive use of personal subsidiary plots (PSP; or household plot of land). These new spheres of employment have become an alternative to employment in state-controlled enterprises, but it is not common. As a rule, employment on private and family farms has a short-term seasonal nature. In 2004, two percent of the youth were employed on private and family farms. Only 1.6% of the youth were involved in entrepreneurship.

PSPs have become the basic source of incomefor many families in rural areas. In times of agrarian crisis, it plays a stabilising role, because it provides food for the family, and a minimal income is obtained by selling the produce from the plot. PSPs soften the consequences of increasing unemployment. Income from PSPs represents over 40% of the budget of rural families. According to our survey, the PSP was the main source of food for more than 77% of the families; for 9% of the families the PSP was the main source of income.

The low level and unreliability of wages have pushed workers to search for additional employment. In 2004, about 14% of all interviewees were engaged in additional employment without an employment contract. For the majority of them the additional employment was in their own settlement. Only about 11 % had additional employment outside their settlement. Among the main forms of additional earning are gathering mushrooms and berries (38 % of the total population and 33 % of the youth) and fishing for sale (21 % and 33 % respectively). Also a large proportion of those who are employed also tend their kitchen gardens (14.3%). The main reasons for the youth's additional employment are an insufficient salary at their main place of work (50 %), available free time (24 %) and as a hobby (12 %).

A profile of rural Karelia's unemployed youth

Rural enterprises solved the problems that arose during the transition by reducing their labour force. The reduction of employees in rural enterprises touched, first of all, the youth, as they were a less competitive group because they lacked sufficient experience, and because of the discrepancy between their vocational training and the requirements of the labour market. Such conditions can lead to a situation when a revival of industrial production needs highly skilled workers, but the labour market will not be able to satisfy those requirements (Elchaninov 2004). Sociological surveys allow us to construct a social portrait of youth unemployment. On the whole, observations strongly suggest that young people are traditionally a vulnerable group in labour markets.

According to federal statistics for the whole of Russia, 30.6% of those listed as officially unemployed in 2004 were young people (Obsledovanie naselenia po problemam zanatosti, 2005). According to our survey, the figure was 39%. In the Republic of Karelia, the overall level of unemployment in rural areas was 10.9%, with the youth making up 28.2% of the unemployed.

The educational level of the rural unemployed in the whole of Russia is much lower than in the Republic of Karelia. In 2004, 43.6% of the population of Russia had a vocational education whilst the figure for the Republic of Karelia was 50,5%. As for people with a higher education, there is a big difference in the level of unemployment in the countryside on the one hand, and in the Republic as a whole on the other. The ratio of these parameters is 2.3% and 5.4% respectively. Furthermore, there is a high percentage of uneducated people (that is, without a general secondary education) among the unemployed population: 26.4 % in rural areas and 21.2 % for the Republic as a whole (Frolova & Arefjeva 2004).

As was already noted, university graduates do not aspire to work in rural settlements. Therefore in the structure of rural unemployed a share of university graduates among the youth is lower than in the Republic level: in 2004 it was 2.0% and 3.5 % accordingly. The professional skills of those who have returned to the village after graduating from educational institutions have remained unused and this is reflected in the growth of unemployment among graduates (Annenkov, Zavodovskji & Frolova 2004).

As far as the educational composition of the unemployed is concerned, the largest group is the group with a general secondary education. This group represented more than one third of the total number of unemployed in 2004 (31.1% in general and 30.3% among the youth). The second largest group are people with a vocational secondary education (22.7% and 18.9% respectively). Another big group among unemployed youth are those with no general secondary education (27%). The proportion of people with higher education is smaller among the unemployed.

According to our survey, among the main causes of youth unemployment is (Table 13-2) firstly, the continuing reduction of the staff, or liquidation of enterprises (18.8% in 2003) although this had fallen considerably in comparison with 2002 when it was 30%. This youth employment can be explained by a reduction in employment in the main sectors of goods production and in a number of traditional branches in the non-productive sphere which in turn has been caused by a reduction in the volume of manufacture in connection with the general crisis of the Russian economy.

Another reason is the increased tendency among young people to leave work voluntarily (37.5%). This has dramatically increased in comparison with 1998. It is possible to explain by the existence of a certain overestimated requirements for workplaces by the young people, on the one hand, and the level of salaries and family reasons (such as caring for children and sick relatives), on the other. According to Frolova and Arefjeva (2004), the share of those who have left work of their own free will has slightly decreased: it was 24.6% in rural areas and 30.1% for the Republic of Karelia as a whole in 2004.

Table 13-2 Main causes of youth unemployment in Karelia, in percent

Year	Never had work	Quit work of own will	Reduction of the staff / liquidation of enterprises	Breach of the law	After the long unoccupied period	Other
1998	48.6	8.6	17.1	-	20.0	5.7
1999	71.4	8.6	5.7	2.9	11.4	-
2000	39.3	39.3	10.7	-		10.7
2002	20.0	40.0	30.0	-	-	10.0
2003	18.8	37.4	18.8	18.8	-	6.2

Source: Surveys data

After the abolition of the centralized system of distribution of graduates in 1990, the youth had no guarantee of employment after graduating from an educational institution. The current educational system does not meet the demands of employers. The struggle for survival of Russian enterprises and the transfer of enterprises to the private sector have led to a toughening of requirements regarding workers' professionalism and an increased emphasis on length of service. All this has considerably reduced the opportunities for employment for young people who are entering the labour market for the first time. This explains the existence of the group who have never had work. In

2004 this group represented 18.8% of the total, and had been at its highest level of 71.4% in 1999. One of the reasons for the reduction in this group has been the mass migration of young people from the countryside. Work still remains a source of existence and an obligatory attribute of life.

As the youth has no clear social and labour orientation, periods of unemployment play a very serious role. Given the limited amount of jobs in rural areas, unemployment tends to be for prolonged periods. The average period of unemployment is higher in rural areas than in the Republic of Karelia as a whole: in 2003 it was 4.34 months in rural areas, and, in the Republic of Karelia, 3.48 months) (Elchaninov 2004). According to our surveys in 2000, 40% of the youth had suffered long-term unemployment from six months to two years. In 2004, that figure fell, but, at the same time, the number experiencing short-term unemployment (from one to three months) had increased. Rural unemployment is especially dangerous for the youth. When a young person loses his/her job and has few prospects of finding another one, they lose the habit of working and an active attitude, and, as consequence, they become demoralized.

Our sociological survey also suggests that the ways young people used to look for a job are still rather old-fashioned. In 2003, 8.3% of unemployed young people resorted to enquiring for jobs through their friends and relatives. In 2000, the figure had been even higher at 14.3%. This way of job seeking is beginning to be less popular. Employers concentrate first of all on whether the personal and professional qualifications and qualities of the candidate fit the requirements of the job on offer. A high percentage of job seekers turned directly to enterprises asking for work (50.1 % in 2003). Recently the tendency to select employees on a competitive basis after the publication of job advertisements in newspapers has appeared. According to our survey, it was only 8.3% in 2003. It is also necessary to note that the number of those who turned to bureaus of employment has increased from 14.3% in 2000 to 33.3% in 2003. The low competitive characteristics (such as lack of experience) of the youth compel them to turn to bureaus of employment (Fig. 13-3). Their main aim in doing so is to receive social benefits. There are such programmes as "Labour adaptation" and "Employment of citizens requiring social protection". Bureaus of employment conclude contracts with organisations and enterprises. Employment protection is carried out by specialised trade unions: e.g. the mason, the stove-maker, the confectioner, the dispatcher, the electrical engineer, the seamstress, the security guard. They provide assistance to the unemployed and offer consultations and supply information to them.

For young people in particular there are an annual job fair advertising vacancies and job-training opportunities. For a long time, there was also a programme offering "youth practice" in one's chosen speciality, which has now been closed by the government. Under this programme, the labour office paid a certain sum of money to an employer for taking on a worker, who then worked for six months and received experience, skills and a record in a special work-record card. Now there is a programme called "The First Workplace", but it is intended only for graduates for initial vocational training with an age limit of 18-20 years.

Fig. 13-3 Most common ways of job seeking among the youth in Karelia

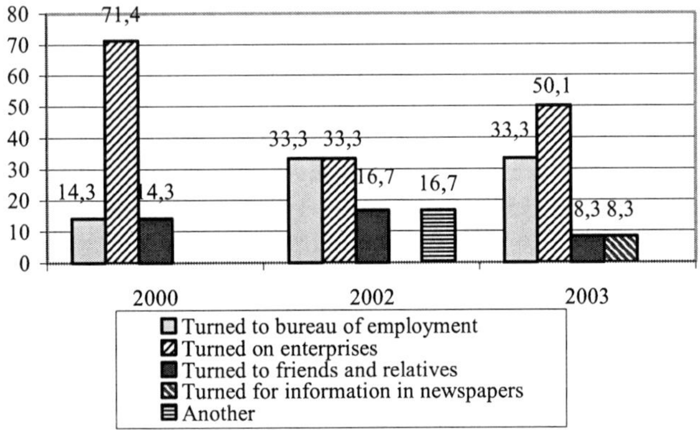

Source: Surveys data

Another way of looking for a job is to use employment agencies. Specialized employment agencies provide a free-of-charge consultation with an expert about job opportunities. Agencies also put an applicant's resume free-of-charge into their information bank. Employers turn to employment agencies when they have many vacancies and are too busy to cope with the stream of applicants. There are also cases when it is necessary to find a new employee by a certain deadline or when a position requires some kind of specialist knowledge or skill.

Besides employment agencies there are also job fairs which offer vacancies and arrange direct contacts between job seekers and the employers. Another way of looking for a job is through the Internet. But unfortunately these ways of job seeking, as a rule, are not available for inhabitants in rural areas.

Youth unemployment in rural areas is certainly a social problem. People who remain unemployed for long periods lose out on economic opportunities and their qualifications and competitiveness also lose value. For many people in this situation, their basic source of existence is social benefits, their parents' pension or casual earnings.

There is mass migration of young people from the countryside to the cities, where there are more opportunities to receive education and enter a profession, and where they can realise their aspirations to earn a living. The basis for this mass migration is to be found, first of all, in socio-economic factors (wage levels, work conditions, problems with accommodation), and socio-psychological factors such as, for example, the prestige that comes from being employed. Also among the main factors which have an influence on youth migration are the limited amount of jobs and, hence, unemployment.

The absence of normal living conditions, poor quality housing and low wages all serve to discourage young people from moving to the countryside. The growth rate of wages in agriculture is far below that of other branches of the economy. Pay levels in agriculture are three times lower than those found in industry. Youth migration to the cities will intensify if radical measures are not taken. It is necessary to develop a programme to attract youth to rural areas which might, for example, include measures for raising the status of teachers and measures to solve the housing shortage, for example, by allocating wood and sites for housing for young families.

Currently some enterprises in rural areas are trying to solve these problems. Enterprises are turning to schools with proposals to conclude agreements to train school leavers in professional educational institutions on condition that they will then return to that enterprise.

Conclusion

The results of our research demonstrate that Karelia's rural labour market is characterized by unemployment, low wages, and a lack of choice both in professional career paths and blue-collar employment.

The most important steps needed for solving youth problems as well as other complex problems affecting rural communities, include the restoration and development of the social infrastructure of villages, the improvement of the material equipment of agricultural enterprises, and the development of social partnerships. Special attention should be given to youth training and various mechanisms to attract and keep young people in the countryside such as: supporting rural schools, developing the enterprise/school contract system of training, improving the provision of housing and increasing wages.

For the preservation and development of rural schools it is necessary:

(1) to create the legal and economic conditions for the provision of free-of-charge full secondary education and free-of-charge education at other levels;
(2) to maintain rural schools;
(3) to create educational and cultural centres in rural areas;
(4) to organize a system of school buses;
(5) to develop a system of distant education; and

(6) to carry out a comprehensive support programme for rural schools (information about, and maintenance of, educational equipment, optimisation of network on the basis of educational and cultural centres) (Velikyi & Zaikina 1999).

To solve the problem of the disparity between the educational qualifications of the youth and the requirements of the labour market, demands different approaches. It is possible to achieve this goal through the early introduction of vocational (career) guidance in schools. It is especially important for secondary school pupils because it is at this stage of their schooling that choices about future careers and jobs become particularly acute and relevant. Therefore, it is very important to create a special agricultural educational programmes and jobs, which would provide opportunities for rural school graduates to appreciate the various attractions of a job or career in agriculture.

In a modern economy, a system of vocational guidance should play a more active role in the formation of the labour force. Such a system has already been created in many countries with advanced market economies. The period of vocational guidance in Western Europe (e.g. Holland, Germany) lasts from between two and four years. Centres for practical training where young people choose a profession, listen to lectures and take tests also function in these countries. As a result, the youth enters the labour market with good labour skills, which considerably increases their chances of finding a good job. For Russia it is very important that similar systems are generated, first of all, at the level of enterprises and municipal districts. A centre of vocational guidance should be created in every rural municipal district (Fedotova 2001).

Now, the rural labour market requires state support, more than ever, both with particular measures and in ensuring the precise coordination of the efforts of ministries, departments and other organizations which have responsibility for developing and realizing employment policy in the agricultural sector.

To solve the employment problem in rural areas, it is necessary to use a sophisticated approach. Initially, there should be a revival of the rural economy, which is impossible without investments across the various sectors of agricultural economic activity (farming, the agro-industrial complex, the timber industry and the mining industry). It is necessary to develop alternative agricultural (PSP) and non-agricultural spheres of employment (a revival of national trades, the development of tourism in rural areas, etc.). Now, the population in rural areas is interested in the development of production and distribution cooperatives, which would collect milk and meat and to deliver it to processors and to markets.

In parallel with these measures, it is necessary to encourage industrial activity and develop mechanisms for reserving workplaces for qualified young personnel.

Ministerial plans aimed at tackling youth unemployment, and the activation of an employment policy should be based on comprehensive and detailed information, in the first instance, the accurate monitoring of employment and unemployment. The elaboration of such measures will facilitate new types of economic behaviour and support the transition to a market economy.

Without a resolution of these problems, Karelia's villages will become backwaters inhabited by illiterate youth, the chronically unemployed, and other marginal elements. Farms will either become unprofitable subsistence family endeavours providing the most basic and rudimentary of living standards or will simply fade away.

References

All-Russian population census of 2002 http://www.gov.karelia.ru/gov/Different/karelia.html

Annenkov M., G. Zavodovskji & E. Frolova (2004) Obzor registriruemogo rynka truda selskih naselennyh punktov Respubliki Karelia za period 2001-2003 [Review of register labour market of rural settlements of the Republic of Karelis during 2001-2003], in *Spros I predlogenie na rynke truda i rynke obrazovatelnyh uslug v Regionah Rossii* [Demand and supply in labour market and market of educational services in the Russian Regions]. Sbornk dokladov po materialam Vserossiskoi nauchno-prakticeskoi Internet-conferenzii [Papers' collection on the base of all Russian scientific Internet-conference]. Vol 2, Petrozavosk, 3-13.

Elchaninov P. (2004) Problemy trudovoi zanatosti selskoi molodegi [Employment problems of rural youth]. *Sociologicheskie issledovania.* Vol 2.

Fadeeva, O. (1999) Sibirskoe selo: al'ternativnye modeli adaptazii (Siberian village: alternative models of adaptation), in *Krestjanovedenie. Teoriaj. Istoria. Sovremennost'* [Peasant studies. Theory. History. Contemporaneity], ed. by V. Danilov & T. Shanin. MVShSEN, Moscow.

Fedotova, M. (2001) Kadrovyi potential sela [Personnel potential of a village]. *Sociologicheskie issledovania*, Vol. 2, 120-21.

Frolova E. & A. Arefjeva (2004) *Pologenie na rynke truda selskih naselennyh Respubliki Karelia za period 2001-2003 godov* [Position on a labour market of rural settlements of the Republic Karelia for the period 2001-2003]. Nekotorye aspekty rynka truda Respubliki karelia / Department FGSZN po RK. – Petrozavodsk, 20-33.

Kalugina, Z. (2001) *Paradoksy agrarnoi reformy v Rossii: sociologichesky analis transformatsionnyck prozessov* [Paradoxes of an agrarian reform in

Russia: the sociological analysis of transformational processes]. IEiOPP SO RAN, Novosibirsk.

Kon, I. (1988) Sociologia molodegi [The sociology of youth]. *Kratkij slovar po sociologii*, Moscow, 353-54.

Mezentseva, E. (2000) *Outsiders in the Labour Market: Russian Men and Women Facing Unemployment.* http://www.datacom.bg/nbgen/CONTENTS.html

Nikonov, A. (1995) *Spriral mnogovekovoi dramy: agrarnaja nauka I politika Rossii (18-20 veka).* Moskva, Enciclopedia rossiiskih dereven [The spiral of Long Drama: Agrarian Science and Politics in Russia (18-20 centuries)]. The encyclopedia of Russian villages publishing house, Moscow.

Obsledovanie naselenia po problemam zanatosti [Inspection of the population on the problems of employment] / Federalnaya slugba gosudarstvennoi statistiki, Moscow, February 2005. 124.

Patsiorkovsky, V. (2003) *Sel'skaja Rossija: 1991-2001* [Rural Russia: 1991-2001]. Finansy and statistica, Moscow.

Prokopov, F. & T. Maleva (1999) *Politika protivodeistvija bezrabotitse* [The policy of counteraction to unemployment]. ROSSPEN, Moscow.

Rimashevskaya, N. (2003) *Chelovek I reforma. Sekrety vysivanija* [The person and reforms. Secrets of survival]. RIZ ISEPN, Moscow.

Shanin, T., V. Danilov & A. Nikulin (eds.) (2002) *Refleksivnoe krestjanovedenie. Desjatiletie issledovanija selskoi Rossii* [Reflective peasant studies. Decade of the study of rural Russia]. MVShSEN, ROSSPEN, Moscow.

Sergienko, A., Z. Kalugina, L. Rodionova, O. Fadeeva & I. Muronova (2004) Economiceskoe povedenie naselenia I socialnye exclusii na selskom rynke truda, [Economic behaviour of population and social exclusion on the rural labour market], in *Socialnaja politika: realii XXI veka* [Social policy: realities of the XXI century]. Nezavisimyi institut socialnoi politiki [Independent Institute of Social Policy] Vol 2,160-97.

Velikyi, P. & A. Zaikina (1998) Chennosty zhiznennoi perspectivy [Values of life's perspective]. *Vyshee obrazovanie v Rossii [Chelovetceskie resursy].* Vol. 4. http://www.pmuc.ru/jornal/number4/index.html

LIST OF CONTRIBUTORS

Dr Robert Ackrill is Reader in European Economics at Nottingham Business School, Nottingham Trent University. As well as working on the implementation of rural development policies in the EU's new member states and applicant countries, he is researching aspects of the EU budget, including the links between it and the CAP. Recent publications include "Historical Institutionalist Perspectives on the Development of the EU Budget System", published in the *Journal of European Public Policy* and co-authored with Adrian Kay of Griffith University, Australia; "EU Enlargement, the CAP and the Cost of Direct Payments: A Note", published in the *Journal of Agricultural Economics*.

Dr Alexander Bedny is Researcher in Sociology at the Centre for Institutional Development of Agriculture, Lobachevski State University of Nizhni Novgorod. His current research interests concern institutional factors of agricultural development in Russia. His recent publications include "Institutional Determinants of Agricultural Enterprises Performance" published in *Organisation in Focus of Sociological Studies* (Nizhny-Novgorod).

Maria Dyakonova is Researcher at the Institute of Economics, Karelian Research Centre, Russian Academy of Sciences (Institute of Economics KRC RAS). She is researching aspects of labour market and education in the Republic of Karelia, Russia. Recent results are published e.g. in "Interregional and International Labour Migration of Citizens in Republic Karelia: Problems and Ways of the Decision" (*The employment service*; in Russian).

Dr Leo Granberg is Professor of Rural Studies in Social Sciences at the Ruralia Institute, University of Helsinki. He is specialist in European rural policy and rural development. He has studied cross-regional business relations in the Barents-region, rural tourism, changes in agriculture and food system as well as development potential of local communities in Lithuania, Russian Karelia and in the Republic of Sakha (Yakutia). He has co-edited the books "Green Ring" (Ashgate), together with I. Kovách and H. Tovey and "Actors on the changing European Countryside" (Hungarian Academy of Sciences) together with I. Kovách.

Maarit Heinonen is Researcher in Sociology at the Aleksanteri Institute, University of Helsinki. She has recently studied multifunctional farm strategies of the eight post-socialist EU new member states as a part of the EU-funded project entitled "Capitalisation of reasearch results on the multifunctionality of agriculture and rurals areas (Multagri)". She acted as a conference co-ordinator of the fifth Aleksanteri Conference in 2005. Currently she is studying socio-cultural value of biodiversity in agriculture.

Inna Kopoteva is Researcher in Socio-Economic Geography at the Aleksanteri Institute, University of Helsinki. She has conducted a number of studies in the Baltic countries and Russia. The recent research is connected to the development and implementation of administrative and municipal reforms in rural Russia.

Dr Katalin Kovacs is working as Senior Researcher and Head of Department in a research institute called Centre for Regional Studies, Hungarian Academy of Sciences. She has conducted sociological and social anthropological research in rural areas. Lately her interest has shifted towards transformation of agriculture, the fall of producer cooperatives and the parallel collapse of the socialist model and the rise of post-socialist, intermediate form of small-scale farming. She has published several case studies and articles on this theme. She is also increasingly involved in rural development research, planning and action.

Karina Lukin is PhD student at the Department of Cultural Studies, University of Helsinki. She is writing her dissertation titled "The History of Landscape in the Kolguev Island" which will deal with the practices of talking about local important places and their histories and in the ways these discourses create meaningful networks of places, a landscape. Besides historical anthropology and landscape studies she has studied Nenets politics of belonging. Her recent publications include "Nenets Folklore in Russian. The Movement of Culture in forms and languages", published in the *Studies in Folk Culture*.

Aine Macken Walsh worked as a researcher on an EU 5th Framework Project entitled "the Integrated Development of Agricultural and Rural Institutions in Central and Eastern Europe (IDARI)" from 2002-2006. As part of her work on this project and also for her PhD dissertation, she conducted a study on governance and rural development in Lithuania, taking a rural partnership programme as a case-study focus. She is currently employed as a rural sociologist at the Teagasc Rural Economy Research Centre, Ireland.

Dr Jouko Nikula is Senior Researcher in Sociology at the Aleksanteri Institute, University of Helsinki. He is specialized in the study on entrepreneurship and middle classes in post-socialist rural areas. He has conducted a number of studies in the Baltic countries and Russia on the strategies of adaptation of rural enterprises and rural development. Results of the studies have been published in "Restoration of Class society in Russia?" (Ashgate); "Decollectivisation, Destruction and Disillusionment – A community study in Southern Estonia" (Ashgate).

Dr Ingrid Oswald is Senior Researcher in Sociology at Humboldt University Berlin and vice-director of the Centre for Independent Social Research (CISR) in St. Petersburg. Her research projects include urban and regional studies as well as migration and ethnic relations in Eastern Europe. Her resent publications include "The 'public-private' sphere in Soviet and post-Soviet society. Perception and dynamics of 'public' and 'private' in contemporary Russia" published in *European Societies* (co-authored with V. Voronkov); "The Descendents of the 'homo sovieticus'. Ethnic Orientations after the Decay of the Soviet Union" (in German) published by LIT.

Dr Nathalie Ortar is Research Fellow in Anthropology at the National School of civil engineering (ENTPE) in Vaulx-en-Velin cedex. Her research projects include urban and regional studies, the meaning given to the dwelling in a migration context in France and Russia.

Dr Arunas Poviliunas is acting as Associated Professor in Sociology at Vilnius University. He is specialized on aspects on social inclusion and development of rural communities in post-socialist countries. His most recent articles (with co-writers of A. Juska and P. Pozzuto) are "Rural Grass-Roots Organizing in Eastern Europe: The Experience from Lithuania" published in the *Community Development Journal* and "Resisting Marginalization: The Rise of the Rural Community Movement in Lithuania" published in the *Sociologia Ruralis.*

Irina Râmniceanu has been a Researcher at the European Institute of Romania and she is a Teaching Assistant at the Academy of Economic Studies (Bucharest). She holds a PhD on the implications of introducing the Common Agriculture Policy in the New Member States and Romania. Her research activity is focused both on the agricultural and rural dimension of the European integration process and on international trade and competitiveness issues. Her most recent papers include "Mapping Agri-Food Competitiveness on the EU Market. Evidence from the New Member States and Romania"; "Questioning Rural Development in an Enlarging EU. The Case of Romania", all published in the Working Papers Series of the European Institute of Romania during 2004-2005.

Dr Eugenia Serova is acting as President of the Analytical Centre on Agri-Food Economics and as Professor and Chair of the Higher School of Economics. She is specialist on agrarian policy and rural labour issues in Russia as well as aspects on transitional agriculture and reforms. She has published research results e.g. "*Agri-Food Economy: Today and Tomorrow*" (ed. by F. Lees and B. Milner; University Press of America); and "GATT Uruguay Round Agreement on Agriculture and Impact of Russia's Entry in the WTO on Agri-Food Sector" with co-author N. Karlova is published in the *Review of Agricultural Economics.*

Dr Ivaylo Vassilev is Research Associate at Northampton Business School, University of Northampton. His main interests are in the areas of transformations in Eastern Europe, business strategy, globalisation, and social theory, particularly around issues of trust. Some forthcoming publications include: "Globalisation and Industrial Change in the Clothing Industry of Transcarpathia, Western Ukraine: A Micro-Level View", *Environment and Planning A*, (co-authored with C. Kalantaridis and S. Slava), "Entrepreneurship and Institutional Change in Post-Socialist Rural Areas: Some Evidence from Russia and the Ukraine", *Journal of East European Management Studies* (co-authored with C. Kalantaridis and L. Labrianidis.

INDEX

S

T

U

W

Y